Founda Science
A Prim ng and
Studying Ḥadīth

Mohammad Akram Nadwi

Translation and critical editing by
Dr. Abu Zayd

Quran Literacy
PRESS

ISBN 978-1-7338374-3-9

Published by:

Quran Literacy Press
1320 Hamilton St
Somerset, NJ 08873
Quranliteracy.org
quranliteracypress@gmail.org

Quran Literacy
PRESS

Front Cover Image: Second page, Abū Dharr manuscript of Ṣaḥīḥ Bukhārī, Süleymaniye Library of Islamic Manuscripts, Istanbul.

Cover design: Juwairia Ansari

Proofreading: Usman Khan, Moiz Mohammed

Co-publishers: Al-Salam Institute (alsalam.ac.uk)

ASI
PRESS

www.alsalam.ac.uk

Contents

Translator's Foreword

Within Islamic disciplines ḥadīth can be extremely daunting and complex—at least it was for me. Ḥadīth detractors aside, for those who place ḥadīth at the center of their epistemology, there are vastly different approaches. For some, ḥadīth is sacred text which places the entire ḥadīth corpus at one's disposal to draw on for their discourse and ideas, which can be incredibly empowering. It can also lead to tremendous amounts of conflicting information on all topics, increasing the levels of confusion and controversy in the Muslim public sphere. There are also more cautious approaches, with differing methods to sift out sound from unsound reports. These methods often place them on opposing sides very much like enemy combatants in a battlefield. How does one make sense of it all? What does one do when one scholar confidently deems a ḥadīth authentic and uses it to build an entire methodological framework, while another deems the same ḥadīth weak, or even fabricated, demolishing that entire edifice? Is it simply a matter of trust? Which books does one rely on, and what parameters should one follow? There are an endless series of questions that cross the minds of students of ḥadīth.

I grappled with many of these questions over the years, as I am sure many of you have as well. Thankfully, with ongoing study, research, and exposure to multiple teachers, I developed answers to some of these fundamental questions, answers which continued to be adjusted over time with new ideas from new teachers and new books. A defining moment in my ḥadīth journey came when I met my beloved teacher Shaykh Mohammad Akram Nadwi. A prolific scholar with a grasp of multiple intellectual traditions, I was most impressed by his deep ḥadīth insights. Those were the sessions that opened my eyes, wherein he vigorously challenged—one might even say, demolished—many notions I had taken for granted while affirming some consistent principles I had learned over time. If my meager knowledge of ḥadīth can be likened to a structure sculpted over time, Shaykh Akram provided remodeling and finishing touches, through the chisel of his critical eye and deep insights.

Shaykh Akram's ḥadīth scholarship is manifested in various specific projects, which must be highlighted here, in order to understand the position of the current book in your hands.

The first is his life-long research which placed him squarely on the global intellectual map and produced his magnum opus: a 43-volume biographical work on female ḥadīth transmitters entitled *al-Wafā᾽ bi Asmā᾽ al-Nisā᾽*. This project spanned decades and took a scholar with humble origins in rural India to far corners of the world in dusty libraries and storehouses in order to comb through ancient manuscripts and uncover the role of the forgotten other-half of the ummah within our intellectual tradition. In that, the research addressed a pressing issue in modern times, one that has consumed many a mind and inspired many a scholar to devise their own solutions.

This very issue, interestingly enough, inspired arguably the greatest legacies for two of my greatest teachers. Maulānā Yūsuf Iṣlāḥī—the Qur᾽ānic scholar and pioneering patron of many Islamic communities in the West—grappled with this issue and lamented the lack of exclusively female seminaries in the history of Islam. This led him to establish one of the first such Islamic educational institutions for women in India: Rampur's al-Jāmi῾at al-Ṣāliḥāt.

When Shaykh Akram's work finally saw the light of day last week—there was no publisher previously willing to produce such a voluminous work—I sent a congratulatory video message to my teacher. In it, I mentioned that his work reminded me of Ibn Khaldūn's famous remark that a good commentary on Ṣaḥīḥ Bukhārī was a debt owed to the Muslim ummah (it had not been done in his time), and another scholar's famous answer shortly thereafter, that *Fatḥ al-Bārī* of Ibn al-Ḥajar was the fulfillment of that debt. Shaykh Akram's work had fulfilled a great debt owed to the world, and we were all the richer for it.

This research was invaluable in developing his taste and critical eye in ḥadīth science. He admits in chapter 28:

> For my work on female ḥadīth narrators, *al-Wafā᾽ bi asmā᾽ al-nisā᾽*, I had to consult countless biographical and historical works, works on ḥadīth and isnād, unpublished manuscripts, and registers of attendance and audition (samā῾). I wound up spending a good

portion of my life buried in these works, which increased my connection with ḥadīth.

The second manifestation of Shaykh Akram's brilliant ḥadīth scholarship appears in his intensive engagement with the Ṣaḥīḥ of Imām Bukhārī, which he has taught for years to advanced students in the UK. I spent some time in my ʿālimīyyah program studying chapters with him in exhaustive detail and by far, these were some of the most valuable lessons I ever attended in my entire life. His deep insights into rijāl (transmitter-criticism), the deeper meanings of the ḥadīth (fiqh al-ḥadīth), the subtle defects of reports hidden to most (ʿilal), and his ability to draw on Bukhārī's own understandings revealed his true position as an erudite master of ḥadīth.

This work leads us to a third expression: *al-Madkhal ilā Ṣaḥīḥ Bukhārī* (forthcoming), which summarizes the insights from these classes in order to produce a specific introductory work for those interested in studying Bukhārī's Ṣaḥīḥ. I have already been tasked by my teacher to translate this next, and I look forward to that project, inshāʾAllāh.

The fourth expression of Shaykh Akram's ḥadīth scholarship will be expressed in his current major research project: producing a critical commentary on Ṣaḥīḥ Muslim. In my view, this work has the potential of overtaking *al-Wafāʾ bi Asmāʾ al-Nisāʾ* to become his most valuable contribution to Islamic scholarship. The following are five major distinctions of this work, much of which has already been completed:

1. The division of the Ṣaḥīḥ with new chapter headings that are consistent with Imām Muslim's original intent and that reflect the beauty of the original work as a masterpiece of ḥadīth craftsmanship
2. A deep analysis of those narrations that Muslim included which Bukhārī had rejected
3. An analysis of those narrations exclusive to Bukhārī which Muslim had rejected
4. A brief and original commentary of the ḥadīth contents

5. A critical analysis and arrangement of Muslim's Muqaddimah (introduction), which is an important independent reference in ḥadīth methodology

The fifth manifestation is *al-Madkhal ilā Sunan al-Tirmidhī* (also forthcoming), a primer on introducing students to a deeper appreciation of Tirmidhī's classical Sunan work. The Sunan features prominently in Shaykh Akram's teaching, and he is keen to point out the need to understand the unique aims and methods of each work. As a student of Bukhārī, Tirmidhī shared his commitment and approach to ḥadīth authenticity, and yet he authored a work with different aims. Shaykh Akram reminded us once in class, 'the greatness of Tirmidhī is that he knew Bukhārī, Muslim and Abū Dāwūd very well, and yet he felt the need to compile a fourth work and was not afraid to make an additional contribution.' The Sunan is designed to reproduce all ḥadīth reports used by jurists, demonstrate their practical application across juristic schools, and provide valuable post-ḥadīth comments on the gradings of these reports.

The final manifestation of Shaykh Akram's ḥadīth expertise lies in two introductory works designed to serve as a preamble to the above mentioned five scholarly projects. The first is *Introduction to the Methodology of Ḥadīth Evaluation* (Mabādiʾ fī Uṣūl al-Ḥadīth wa al-Isnād), published in 2019 by Al-Salam Institute Press under their Islamic Sciences Text Series. It is the more basic of the two works and focuses primarily on ḥadīth terminology (muṣṭalaḥ).

The second of these works is the current book, which represents a more advanced primer to the general ḥadīth sciences. It is a collection of Shaykh Akram's insights on various topics pertaining to this complex field. The book appears to be have been hand-picked, by the driving of fate, from all the insights and answers I gathered myself from my teacher's lessons over time in response to my own queries. His selection reveals his acumen as a master teacher, who knows well what lessons his students need in order to advance their journey in a meaningful way. I had long compiled my own notes on these lessons and shared them with students, and Shaykh Akram here had provided a far superior selection crafted by his own eloquent pen, and for that I am grateful.

It should be noted that the chapters, though arranged within six topical units, stand independently and can be read separately in no particular order. My translation style should now be familiar to readers of Shaykh Akram's more recent English works. My aim is always to convey the best sense of the author's words in English and not to follow a literal word-focused approach. The subdivisions of chapters are my own work. I have provided ample footnotes to add needed clarifications, biographies of some—not every—individual, and the occasional insights from Shaykh Akram's classes or from my discussions with him. I have provided isnād charts when discussion of transmitters is dominant, and I hope these are useful to the reader to follow the text. The word *Sunnah* is capitalized when it refers to the generality of the Prophet's example and in lowercase when referring to specific Prophetic practices. I have refrained from the use of any abbreviations, even in a work as technical as this one, in order to render a more flowing text. Qurʾānic translations follow no particular method, but among my preferred ones are Abū al-Aʿlā Mawdūdī's *The Meaning of the Qurʾān* and Muḥammad Asad's *The Message of the Qurʾān,* which I use as a base and take the liberty to further modify as I deem fit. In the end, it should be noted that this is a translation of Shaykh Akram's work and as such, any mistakes found are bound to be mine.

I must thank all those involved in this translation effort, starting with my family and children, whose valuable time I have continuously sacrificed in pursuit of my endeavors. I only pray that God's grace blesses them and safeguards their faith and future, making up for all the lost parenting time. I take comfort in my conviction that His grace and mercy are far superior to any of my own efforts at tarbiyah and upbringing. I thank my proofreaders Usman Khan (for taking valuable time out of his PhD studies at Princeton University) and Moiz Mohammed (for placing his reckless pursuits on pause, even if briefly). Finally, I thank Professor Shaykh Issam Eido of Vanderbilt University for graciously agreeing to write the academic foreword to this work.

This translation effort took the better part of the pandemic year of 2020. It was the unique, God-created circumstances of this trying time which placed the world on pause and forced us to be confined to our homes for an entire year—and still counting—that created the opportunity and space for me to complete this project. No matter what happens, it is always good for the believers.

How amazing is the matter of the believer, for all his affairs are good! In prosperity, he is grateful, and that is good for him. In adversity, he is patient, and that is good for him. (Ṣaḥīḥ Muslim)

Abu Zayd Obaidullah Anwar Choudry
Piscataway, New Jersey
January 28, 2021

Foreword by Issam Eido

In 2009, a female PhD student from Princeton University came to Damascus to study with me ḥadīth sciences and the genre of al-samāʿāt focusing on the role of female narrators during the Islamic medieval age. At that time, I was already familiar with Akram Nadwi's general work and scholarly efforts, but it was the first time I came to know about his ongoing project on ḥadīth transmission and the role of female narrators. I realized how promising this project would be and its potential impact on reframing our reading of Islamic intellectual history.

During my study of ḥadīth sciences I was fortunate to meet with giant scholars such as Shaykh ʿAbd al-Fattāḥ Abū Ghudda and Nūr ad-Dīn ʿItr, as well as many seekers of ḥadīth sciences who came from Syria, India, Pakistan, Turkey and the Western World. The impression I have collected during this long period is that the Indian subcontinent has produced and given our modern world serious and productive scholars in the field of ḥadīth studies who have been able to reform, reproduce, and reframe the field from within. Without any hesitation, one of these scholars is Shaykh Akram Nadwi who is representing a new episode in this long series. His intellectual life and scholarly works are expressive and full of real stories and incidents that inspire the seekers of knowledge in general and the students of ḥadīth in particular.

A couple of things can be mentioned here about the significance of his character. Among them is his connecting with real scholars of the discipline whether they are his shuyūkh or his colleagues, his capability to reframe complicated issues in the field following a brilliant and simple way that can at one time teach beginners and provoke advanced seekers, his humility and sincere advice he gives to his fellows and students, his vast and comprehensive knowledge covering different fields and disciplines, and his uniqueness in terms of understanding both traditional knowledge and western scholarship. These characteristics represent and reflect his new scholarly work *Foundation to Ḥadīth Science: A Primer on Understanding & Studying Ḥadīth.* It is a work that can be an important step for beginners, and a source for serious and complex dialogue among advanced students and scholars.

In this work, Nadwi, generously, represents seven major elements: 1-clarifying and confirming specific ḥadīth issues that many student are used to discussing and debating such as mursal, tadlīs, mudraj, munkar, etc., with brief and clear words and examples, 2- reestablishing and fixing some issues that have occupied students' minds for decades, even centuries, by providing a new approach based on evidences, such as his approach to riwāya, types of ḥadīth books, the meaning of shādhdh, the ranks of knowledge, the preference of Muslim's Ṣaḥīḥ over al-Bukharī, 3- reframing some technical issues and giving a clear taxonomy for terms such as ṣaḥiḥ, ḥasan, and ḍaʿīf, 4- providing new viewpoints on a couple of issues seekers need to hear such as the Ḥanafi school and ḥadīth, and the significance of Abū Hurayra's ḥadīth, 5- summarizing and giving concise information on a couple of ḥadīth matters citing unparalleled and appropriate quotations; 6- sincere advices and recommendations for seekers of ḥadīth based on his personal and scholarly communications with his shuyūkh and colleagues, in particular those who are living in the Muslim word and are known for seriousness, sincerity, and humility; and 7- finally, though the style he chose to write in is a very traditional one (based on Q/A), it can be a creative way to motivate readers to engage in reading and forget the time.

However, I must point out that though the book targets both beginners and advanced students, it can confuse some learners who are not equipped with enough ḥadīth studies and do not have a solid background on some issues mentioned in the book such as the Ḥanafi principles of ḥadīth, and the sub-ranks between ṣaḥiḥ, ḥasan, and ḍaʿīf. In addition, there are a couple of places in the book that need more clarification and evidence; leaving them without clarification perhaps causes some avoidable argument among students, for example the ranks of knowledge and the impact of Muslim praxis on the ḥadīth authentication process. Additionally, there are some issues mentioned in the book which I, personally, would contend with the author, in particular his viewpoints on the Ḥanafi school and ḥadīth, and the definition of ṣaḥīḥ which needs more deep discussion in terms of differentiating between the definition itself and the usages of ṣaḥiḥ in the early period of Islam. Moreover, it would be important for the learners to know who are meant by early (mutaqaddim) and late (mutaʾakhkhir) ḥadīth scholars so that one can grasp the border line between these two eras and their related issues.

Finally, the book is an important source for students of ḥadīth, beginner or advanced (muqtaṣid and mujtahid), replete with much information and creative thoughts on ḥadīth studies in particular and Muslim intellectual history in general.

Issam Eido,
Senior lecturer, the Department of Religious Studies, Vanderbilt University
Author of *Manhaj Qabūl al-Akhbār ʿinda Al-Muḥaddithīn* (Ḥadīth Scholars' Criteria of Ḥadīth Criticism)
Nashville, Tennessee
January 22, 2021

Author's Introduction

Over twenty years ago I authored a booklet entitled: *Foundations in the science of Ḥadīth and Isnād*, which was quite well-received, undergoing a number of publications and being used in schools across the Middle East, India, Pakistan, Europe and the United States. After that, I devoted myself to working on a commentary on Ṣaḥīḥ Muslim in a unique manner. I wrote an introduction to the work that highlighted the distinctions of the Ṣaḥīḥ as well as Imām Muslims' methodology.

It became apparent to me during the course of my teachings at Al-Salam Institute (Oxford and London), Cambridge Islamic College, my lectures throughout the United Kingdom and beyond, and my rubbing shoulders with scholars and students of knowledge, that most students and researchers fail to understand properly the methodology of the books of ḥadīth. These books are the primary and fundamental sources, and for many, the most critical and important part of their ḥadīth study. This realization prompted me to author an introduction to Ṣaḥīḥ Bukhārī and Sunan Tirmidhī. It is my hope that these three works—my commentary on Ṣaḥīḥ Muslim and these two introductions—will fill in some gaps in our understanding of the science of ḥadīth.

While working on these three projects, I found myself repeating certain themes and ideas. Surely, repetition is a flaw and a tiresome matter. I decided to single out these general ideas in a separate work that would head the other three. It is this work that I place today in the hands of readers and title *Tamhīd 'Ilm al-Ḥadīth.*

This introductory work includes articles I authored at various times concerning ḥadīth issues. I authored them in question-and-answer format in order to make it easier for students to follow the points of discussion. I have modified some of these articles in order to fit this new work, which includes a number of essential issues every serious student needs to grasp before embarking on a study of ḥadīth.

I divided the work into six chapters. The first includes clarifying the concept of sunnah and ḥadīth, how the sunnah explains the Qur'ān in various ways, the differences between sunnah and ḥadīth, between ḥadīth and philosophy, and between ḥadīth and fiqh. I have mentioned the preservation of ḥadīth among the Companions and successive generations in memory and writing, and summarized the history of ḥadīth documentation.

The second chapter is about essential principles. I did not focus on defining terminologies, which is the subject of my previous book Introduction to the Methodology of Ḥadīth Evaluation (Mabādiʾ fī Uṣūl al-Ḥadīth wa al-Isnād).[1] Rather, I have explained important points in understanding the notions of sound and weak reports, the practice of reading and hearing ḥadīth, and the concept of ijāzah. I have discussed the notion of hidden defects and presented critical remarks about the text *Nukhbat al-Fikr* because of its importance in this field. I ended that with a discussion on principles of ḥadīth according to the Ḥanafī school of jurisprudence.

The third chapter has to do with the books of ḥadīth, where I mentioned the most important of these works, especially the Muwaṭṭaʾ and the six primary works (uṣūl al-sittah). I discussed the meaning of the term *kitāb* and the issue of the soundest book, objecting to Abū Ḥanīfah's *Kitāb al-Āthār* as a candidate. I ended with a discussion on the narration of these books by isnād.

The fourth chapter is about the people of ḥadīth, which includes a discussion on the Companions of the Prophet ﷺ from whom ḥadīth is taken. I have defended ʿĀʾishah and Abū Hurayrah, discussed the ḥadīth about revival, and the virtues of those who pursue ḥadīth.

The fifth chapter is about devoting oneself to ḥadīth and includes two general pathways to studying ḥadīth. I have mentioned the right approach and discussed ḥadīth assemblies.

The sixth and final chapter discusses important reminders, warnings and advice to students that are indispensable for their ḥadīth studies.

In the end, I call on God to accept this work in a good way and allow it to be beneficial to His servants, and all praise is for God, the Lord of the worlds.

Mohammad Akram Nadwi
29 Dhū al-Ḥijjah, 1441
August 19, 2020

[1] Published by Al-Salam Institute Press in 2019 under their Islamic Sciences Text Series.

PART 1: SUNNAH AND ḤADĪTH

The Sunnah Only Clarifies the Qurʾān

Do you agree with those who say that the Sunnah only serves to explain the Qurʾān? Who am I to agree or disagree with the great Imāms of the ummah? I am merely a student who stole a seat at their table, who seeks to learn something from them, and share a bit of their light. The profound meaning of Sufyān b. ʿUyaynah's (d. 198/815)[1] statement never ceases to amaze me: 'The Sunnah is an explanation of commands and prohibitions.'[2] Also, there is the statement of Imām Shāfiʿī (d. 204/820) and others who said: 'Surely, the Sunnah is an elaboration of the Qurʾān.'[3] I testify to the truthfulness of what they said and will never swerve from the strength of their view nor from the rightness of their understanding.

But haven't you differed from them in other matters? I differed from some of them only by inclining to others of their same ranks in knowledge, piety, righteousness, and guidance. They were a group that sincerely strove to their best ability for the sake of God alone, earning two degrees of reward when they were correct and one when they were mistaken.

Is their view that the Sunnah is an explanation of the Qurʾān self-sufficient and able to stand on its own? Yes, it is, for it affirms the very message of the Qurʾān itself: ﴾*So that you may explain to the people what was revealed unto them*﴿ .[4] If one were to fully comprehend the manner in which the Sunnah explains the Qurʾān, it would increase a person's understanding of God's Book and this religion. Who could deny that deep insight into the nexus of the Qurʾān and Sunnah would lead to the most solid evidence and proofs?

What are the various aspects in which the Sunnah explains the Qurʾān? They are five:

---

[1] Sufyān b. ʿUyaynah (d. 198/815) was the great jurist and ḥadīth scholar of Makkah, and originator of the *first ḥadīth tradition* ('ḥadīth musalsal bil-awaliyyah')—which continues to this day—of narrating to students the ḥadīth of mercy before any other.

[2] Ibn Taymiyyah, *Majmūʿ*, vol 3, pg 2056.

[3] See the beginning of Shāfiʿī's *al-Risālah*.

[4] Qurʾān 16:44.

1. **Elaboration** (*bayān tafsīrī*): This is what appears in the Sunnah to affirm or facilitate an understanding of what is already in the Qur'ān. So the statement of the Prophet ﷺ: 'A Muslim is a brother to a Muslim'[5] is an affirmation of God's statement: ﴾*Surely the believers are brothers.*﴿ [6] Also, the Prophet's teaching of the rules pertaining to menses is facilitating an understanding of God's statement: ﴾*They ask about the monthly course. Say, 'It is a state of impurity'; so keep apart from women during their monthly course and do not go near them until they are clean.*﴿ [7] The ḥadīth of Jibrīl[8] is an affirmation and approximation of the meanings of īmān and islām as mentioned repeatedly in the Qur'ān.

2. **Application** (*bayān taṭbīqī*): This is the Prophet's application of the teachings of the Qur'ān in his own lifetime. This is explained by what Bukhārī relates from 'Ā'ishah, God be pleased with her, who said: 'The Prophet would frequently say in his bowings and prostrations: 'Glory be to you God, our Lord, and all praise; God forgive me.''[9] 'Ā'ishah continued: 'He was simply applying the Qur'ān.'[10] In other words, this supplication of his was an application of God's words: ﴾*Then extol the praise of your Lord and pray to Him for forgiveness.*﴿ [11] And the various ḥadīth reports from the Companions concerning the Ḥajj of the Prophet ﷺ are an application of God's statement, among others, concerning Ḥajj: ﴾*Pilgrimage to the House is a duty owed to Allah by all who can make their way to it.*﴿ [12] The ḥadīth of the prayer of Jibrīl[13]

---

[5] Ḥadīth of Ibn 'Umar related by Bukhārī in Kitāb al-maẓālim wa al-ghaṣb—Bāb lā yaẓlimu al-muslimu al-muslima wa lā yuslimuhu; and by Muslim in Kitāb al-birr wa al-ṣilah wa al-ādāb—Bāb taḥrīm al-ẓulm.

[6] Qur'ān 49:10.

[7] Qur'ān 2:2

[8] Related from 'Umar by Muslim, and from Abū Hurayrah by Bukhārī and Muslim

[9] In Arabic: *subḥānakallāhumma rabbanā wa biḥamdik, Allāhummaghfirlī.*

[10] Ṣaḥīḥ Bukhārī: Kitāb al-adhān—Bāb al-tasbīḥ wa al-du'ā' fī al-sujūd. The expression used by 'Ā'ishah was: *yata'awwalu al-Qur'ān* (from the word *ta'wīl*).

[11] Qur'ān 110:3.

[12] Qur'ān 3:97.

[13] Related by Mālik in his Muwaṭṭa' and reproduced by Bukhārī and Muslim. Malik relates from Zuhrī that 'Umar b. 'Abd al-'Azīz delayed the prayer once. Afterwards, 'Urwah b. al-Zubayr came and informed him that Mughīrah b. Shu'bah did the same one day in Iraq, after which Abū Mas'ūd al-Anṣārī

alongside the Prophet is an explanation of the times of prayer mentioned in God's Book. Most of the specific sunnah practices that are reported concerning purity, prayer, fasting, charity, Ḥajj, marriage, divorce and all other practical religious matters belong to this type of Sunnah.

3. **Specifying Limits** (*bayān ḥudūdī*): This is where the Prophet ﷺ through his sunnah demonstrated the exact limits of certain commands that appear in the Qur'ān, in terms of their maximum, minimum, and allowable extents. For instance, the Qur'ān commands the washing of the body parts in ablution (wuḍū'),[14] while the sunnah clarifies the detail that washing the body parts in ablution once is the minimum amount, three times the maximum, and two also acceptable. Muḥammad b. al-Ḥasan al-Shaybānī (d. 189/805) states: Abū Ḥanīfah relates to us from Ḥammād from Ibrāhīm from al-Aswad b. Yazīd from 'Umar b. al-Khaṭṭāb that he performed ablution and washed his hands twice, gargled twice, rinsed his nose twice, washed his face twice, his elbows twice, forward and backwards, and then wiped his head twice and washed his feet twice. Ḥammād then said: Once suffices if it is done completely. Muḥammad commented: And this is what we follow.[15]

4. **Perfecting Commands** (*bayān takmīlī*): The Prophet ﷺ was keen to obey his Lord in the most complete and perfect manner possible. His Lord ordered him in ablution to wash three body parts and wipe his

objected to him by saying: What's this, Mughīrah? Don't you know that the angel Jibrīl came down and led the Prophet in prayer. Then he prayed again, leading the Prophet. Then he prayed again, leading the Prophet. Then he prayed again, leading the Prophet. Then he prayed again, leading the Prophet. Then Jibrīl said, 'This is what you have been ordered to do.' 'Umar b. 'Abd al-'Azīz said to 'Urwah, 'Be sure of what you relate, 'Urwah. Was it Jibrīl who established the time of prayer for the Messenger of God?' 'Urwah said, 'That's how Bashīr b. Abī Mas'ūd used to relate from his father.'

[14] ﴾*Believers! When you stand up for Prayer wash your faces and your hands up to the elbows, and wipe your heads, and wash your feet up to the ankles. And if you are in the state of ritual impurity, purify yourselves (by taking a bath). But if you are either ill, travelling, have satisfied a want of nature or have had contact with women and find no water then have recourse to clean earth and wipe your faces and your hands therewith. Allah does not want to lay any hardship upon you; rather He wants to purify you and complete His favours upon you so that you may give thanks.*﴿ (Qur'ān 5:6)

[15] *Kitāb al-Āthār*, pg 1-2. This is the very first ḥadīth of this book.

head,[16] but he chose, when washing his face, to gargle, clean his mouth with siwāk,[17] and rinse his nose in order to perfect the command of washing. As another example, it is related in the Ṣaḥīḥayn[18] and other sources from Maymūnah the wife of the Prophet ﷺ who said: 'I placed water for the bath of the Prophet. He washed his hands twice or thrice and then poured water on his left hand and washed his private parts. He rubbed his hands over the earth (and cleaned them), rinsed his mouth, washed his nose by putting water in it and blowing it out, washed his face and both forearms and then poured water over his body. Then he withdrew from that place and washed his feet.'[19] This was a practice that perfected God's commands: ﴾*And if you are in the state of ritual impurity, purify yourselves*﴿;[20] and His statement: ﴾*. . . or while you are defiled—save when you are travelling—until you have washed yourselves.*﴿ [21]

5. **Prophetic Understandings** (*bayān istinbāṭī*): A great many of the Prophetic sunnah practices represent his own understanding of and extractions from God's Book. For instance, his statement: 'The best of generations is my generation, and then those that follow them';[22] is derived from God's statement: ﴾*And of those who led the way—the first of the Emigrants (Muhājirūn) and the Helpers (Anṣār)—and those who followed them in the best possible manner, God is well-pleased with them and*

[16] Qur'ān 5:6.

[17] The siwāk refers to the cleaning stick used by Muslims to brush their teeth. It has been recommended in numerous Prophetic ḥadīth.

[18] This term refers to Ṣaḥīḥ Bukhārī and Muslim.

[19] Ṣaḥīḥ Bukhārī: Kitāb al-ghusl—Bāb al-ghusl marratan wāḥidah; Kitāb al-ghusl—Bāb tafrīq al-ghusl wa al-wuḍū'; Kitāb al-ghusl—Bāb tafrīq al-maḍmaḍah wa al-istinshāq fī al-janābah; Kitāb al-ghusl—Bāb man afragha biyamīnihī 'alā shimālihī fī al-ghusl; Kitāb al-ghusl—Bāb man tawaḍḍa'a fī al-janābah thumma ghasala sā'ira jasadihī; Kitāb al-ghusl—Bāb man nafḍ al-yadayn min al-ghusl 'an al-janābah; Kitāb al-ghusl—Bāb al-tasattur fī al-ghusl 'inda al-nās; Ṣaḥīḥ Muslim: Kitāb al-ḥayḍ—Bāb ṣifat ghusl al-janābah.

[20] Qur'ān 5:6.

[21] Qur'ān 4:43.

[22] Ṣaḥīḥ Bukhārī: Kitāb al-shahādāt—Bāb lā yash-had 'alā shahādat idhā ush-hid; Kitāb faḍā'il al-ṣaḥābah—Bāb faḍā'il aṣḥāb al-nabī; Kitāb al-riqāq—Bāb mā yuḥdhar min zaharat al-dunyā wa al-tanāfus fīhā; Kitāb al-aymān wa al-nudhūr—Bāb ithm ma lā yafī bi al-nudhur; Ṣaḥīḥ Muslim: Kitāb faḍā'il al-ṣaḥābah—Bāb faḍl al-ṣaḥābah thumma aladhīna yalūnahum.

they are well-pleased with God.} [23] The expiation for the one who broke his fast in Ramadan was specified by the Prophet[24] and derived from the punishment for the practice of ẓihār in the Qur'ān.[25] Deliberately breaking the fast in Ramadan involves making lawful what God forbade, while ẓihār involves forbidding something lawful. Since both acts of forbidding or allowing are meant exclusively for God, the Prophet considered the two equivalent for the purposes of expiation. No doubt equating two identical matters is the best form of independent reasoning (ijtihād). This is supported by God's statement: {*We have revealed to you this Book with the Truth so that you may judge between people in accordance with what God has shown you.*} [26]

Does it harm a person to be unaware of these aspects? Yes, indeed it does, for the one who does not strive to properly reconcile the Qur'ān and Sunnah will fall into a number of errors: either interpreting the Qur'ān through means other than the Sunnah, considering the Sunnah to be independent of the Qur'ān, or considering both insufficient for full guidance thereby causing them to resort to baseless analogies and conjecture. Had these people understood the firm, inseparable link between these two sources, they would not have been afflicted by these far-fetched opinions. They would not have missed out on realizing the benefits that God has mandated upon His servants or considering elements of the Sharī'ah contradictory.

What would you advise us with? I advise you and myself to hold onto the Book of God and the Sunnah of His Messenger ﷺ, properly reconciling the two and sincerely implementing their mandates upon individuals and societies. And be

---

[23] Qur'ān 9:100.

[24] This is found Ṣaḥīḥ Bukhārī: Kitāb al-ṣawm—Bāb idhā jāma'a fī Ramaḍān; Kitāb al-ṣawm—Bāb al-mujāmi' fī Ramaḍān; Kitāb al-hibah wa faḍlihā—Bāb idhā wahaba hibatan faqabaḍahā al-ākhar wa lam yaqul qabilt; Kitāb al-nafaqāt—Bāb nafaqat al-mu'sir 'alā ahlih; Kitāb al-adab—Bāb al-tabassum wa al-ḍaḥak; Kitāb al-adab—Bāb mā jā'a fī qawl al-rajul waylak; Kitāb kaffārat al-aymān—Bāb qawlihī qad faraḍallāhu lakum taḥillat; Kitāb kaffārat al-aymān—Bāb man a'āna al-mu'sir fī al-kaffārah; Kitāb kaffārat al-aymān—Bāb yu'ṭī fī al-kaffārah 'asharat masākīna qarīban kāna aw ba'īdan; Ṣaḥīḥ Muslim: Kitāb al-ṣawm—Bāb taghlīẓ taḥrīm al-jimā' fī nahār Ramaḍān.

[25] An unlawful pagan form of divorce in which the husband said to his wife, 'You are to me like my mother's back.' The Arabic term for back, *ẓahr*, gives rise to the term ẓihār. It is referred to in the Qur'ān 58:2-4.

[26] Qur'ān 4:105.

wary of conjecture and baseless speculation in God's religion, for such conjecture is the falsest of speech. And you should know that the ijtihād of jurists is nothing but an extension of the ijtihād of the Prophet ﷺ and a sub-type of his own extractions from the Book of God. Whoever conforms to this type of reasoning is correct, and those who do not are mistaken. How excellent is what God said: ﴾*Those who strive hard in Our cause, We shall surely guide them to our ways.*﴿ [27]

[27] Qur'ān 29:69.

Qur᾿ān and Sunnah

Clarify for us the true connection between the Qur᾿ān and the Sunnah. Islamic groups and sects have differed greatly over their stance towards the Sunnah and over the nature of its link with the Qur᾿ān. What is your position on that? This is an excellent and beneficial question. I will first present the popular positions from past to present concerning the Sunnah of the leader and master of the prophets and messengers, the beloved of the Lord of the worlds ﷺ. I will then comment on them in a fair and balanced way, without being extreme or excessive. I summarize these positions into five groupings.

Group One: Qur᾿ān Only

The first group confines itself to the Qur᾿ān as entirely independent from the Sunnah in a way that leaves room for injustice and indiscretion, not to mention a fair bit of arrogance. This view is faulty, opposing both revelation and reason. As for revelation, God commands the believers to obey, follow and emulate the example of the Prophet ﷺ in numerous verses, while sternly warning those who oppose his instructions.

From the standpoint of reason, can it be imagined that the Qur᾿ān be acted upon without those things which would explain the meanings and applications of its verses? It would be the height of delusion to take its meanings from other than the Prophet ﷺ, whom God entrusted with this task and favored over the rest of creation. The Prophet ﷺ stated in a sound ḥadīth: 'Surely I have been given the Book along with something like it. Soon a time will come when a man reclining on his couch will say, '*Stick to the Qur᾿ān alone. Whatever it deems permissible, treat it as permissible. Whatever it deems forbidden, treat it as forbidden*.'"[1] Here, 'something like the Qur᾿ān' refers to the Prophet's interpretation and application of the Qur᾿ān. His interpretation reveals the truth in an impartial manner, and his application is both accurate and protected from error.

[1] Sunan Abū Dāwūd. Kitāb al-sunnah: Bāb fī luzūm al-sunnah.

Numerous reports have reinforced the obligation of following him and warned against opposing him in any way. I do not believe that this weak view deserves any response more than this.

Group Two: Qur'ān and Mutawātir Sunnah Only

The second group accepts widespread sunnah reports concerning prayer, pilgrimage, and its likes, while turning people away from sunnah practices that are not widespread or those based upon solitary reports, even if these reports are otherwise sound and narrated by trustworthy and accurate experts. This is the approach of many proponents of the Muʿtazilite creed[2] as well as contemporary reformists. It is also a deviant view that deprives Muslims from the divine mercy which was placed in the ways and manners of the Messenger ﷺ. How can it be that they reject what has come from the protected Prophet ﷺ while mandating that people accept their own fabricated views and interpretations? This group resembles the previous one in contradicting overt logic and reason, and in that, it is more akin to fleeting, whimsical thoughts.

Group Three: Qur'ān and Non-Contradictory Sunnah Only

The third group accepts those sunnah practices and reports that do not conflict with Qur'ānic verses in any way. This view appears to be sound but in practice winds up serving as a means to abandon those aspects of guidance and truth which contradict one's own whims, desires and traditions. How many sound reports have been rejected by ignorant and foolish individuals on the supposition that they contradict the Qur'ān, whereas—were they to examine them more deeply or refer to those with expertise and keen understanding—they would have soon realized that Qur'ānic verses and the Sunnah of the chosen Prophet ﷺ reinforce one another and exist in perfect harmony and cohesion?

[2] The Muʿtazilah (often known as 'Rationalists') were a theological school founded by Wāṣil b. ʿAṭā' (d. 131/748) that believed in the all-pervasive justice of God as the master principle in creation, which led them to believe, among other things, that the Qur'ān is created, that evil-doers will necessarily be punished with the Fire and doers of good rewarded with Paradise, that God's attributes are metaphorical, and that God cannot be seen in the Afterlife. Of course, there is no absolute uniformity in any group.

Either their understanding of Qur'ānic verses is defective or they fail to comprehend the Sunnah, or a combination of both.

Group Four: Qur'ān and Sunnah Equal

The fourth group represents the pious scholars of mainstream Sunnī Islam[3] who honor the Sunnah as it rightly deserves but wind up sometimes going to extremes and crossing bounds. In their veneration of the sanctity of the Sunnah, they equate it to God's Book, either literally or in practice. Some of them refer to the Qur'ān and Sunnah as two equal primary sources or make statements such as: 'The Sunnah judges over the Book,' or 'The Qur'ān is more in need of the Sunnah than the Sunnah is in need of the Qur'ān.' They are mistaken in their use of these expressions, as well as their meanings. This approach leads to instituting changes in some details of religion and reversing some of its priorities.

Who are these scholars that you are referring to? My respect for them prevents me from mentioning their names. I hate that people develop a bad opinion of them that would prevent them from benefiting from them.

Can you provide for us examples of some mistakes that result from considering the Qur'ān and Sunnah to be equivalent? These mistakes are many, but my heart does not accept that I list them, for that is equivalent to naming these scholars.

We are surprised that you have reached the level of audacity to disparage the scholars of Islam, who are the pillars and the support of the faith. I seek God's refuge from denying their merit, from not benefiting from them, or from detracting from their status in any way! By God, I love them from the bottom of my heart, for loving them is a part of faith. I pray to God to place me among their ranks and raise me with them in the next life, for they are the best and most righteous of God's creation, God be pleased with them and raise their ranks. However, they are not immune from mistakes. They have taught us that the views of every single person can be accepted or rejected except for the Seal of the Prophets ﷺ. They have taught us that the truth is more worthy of being followed.

So what is the correct position regarding this issue? It is as follows:

[3] Ahl al-sunnah wa al-jamā'ah is the classical term for the mainstream Muslim body.

Group Five: Qur'ān as Source, Sunnah as Branch

The fifth group is that of the Companions and Followers,[4] and those expert scholars after them who followed their approach. They were many in the past, and a few in the present. They believe that the Qur'ān is entirely clear and lucid while needing some detail and elaboration, most of which is contained within the Qur'ān itself and some of it in the Sunnah. They affirm that the Qur'ān is the foundation while the Sunnah is its branch, that the Qur'ān contains universal principles while the Sunnah contains details and particulars. The true relationship, therefore, of the Qur'ān and Sunnah is between that which is definitive and decisive, and its elaboration; between a source and its branch; or between a universal idea and its components.

Which of the groups do you adhere to? What is obligatory upon me and those who understand this religion is to choose the fifth view, which is the correct one and the one advocated by the Qur'ān and Sunnah itself. It is the view adopted by the Companions and Followers, and the one that is supported by sound reason, correct thinking, and deep examination.

What is your position regarding those reports which contradict God's Book? There can never be a clash between the Book of God and what is soundly established in the Sunnah and ḥadīth reports.

Does not the sound ḥadīth ('There is no prayer without al-Fātiḥah,')[5] contradict the verse: {And recite whatever is easy [in prayer].}[6]? Or the ḥadīth that: 'Whatever is established by birth is also established by breast-feeding,'[7] contradict the verse {. . . and your milk-mothers and your milk-sisters . . .}[8]? Does not the ḥadīth that 'Do not marry

---

[4] The Tābiʿūn, 'Followers' or 'Successors,' are the generation of Muslims that learned from the Companions.

[5] Ṣaḥīḥ Bukhārī: Kitāb al-adhān—Bāb wujūb al-qirā'ah li al-imām wa al-ma'mūm fī al-ṣalawāt kullihā fī al-ḥaḍar wa al-safar; Ṣaḥīḥ Muslim: Kitāb al-Ṣalāh—Bāb wujūb qirā'at al-Fātiḥah fī kulli rak'ah.

[6] Qur'ān 73:20.

[7] Ṣaḥīḥ Bukhārī: Kitāb al-shahādāt—Bāb al-shahādah 'alā al-ansāb wa al-raḍāʿ al-mustafīḍ; Kitāb farḍ al-khumus—Bāb mā jā'a fī buyūt azwāj al-nabī; Kitāb tafsīr al-Qur'ān—Bāb sūrah al-Aḥzāb; Kitāb al-nikāḥ—Bāb wa ummahātukum al-lātī; Kitāb al-nikāḥ—Bāb lā tunkiḥu al-mar'ah 'alā 'ammatihā; Kitāb al-nikāḥ—Bāb mā yuḥillu min al-dukhūl; Kitāb al-adab—Bāb qawl al-nabī taribat yamīnuk; Ṣaḥīḥ Muslim: Kitāb al-raḍāʿ—Bāb yaḥrumu min al-raḍāʿah mā yaḥrumu min al-wilādah.

[8] Qur'ān 4:23.

a woman and her maternal or paternal aunt at the same time' [9] *contradict the verse: {[Forbidden to you] is to have two sisters [as your wives] at one and the same time}* [10]*? Are there not so many similar examples?*

There is no contradiction in these examples at all, except for those who don't examine them deeply and rush to judgement instead. They fail to relate evidence and examples properly with one another or distinguish what is contradictory from what is merely different.

[9] Ṣaḥīḥ Bukhārī: Kitāb al-nikāḥ—Bāb lā tunkiḥu al-mar'ah 'alā 'ammatihā; Ṣaḥīḥ Muslim: Kitāb al-nikāḥ—Bāb taḥrīm al-jam' bayna al-mar'ah wa 'ammatihā aw khālatihā fī al-nikāḥ.

[10] Qur'ān 4:23.

Sunnah and Ḥadīth

What is the meaning of sunnah? The technical meaning of the term is the path in worship and religious affairs that was established by the Prophet ﷺ and then pursued by the Rightly Guided Caliphs, the rest of the Companions, and the leading figures in the generations that followed them.

And what is the meaning of ḥadīth? Technically, it is a report comprised of the words of the Prophet ﷺ, his actions, tacit approvals, personal characteristics, or other matters.

And what is the real connection between them? Is it a successive, sequential relationship, or an explanatory one in which one elaborates on the other? From one aspect, the relation between them is that of specification (i.e. general versus specific). In this way, some of the sunnah is also ḥadīth, while some ḥadīth is also sunnah. In other words, ḥadīth could be considered broader than sunnah in one way, while sunnah could be broader than ḥadīth in another.

In fact, much of what is reported concerning the Prophet's statements, actions, approvals or descriptions actually represent ḥadīth and not sunnah, while much of has been passed on by the early generation of jurists of various regions, in terms of practices concerning prayer, charity, pilgrimage, edicts and rulings, represent sunnah and not ḥadīth or reports.

Can you give us an example? Examples abound in books of ḥadīth and fiqh.

Three Examples of Sunnah

An example of sunnah is what Mālik relates from Ḥumayd al-Ṭawīl from Anas b. Mālik who said: I prayed behind Abū Bakr, ʿUmar and ʿUthmān, and none of them recited *bismillāh al-raḥmān al-raḥīm* when they began their prayers.[1] Bukhārī and Muslim, as well as other experts of ḥadīth, also related this.[2] It is

[1] Muwaṭṭaʾ: Kitāb al-ṣalāh—Bāb al-ʿamal fī al-qirāʾah.

[2] Bukhārī: Kitāb al-adhān—Bāb mā yaqūlu baʿda al-takbīr; Muslim: Kitāb al-ṣalāh—Bāb ḥujjah man qāla lā yujharu bi al-basmalah.

additionally supported by a ḥadīth of Abū Hurayrah in which he reports that the Prophet ﷺ said: God says: 'I have divided the prayer into two halves between Myself and My servant, and for my servant is what he asks for.' When the servant states, 'Praise belongs to God, Lord of the worlds,' God replies, 'My servant has praised me . . .'[3]

Another example of sunnah is what Yaḥyā b. Yaḥyā al-Laythī relates in the Muwaṭṭaʾ: I heard Mālik say concerning the six days of fasting after the Eid al-Fiṭr following Ramadan, 'I have not observed any person of knowledge and understanding fast these days, and such a report has not reached me from any of the early authorities. Rather, the people of knowledge considered the practice makrūh (detested) fearing that it would become an innovated practice or that ignorant ones would add to Ramadan that which did not belong to it.'[4]

Yet another example is that Abū Dāwūd relates from Ṭawūs, who said: I asked Ibn ʿUmar about praying two rakʿahs before Maghrib and he replied, 'I have not seen anyone in the era of the Prophet ﷺ pray these.'[5] ʿAbd al-Razzāq[6] relates in his Muṣannaf from Ibrāhīm al-Nakhaʿī who said: 'Neither Abū Bakr, nor ʿUmar, nor ʿUthmān ever prayed two rakʿahs before Maghrib.'[7]

[3] Ṣaḥīḥ Muslim: Kitāb al-ṣalāh—Bāb wujūb qirāʾat al-Fātiḥah fī kulli rakʿah.

[4] Muwaṭṭaʾ: Kitāb al-ṣiyyām. For elaboration, see Dr. Nadwi's article 'Fasting Six Days of Shawwal', UK: Al-Salam Institute. [https://alsalam.ac.uk/shawwal/]

[5] Sunan Abī Dāwūd: Kitāb al-ṣalāh—Bāb al-ṣalāh qabl al-Maghrib.

[6] ʿAbd al-Razzāq al-Ṣanʿānī (d. 211/826) was an early ḥadīth scholar of Yemen and author of many works, of which only the Muṣannaf survived.

[7] Muṣannaf ʿAbd al-Razzāq: Kitāb al-ṣalāh—Bāb al-rakʿatayn qabl al-Maghrib.

Three Examples of Ḥadīth

Examples of ḥadīth (which are not sunnah) include what was related by Nasā'ī in his Sunan:

BOOK OF OPENING PRAYER—CHAPTER: THE READING OF BISMILLĀH AL-RAḤMĀN AL-RAḤĪM Muḥammad b. ʿAbdullah b. ʿAbd al-Ḥakam informed us from Shuʿayb: Layth informed us: Khālid informed us from Saʿīd b. Abū Hilāl from Nuʿaym al-Mujmir, who said:

I prayed behind Abū Hurayrah, and he recited *bismillāh al-raḥmān al-raḥīm* and then recited al-Fātiḥah until he reached *ghayri al-maghḍūbi ʿalayhim wa lā al-ḍāllīn,* after which he said: *Āmīn,* and the people also said: *Āmīn.* And every time he prostrated he said: *Allāhu Akbar,* and whenever he got up from sitting after two rakʿahs, he said: *Allāhu Akbar.* And he said at the end of the prayer after salām, 'By the One in Whose Hand is my soul, my prayer most closely resembles that of the Prophet among you.'[8]

سنن النسائي - كتاب الافتتاح - باب قراءة بسم الله الرحمن الرحيم

أَخْبَرَنَا مُحَمَّدُ بْنُ عَبْدِ اللهِ بْنِ عَبْدِ الْحَكَمِ، عَنْ شُعَيْبٍ ، حَدَّثَنَا اللَّيْثُ، حَدَّثَنَا خَالِدٌ، عَنْ سَعِيدِ بْنِ أَبِي هِلَالٍ، عَنْ نُعَيْمٍ الْمُجْمِرِ، قَالَ: صَلَّيْتُ وَرَاءَ أَبِي هُرَيْرَةَ، فَقَرَأَ: بِسْمِ اللهِ الرَّحْمَنِ الرَّحِيمِ، ثُمَّ قَرَأَ بِأُمِّ الْقُرْآنِ، حَتَّى إِذَا بَلَغَ: غَيْرِ الْمَغْضُوبِ عَلَيْهِمْ وَلا الضَّالِّينَ، فَقَالَ: آمِينَ، فَقَالَ النَّاسُ: آمِينَ، وَيَقُولُ كُلَّمَا سَجَدَ: اللهُ أَكْبَرُ، وَإِذَا قَامَ مِنَ الْجُلُوسِ فِي الاِثْنَتَيْنِ قَالَ: اللهُ أَكْبَرُ، وَإِذَا سَلَّمَ قَالَ: وَالَّذِي نَفْسِي بِيَدِهِ إِنِّي لَأَشْبَهُكُمْ صَلَاةً بِرَسُولِ اللهِ صَلَّى اللهُ عَلَيْهِ وَسَلَّمَ.

Another example is that which Muslim narrated in his Ṣaḥīḥ:

[8] Sunan al-Nasā'ī: Kitāb al-iftitāḥ—Bāb qirāʿat bismillāh al-Raḥmān al-Raḥīm.

BOOK OF FASTING—CHAPTER: RECOMMENDATION OF FASTING SIX DAYS OF SHAWWĀL FOLLOWING RAMADAN Yaḥyā b. Ayyūb, Qutaybah b. Saʿīd and ʿAlī b. Ḥujr all reported to me: from Ismāʿīl: Ibn Ayyūb said: Ismāʿīl b. Jaʿfar related to us: Saʿd b. Saʿīd b. Qays related to me from ʿUmar b. Thābit b. al-Ḥārith al-Khazrajī from Abū Ayyūb al-Anṣārī, God be pleased with him, who related to him that the Prophet ﷺ said: 'Whoever fasts Ramadan, then follows that with six from [the month of] Shawwāl would be as if he fasted for a lifetime.'[9]

صحيح مسلم - كتاب الصيام - باب استحباب صوم ستة أيام من شوال إتباعا لرمضان حَدَّثَنَا يَحْيَى بْنُ أَيُّوبَ، وَقُتَيْبَةُ بْنُ سَعِيدٍ، وَعَلِيُّ بْنُ حُجْرٍ، جَمِيعًا عَنْ إِسْمَاعِيلَ، قَالَ ابْنُ أَيُّوبَ: حَدَّثَنَا إِسْمَاعِيلُ بْنُ جَعْفَرٍ، أَخْبَرَنِي سَعْدُ بْنُ سَعِيدِ بْنِ قَيْسٍ، عَنْ عُمَرَ بْنِ ثَابِتِ بْنِ الْحَارِثِ الْخَزْرَجِيِّ، عَنْ أَبِي أَيُّوبَ الْأَنْصَارِيِّ رَضِيَ اللهُ عَنْهُ أَنَّهُ حَدَّثَهُ أَنَّ رَسُولَ اللهِ صَلَّى اللهُ عَلَيْهِ وَسَلَّمَ قَالَ: مَنْ صَامَ رَمَضَانَ، ثُمَّ أَتْبَعَهُ سِتًّا مِنْ شَوَّالٍ، كَانَ كَصِيَامِ الدَّهْرِ.

Yet another example is what Muslim narrated:

BOOK OF PRAYER OF THE TRAVELER AND ITS SHORTENING—CHAPTER: TWO RAKʿAHS OF PRAYER BEFORE MAGHRIB Shaybān

صحيح مسلم - كتاب صلاة المسافرين وقصرها - باب استحباب ركعتين قبل صلاة المغرب

[9] Ṣaḥīḥ Muslim: Kitāb al-ṣiyām—Bāb istiḥbāb ṣawm sittah min shawwāl ittibāʿan li Ramaḍān. Should the question arise, it should be noted that the chapter headings of Ṣaḥīḥ Muslim are not from Imām Muslim but added by later commentators, such as Nawawī, and do not necessarily reflect Muslim's conclusions.

b. Farrūkh narrated to us: ʿAbd al-Wārith narrated to us from ʿAbd al-ʿAzīz (and he is Ibn Suhayb) from Anas b. Mālik who said: When we were in Madīnah, the moment the Muʾadhdhin made the call to the sunset prayer, the people hastened to the pillars of the mosque and prayed two rakʿahs with the result that any stranger coming into the mosque would think that the obligatory prayer had been observed owing to the number who were praying then.[10]

وَحَدَّثَنَا شَيْبَانُ بْنُ فَرُّوخَ، حَدَّثَنَا عَبْدُ الْوَارِثِ، عَنْ عَبْدِ الْعَزِيزِ وَهُوَ ابْنُ صُهَيْبٍ، عَنْ أَنَسِ بْنِ مَالِكٍ قَالَ: كُنَّا بِالْمَدِينَةِ، فَإِذَا أَذَّنَ الْمُؤَذِّنُ لِصَلَاةِ الْمَغْرِبِ ابْتَدَرُوا السَّوَارِيَ فَيَرْكَعُونَ رَكْعَتَيْنِ رَكْعَتَيْنِ، حَتَّى إِنَّ الرَّجُلَ الْغَرِيبَ لَيَدْخُلُ الْمَسْجِدَ فَيَحْسِبُ أَنَّ الصَّلَاةَ قَدْ صُلِّيَتْ مِنْ كَثْرَةِ مَنْ يُصَلِّيهِمَا.

Another is what Bukhārī relates:

BOOK OF TAHAJJUD—CHAPTER: PRAYING BEFORE MAGHRIB Abū Maʿmar related to us: ʿAbd al-Wārith related to us from Ḥusayn from ʿAbdullah b. Buraydah who said: ʿAbdullah al-Muzanī related to me from the Prophet ﷺ who said: ‘Pray before the Maghrib prayer.’ He said it three times, and in the third, he added, ‘for whoever wants to do so,’ fearing that people would take it as a sunnah practice.[11]

صحيح البخاري - أبواب التهجد - باب الصلاة قبل المغرب

حَدَّثَنَا أَبُو مَعْمَرٍ: حَدَّثَنَا عَبْدُ الْوَارِثِ، عَنِ الْحُسَيْنِ، عَنِ ابْنِ بُرَيْدَةَ قَالَ: حَدَّثَنِي عَبْدُ اللهِ الْمُزَنِيُّ عَنِ النَّبِيِّ صَلَّى اللهُ عَلَيْهِ وَسَلَّمَ قَالَ: صَلُّوا قَبْلَ صَلَاةِ الْمَغْرِبِ. قَالَ فِي الثَّالِثَةِ: لِمَنْ شَاءَ. كَرَاهِيَةَ أَنْ يَتَّخِذَهَا النَّاسُ سُنَّةً.

---

[10] Ṣaḥīḥ Muslim: Kitāb ṣalāh al-musāfirīn wa qaṣrihā—Bāb istiḥbāb rakʿatayn qabl ṣalāh al-Maghrib. Also related in Ṣaḥīḥ Bukhārī: Kitāb al-ṣalāh—Bāb al-ṣalāh ilā al-ustuwānah; Kitāb al-adhān—Bāb kam bayna al-adhān wa al-iqāmah.

[11] Ṣaḥīḥ Bukhārī: Kitāb al-tahajjud—Bāb al-ṣalāh qabl al-Maghrib; Kitāb al-Iʿtiṣām bi al-kitāb wa al-sunnah—Bāb nahy al-nabī ʿalā al-taḥrīm.

When Ḥadīth Clashes with Sunnah

If a ḥadīth clashes with a sunnah, which of them do we prefer? The sunnah takes priority over ḥadīth. The examples we related of the sunnah are prioritized over the ḥadīth that we have reported.

Does that not necessitate that we reject sound reports without justification? No, because the sunnah represents an elaboration of the Book of God and the continuing, inherited tradition passed on from one generation to another, among the golden centuries. Ḥadīth and other reports that conflict with the sunnah, despite their authenticity, carry the possibility of being abrogated, containing errors or alternate interpretations.

Did any of the guided Imāms speak of this? Yes, for in *Tartīb al-Madārik*, Mālik states: I have seen Muḥammad b. Abū Bakr b. ʿAmr b. Ḥazm, who was a judge and whose brother ʿAbdullah happened to be a ḥadīth scholar with prolific reports and a truthful person. I observed that whenever his brother Muḥammad issued a verdict which happened to clash with a ḥadīth, ʿAbdullah would criticize him by saying, 'Isn't there such and such ḥadīth on this issue?' Muḥammad would reply, 'Yes.' ʿAbdullah would ask, 'So why do you not base your verdict on it?' Muḥammad would reply, 'Where do the people stand in relation to this? (meaning what was the consensus of the scholars of Madīnah)'.

Ibn al-Muʿadhdhal says on this issue: I heard a person ask Ibn Mājishūn, 'Why do you sometimes relate a ḥadīth but not act upon it?' He replied, 'So it would be known that I am upon inherited knowledge.' Ibn Rabīʿah said: 'A thousand from a thousand is better than one from one' (i.e., there is strength in numbers).[12] Something similar is related from Ibrāhīm al-Nakhaʿī and Mālik b. Anas, God be pleased with them both.

There are people that consider ḥadīth and sunnah to be synonymous. They may have done so but are not correct. They have greatly harmed fiqh and the way of the jurists.

Can you explain that more clearly? It is forthcoming in the chapter "Between Ḥadīth and Fiqh."

[12] *Tartīb al-madārik*, vol 1, pg 45-6.

CHAPTER 3: SUNNAH AND ḤADĪTH

Do we need ḥadīth to verify the sunnah? Yes. Whenever people ascribe a sunnah to the Prophet ﷺ or his Companions, then it is obligatory to verify that with various means, which include but is not limited to the methodology of the ḥadīth scholars.

Ḥadīth and Philosophy

Clarify for us the real difference between ḥadīth and philosophy. If you are really concerned about this question, know that success from your Lord is close at hand. It is a formidable question but also quite worthy. Not knowing the difference between ḥadīth and philosophy produces gross absurdities and risks great falsehood. Individuals begin to treat ḥadīth as philosophy and place philosophy in the position of ḥadīth, weighing one with the scale of the other. As a result, they are not able to find any real way to distinguish historical reports from philosophical speculation. And how can the truth possibly clarify the firmness of its pillars and the sturdiness of its foundations when scales are muddled, parameters confused and standards unknown?

We are confused as to why that would lead to absurdity, so please explain. Ḥadīth is essentially a type of historical report (khabar), which is one person informing another of the reality of something he saw with his own eyes or heard with his own ears. These reports are related from specific realities (ḥaqāʾiq), which are either seen, heard or otherwise known through the senses.

Philosophy, on the other hand, represents conclusions or premises that are arrived at by practicing analogical reasoning (qiyās) or pursuing the process of deductive reasoning. The philosopher does not inform based upon what he has heard with his own ears or seen by his own eyes, but rather, through what he has 'seen' through his own reasoning and thought processes.

Tell us the difference between ascertaining the veracity of a report versus arriving at a correct philosophical view. The basic way to verify the soundness of a report is to ascertain that the informer (the source of the report) is:

1. truthful and trustworthy in what he has seen or heard, and
2. precise in that reporting.[1]

---

[1] These correspond to the two mainstay requirements for accepting a ḥadīth narrator according to the principles of ḥadīth science: moral uprightness (ʿadālah) and accuracy (ḍabṭ). Specifically, in this context,

The sound report, therefore, is the transmission of a reality in a way that is free of untruths, mistakes or whims.

The path to validate the soundness of a philosophical view, on the other hand, is to verify that it is logical and attained from certain premises arranged in a particular order. What the philosopher posits is not reality itself but, rather, his own understanding of that reality and his deduction therefrom.

Please provide us examples that will lift the veil from the issue and remove the confusion. When a person states, 'Allah says in the Qur'ān, {*He Allah is One*};[2] and {*Is not Allah the best of judges?*}'[3] then this is his report from what he has read in the Book of Allah. What is required from him is simply to be truthful in his reporting.

When another says, on the other hand, that 'Allah is necessarily existent'; or 'Existence is one without being divided into necessary and possible'; or yet another says, 'The right to rule is the most particular distinction of Godhood,'[4] then these are all philosophical statements. What is required from their speakers is that they be logical in what they say and have determined their deductions through rational evidence and sound intellectual precepts.

When a person says that the Prophet migrated from Makkah to Madīnah, then that is a report. When another says that he migrated in order to establish a state, then that is a philosophical statement whose proof is not the same as the proof of the first.

When someone narrates from the Prophet ﷺ the following ḥadīth, for instance:

> By the One, besides Whom there is no other god, verily one of you performs the actions of the people of Paradise until there is but an arm's length between him and it, and that which has been written overtakes him, and so he acts with the actions of the people of the Hellfire and thus enters it; and verily one of you performs the actions of the people

---

it means that the reporter has a basic level of moral fortitude to ensure that he is truthful about his reporting, and the ability to be precise and not mistaken in his reporting (either through proficient memory or accurate written notes).

[2] Qur'ān 112:1.

[3] Qur'ān 95:8.

[4] *Ulūhiyyah*, or "Godhood," is the concept of God's exclusive right to be worshipped.

of the Hellfire, until there is but an arm's length between him and it, and that which has been written overtakes him and so he acts with the actions of the people of Paradise and thus he enters it.[5]

then this is a report. But if one says that a human being is compelled and driven, without any desire or will of his own, then this is philosophy.

What is the absurdity that you alluded to? It is the absurdity of scholastic theologians, many Sufis and jurists, and most of the rationalist followers of the Orientalists[6] and those intruding on their stained and dirty tables. They reject ḥadīth on the basis that they are not logical, though they be sound according to ḥadīth experts, having fulfilled abundant and multiple conditions for the soundness of reports. Some of them reject the ḥadīth concerning Divine attributes and unseen matters on the basis that they contradict their forged principles. Others reject ḥadīth that contradict some of their own deductions, principles and precepts. And others absolved themselves of ḥadīth entirely because they clash with their artificial schools of thought, their whims, the monasticism they invented, or the extremism they stole or borrowed from outside the Muslim tradition.

Many of these people have authenticated reports solely based on the soundness or validity of their meanings and content, though they may be weak or fabricated in their chains. Their philosophizing is captured by this statement of theirs: 'This ḥadīth is weak in chain but sound in meaning.'[7] This represents weighing reports through the scale of philosophy. It is a silly and vile statement, in fact, one of the worst. It is not anyone's right to attribute a statement to the Prophet ﷺ except through a sound chain of transmission that is acceptable to the leaders of this discipline: the capable, brilliant and reliable experts of ḥadīth. A statement being sound in meaning does not make it a ḥadīth of the Prophet ﷺ. How many insightful statements come from philosophers and wise men, or even

---

[5] Ṣaḥīḥ Bukhārī: Kitāb bad' al-khalq—Bāb dhikr al-malā'ikah; Kitāb aḥādīth al-anbiyā'—Bāb qawl Allah wa idh qāla rabbuka li al-malā'ikah; Kitāb al-qadr—Bāb fī al-qadr; Kitāb al-tawḥīd—Bāb qawuluhū walaqad sabaqat kalimatunā; Ṣaḥīḥ Muslim: Kitāb al-qadr—Bāb kayfyah khalq al-ādamī fī baṭn ummihī.

[6] Orientalist is the term used to denote Western scholars who study the East, or "Orient," though it is used primarily for those who studied the Muslim and Arab world through Eurocentric lens.

[7] This statement is quite common among contemporary Muslim scholars and teachers, even making its way into textbooks of certain Islamic universities.

from the other prophets and messengers, and yet our own Prophet ﷺ did not utter them? We do not attribute these to the Prophet ﷺ by virtue of their being the highest wisdom or the soundest meaning. In fact, it has been mass-transmitted from him that he said: 'Whoever attributes to me that which I did not say, let him take his seat in the Fire.'[8]

And there is the statement in His Book: ﴾*And who is more unjust than the one who invented a lie upon God?*﴿[9] There is no doubt that the one who lied upon the Prophet has lied against God.

What do you say concerning the content-criticism of ḥadīth texts? This is a statement of truth by which falsehood is intended. Orientalist scholars popularized it, and many naïve Muslims also accepted it, deliberately or unwittingly. They philosophized ḥadīth and took the idea of textual criticism as a means to reject that which didn't correspond to their whims and diseased tastes. Moreover, they differ greatly among themselves in this alleged critique of theirs, according to various aims, inclinations, and desires. So one "thinker" rejects a group of ḥadīth reports, while another rejects an entirely different portion, with clashing thought processes and conflicting methodologies. They belittle knowledge and guidance, while playing with their own intellects and those of others.

Did not the scholars of reports and historians reject many reports on the basis that they were impossible or unlikely? Of course.

So why didn't the ḥadīth scholars know this principle? They knew it well and implemented it practically, in a manner that amazed the people of knowledge and reinforced their confidence in the principles and craft of ḥadīth experts, with a confidence that approached the level accorded to miracles. They considered some ḥadīth weak based upon their anomalous or contradictory nature, but they did not deviate from objectivity nor did they philosophize matters as others had done. Few are the ḥadīth that are ṣaḥīḥ in their chains while being anomalously transmitted or contradictory in their meanings. Whenever such a matter is found

[8] This represents, according to ḥadīth scholars, the most authentic ḥadīth report on record. It is widely narrated from the Prophet through multiple concurrent channels of transmission, through more chains and routes than any other ḥadīth. See Ṣaḥīḥ Bukhārī: Kitāb al-ʿilm—Bāb ithm man kadhaba ʿalā al-nabī; Kitāb al-janāʾiz—Bāb mā yukrahu min al-niyāḥah ʿalā al-mayyit; Kitāb al-adab—Bāb man summiya bi asmāʾ al-anbiyāʾ; Ṣaḥīḥ Muslim: Muqaddimah—Bāb fī taḥdhīr min al-kadhib ʿalā rasūl Allah.

[9] This appears at least 9 times in the Qurʾān: 6:21, 6:93, 6:144, 7:37, 10:17, 11:18, 18:15, 29:68, 61:7.

in a ṣaḥīḥ ḥadīth it is usually due to a mistake or false assumption on the part of some of the narrators. And who is the one who has never made a mistake? These mistakes are exceedingly rare, even though in some of these instances there are explanations that have fully satisfied certain scholars.

Ḥadīth and Fiqh

Now that we are able to distinguish between the true nature of ḥadīth and philosophy, recognize the scales and parameters of each, please reveal to us the true difference between ḥadīth and fiqh, removing some confusions and misperceptions concerning them.

Ḥadīth are historical reports, while fiqh represents law and philosophy. Ḥadīth in its technical usage is a reporting of the words of the Prophet ﷺ, his actions, approvals, characteristics, or any other matter concerning him. It is also applied to the reports of the Companions and Followers. Fiqh in its lexical usage is knowledge of the practical rulings of the Sharīʿah as deduced from their detailed evidence from the Qurʾān, Prophetic Sunnah, inherited practices, scholarly consensus (ijmāʿ), universal maxims (qawāʿid kulliyah), and the process of analogical deduction (qiyās).

Ḥadīth has its own particular methodology for verification while fiqh has one that resembles philosophy. If you want to know, for instance, about the Battle of Badr, or the description of the Prophet's prayer, or his Ḥajj, you need to establish that through the method of the historians, which is exactly what the ḥadīth scholars did. In fact, ḥadīth experts even surpassed historians in diligence, caution, precision, and accuracy. That is all laid out in the Risālah of Imām Shāfiʿī, the Muqaddimah of Imām Muslim, and other books of ḥadīth sciences.

If you want to know, on the other hand, about the pillars of ṣalāh or its recommended acts, you would need to establish those by proving them from the Qurʾān—specifically, its textual evidences and those of its evidences that are general, inferred or necessitated—and from the practices transmitted from the Prophet to the Companions and Followers, from the consensus of jurists, from the legal maxims which were relied upon by the pious scholars of ijtihād, and from analogical deduction based on finding common rationales and similarities.

Do we need ḥadīth for fiqh? Yes, you would need it if you were to ascribe a statement or view to the past, because in that case it would become a historical report, and the methodology of ḥadīth scholars is best suited for determining the veracity of historical reports. In addition, fiqh would also require an understanding of the Qur'ān, language, medicine, and economics. It would be necessary for the jurist to refer to scholars of tafsīr if the meaning of a verse proved difficult, or to scholars of ḥadīth if there were a need to establish the veracity of a report, or to scholars of language if some Arabic words or expressions appeared problematic. A jurist would also need to refer to physicians if a problem concerning medicine of the physical body were presented to them, or to economists if the issue were one concerning financial matters.

Is it correct to oppose a fiqh ruling with ḥadīth? This matter requires further elaboration. If a jurist built a ruling on evidence from the Qur'ān, transmitted Sunnah, and juristic maxims and principles, then it would not be correct to oppose that with a ḥadīth or report, because ḥadīth and other reports would be in that case peripheral matters that can contain mistakes or ambiguity.

Is it okay to oppose fiqh with reports of trustworthy narrators then? No, because even the trustworthy narrators can err and make mistakes, and because sound reports can carry multiple possibilities [of meaning and application], or even be abrogated. So such reports cannot reach the level where they could nullify rulings.

What is the other side of this explanation? If a jurist had built a ruling on a ḥadīth report and possessed no other evidence—neither from the Qur'ān, Sunnah, transmitted practice or legal maxim—then in that case it could be correct to oppose that with a stronger ḥadīth. In this case, it would be obligatory on the jurist to rely on the principles of ḥadīth scholars in authenticating reports.

Why do later jurists insist on explaining the principles of ḥadīth according to their schools? They are mistaken in that, and I have explained their error in the chapter on principles of ḥadīth according to the Ḥanafī School.

How would we defend the Ḥanafī school when ḥadīth scholars oppose it through ḥadīth? The Ḥanafī school of jurisprudence does not need us to defend it. Rather, we first need to study it deeply in order to fully understand it, and then to present it to others without any distortion, amendment or apology.

Is it warranted for a ḥadīth scholar to talk about fiqh? No, unless they reached the level of expertise of jurists. There were only a few such scholars that combined ḥadīth and fiqh with proficiency, such as Sufyān al-Thawrī (d. 161/778),[1] Mālik and Bukhārī.

So what do you say about ḥadīth scholars that opposed jurists? They were mistaken in that. Let everyone—jurists, ḥadīth experts, tafsīr scholars, grammarians, physicians, economists—confine themselves to their discipline without crossing its bounds.

[1] Sufyān b. Saʿīd b. Masrūq al-Thawrī was a great Kūfan jurist known also for his mastery of ḥadīth sciences, earning him the title 'Amīr al-muʾminīn fī al-ḥadīth.'

Ḥadīth Preservation

It has become a widespread belief among certain scholars and researchers that ḥadīth was preserved only after the second century. This represents a gross ignorance of history. It is possible that this misunderstanding was partly motivated by the report of Bukhārī in which the Caliph ʿUmar b. ʿAbd al-ʿAzīz (d. 101/720) wrote to Abū Bakr b. Ḥazm:[1] 'Search out the ḥadīth of the Prophet ﷺ and write them down, for I fear the decline of knowledge and scholarship.'[2]

The truth is that ʿUmar was seeking to gather and collect ḥadīth reports from the memories and personal writings of scholars into one compilation, as we will expound on later. Prior to this period of official documentation, ḥadīth reports were preserved through memory and various written collections. It is well known that preservation and official documentation are two different matters.

Preserving Ḥadīth Through Memory

Arabs were known for their strong memories, to the point that many of them became renowned for accurately preserving their lineage for generations, some of them even the lineage of their camels and horses. They were known for long odes of poetry, stories and anecdotes. When Islam came to them, these same faculties were used to preserve the reports of their Prophet ﷺ, which represented the foundation of their faith and source of their guidance. They used to listen to his words and speeches and ask him when something was not clear to them. They did this in compliance with the Qurʾānic command: ﴾*Ask the people who possess knowledge if you do not know.*﴿ [3]

---

[1] Abū Bakr b. Muḥammad b. ʿAmr b. Ḥazm al-Anṣārī was a jurist of the Followers whom ʿUmar b. ʿAbd al-ʿAzīz appointed as judge and governor of Madīnah. He died in 120 AH at the age of 84 during the reign of Hishām b. ʿAbd al-Malik.

[2] Ṣaḥīḥ Bukhārī: Kitāb al-ʿilm—Bāb kayfa yuqbaḍu al-ʿilm. This is a muʿallaq, or isnād-less, report, which represents a lower-tier of soundness among the corpus of Ṣaḥīḥ Bukhārī.

[3] Qurʾān 16:43, 21:7.

Inquiry is the key to learning. Zuhrī (d. 124/742)[4] stated: 'Knowledge has many treasures which are only opened by inquiry.'[5] Abū al-ʿĀliyah (d. 90/708)[6] used to say to his neighbor: 'Ask me questions and write down my ḥadīth reports, before you start searching for them from others and not find them.'[7] Ibn Sīrīn used to say: 'Know that knowledge is locked and the keys are asking questions.'[8]

Most senior Companions were well-known to have memorized ḥadīth, including the four Rightly-Guided Caliphs, Ibn Masʿūd, Ubayy b. Kaʿb, ʿĀʾishah, Muʿādh b. Jabal, Abū al-Dardāʾ, Ibn ʿUmar, Abū Hurayrah, Ibn ʿAbbās, Abū Mūsā al-Ashʿarī, Abū Saʿīd al-Khudrī, Jābir b. ʿAbdullah, and Anas b. Malik. There were also many to do so from subsequent generations, from which I will share some illustrations of their renowned memories.

Ḥammād b. Zayd (d. 179/795)[9] relates from ʿAmr b ʿUbayd from Abū al-Zuʿayziʿah the secretary of the Umayyad governor Marwān b. Ḥakam that Marwān asked Abū Hurayra to narrate ḥadīth while secretly recording it from behind a curtain.[10] Later on, after some time, they tested him by asking him to repeat those ḥadīth while the secretary sat behind a curtain again. He was found to repeat all ḥadīth without adding or detracting anything, even sticking to the same order. Imām Dhahabī commented, 'This is real memory.'[11]

Hishām b. ʿAmmār related that al-Walid related to him from Saʿīd that the Caliph Hishām b ʿAbd al-Malik asked Zuhrī to dictate ḥadīth to some of his sons. Zuhrī dictated 400 ḥadīth reports from his memory. After leaving the Caliph, Zuhrī sought out other ḥadīth students and dictated to them these same reports. After a month or so, Zuhrī met the Caliph Hishām again, who complained that he lost that book in which he had written down the ḥadīth.

---

[4] Great ḥadīth expert of Madīnah who was among Mālik's teachers and counted among the six pillars of ḥadīth (madār al-ḥadīth) among the junior Followers.

[5] Al-Rāmahurmuzī, *Al-muḥaddith al-fāṣil*, pg 360.

[6] Abū al-ʿĀliyah al-Riyāḥī Rafīʿ b. Mahrān of Baṣrah (d. 90/708) was a noted early Qurʾānic scholar who read the Qurʾān to Ubayy, Zayd b. Thābit, and Ibn ʿAbbās. It is even said that he recited to ʿUmar. Those who recited to him included Shuʿayb b. Ḥabḥāb, Rabīʿ b. Anas, and Aʿmash.

[7] *Al-muḥaddith al-fāṣil*, pg 360.

[8] Ibid.

[9] Ḥammād b. Zayd was a Persian-origin ḥadīth expert of Baṣrah, Iraq.

[10] Abū Hurayrah did not like his ḥadīth to be written.

[11] al-Dhahabī, *Siyar Aʿlām al-Nubalāʾ*, vol 2, pg 598.

Zuhrī said, 'Don't worry,' and asked for a book and dictated those reports again. Hishām later found his first book, and, after comparing the dictated reports, commented 'He did not miss a single letter.'[12]

Mughīrah b. Miqsam al-Ḍabbī (d. 133/750)[13] stated: 'It never happened that my ears heard something and then I forgot it.' Dhahabī comments on this: 'By God, this is real memory and retention, which doesn't come from studying a book multiple times in order to present it, only to stumble over it, and then having to re-study it in order to memorize it again, only to forget it, or most of it, yet again.'[14]

Abū Bakr b. Shādhān relates that Abū Bakr the son of Abū Dāwūd was visiting Sijistān [sic][15] for some business. When he was asked to narrate ḥadīth, he responded that he did not bring his books. They insisted by saying: 'Does the son of Abū Dāwūd need books?' This excited him and he eventually obliged and wound up narrating 30,000 ḥadīth from his memory. Some in Baghdad were jealous and hired a courier for six dinārs to go to Sijistān and write a copy of all the ḥadīth that were dictated, and bring them back to Baghdad to compare them with the original notes with the ḥadīth experts. Abū Bakr states that they found only six mistakes, three of them his own and three from his teacher (who had dictated them wrong).[16]

There is also an interesting anecdote that reveals the extent of this phenomenon of memorizing ḥadīth among even laypersons. Ibn al-Jawzī (d. 597/1201)[17] relates in his work al-Adhkiyā᾿ that Naṣr b ʿAlī al-Jahḍamī of Baṣrah stated:[18]

---

[12] Al-Fasawī, *Al-maʿrifah wa al-tārīkh*, vol 1, pg 640.

[13] Great jurist, ḥadīth scholar, and junior Follower from Kūfah, who was a student of Ḥammād, Ibrāhīm al-Nakhaʿī, Shaʿbī, and Mujāhid. He was blind and known for his photographic memory. He was deemed trustworthy by Yaḥyā b. Maʿīn and accused of tadlīs by others.

[14] *Siyar,* vol 6, pg 11.

[15] There are two accounts of this story referencing a visit to either Isfahan or Sijistān, but the former is correct.

[16] *Siyar,* vol 13, pg 224-5.

[17] ʿAbd al-Raḥmān b. ʿAlī b. Muḥammad was a Ḥanbalī jurist, scholar and judge from Baghdad who happens to be probably the single most prolific author in our tradition, as Dhahabī affirmed: 'I have not known anyone amongst the scholars to have written as much as he did.'

[18] An analysis of this incident served as the inspiration for al-Khaṭīb al-Baghdādī's humorous work *Al-taṭfīl wa ḥikāyat al-ṭufayliyyīn,* translated by Emily Selove as *The Art of Party-Crashing in Medieval Iraq.*

I had a neighbor who was a party crasher (ṭufaylī),[19] and he was one of the best-looking and best-spoken people, and the best-perfumed and most finely-dressed as well. It was his custom to follow me when I was invited to a gathering, and people did honors to him on my account because they assume that he was my friend.

So it came to happen that Jaʿfar b. al-Qāsim al-Hāshimī, prince of Baṣrah, wanted to celebrate the circumcision of one of his sons, and I said to myself, 'I'm probably going to get an invitation from the Prince, and this man is probably going to follow me again. By God, if he follows me this time, I'm really going to teach him a lesson!'

And I was like that right up until the arrival of the messenger with the invitation.

No sooner had I put on my robe and stepped out the door but I saw the party-crasher waiting for me by the gate of his house, ready to go. I set off, and he followed me. After we entered the prince's house, we sat for a while, and then the food was called out and tables brought, and everybody was pressed around the table because there were so many people.

I proceeded to one of the tables with the party-crasher on my heels, but just as he reached out his hand and began to grab the food, I said: 'Durust b. Ziyād related to us from Abān b. Ṭāriq from Nāfiʿ from Ibn ʿUmar that the Prophet ﷺ said, *He who enters a gathering to which he was not invited and eats their food enters as a thief and leaves as a looter.*'

When he heard that he said, 'By God, I thumb my nose at you, Abū ʿAmr! And there is not one man among this crowd but thinks that you just insinuated something about him! Aren't you ashamed to talk like that at the very table of he who feeds the people, and to

[19] The art of party-crashing earned its name from Ṭufayl b. Zallāl, a famous figure of the Ghaṭafān clan in Kūfah who used to attend parties uninvited, for which he became famous and became known as 'Ṭufayl al-ʿarāʾis' ('Ṭufayl of the parties'). The notion of party crashing was thus named after him. It is also said that his father would carry food out from parties, so this notion was named after the father (zallah). Thus, party-crashing came from the son, sneaking food out from the father.

play the miser with food that isn't even yours? And aren't you ashamed to cite the unreliable ḥadīth transmitter Durust b. Ziyād on the authority of Abān b. Ṭāriq, who is unreliable as well? And yet on his authority you pass judgments that go against the Prophet himself—for the thief's punishment is cutting of the hands and the looter's is as the imām sees fit—but according to this ḥadīth related to us by Abū ʿĀṣim al-Nabīl, on the authority of Ibn Jurayj, on the authority of Abū al-Zubayr, on the authority of Jābir, that the Prophet ﷺ said: *Food for one is enough for two, and food for two is enough for four, and food for four is enough for eight*. And this is a sound isnād.'

Naṣr b. ʿAlī said, 'I was dumbfounded, and no reply came to my mind. When we left the party, he crossed to the other side of the street after he had been walking behind me, and I heard him say:

'He who thinks to begin a war
and suffer no harm, think again!'"[20]

Preserving Ḥadīth Through Writing

At the same time, it is a fact that not every individual is endowed with strong memory, and so the majority of people must rely on writing for their knowledge. Muʿāwiyah b. Qurrah stated: 'Whoever does not write knowledge down will never be considered a true scholar.'[21] Ismaʿīl b. ʿAbd al-Malik relates: 'I was sitting with ʿAṭāʾ b. Abī Rabāḥ when someone came and narrated a ḥadīth, and he immediately informed his son to write it down.'[22] Sufyān al-Thawrī relates from Manṣūr that he said to the great jurist Ibrāhīm al-Nakhaʿī: 'The ḥadīth of Sālim b. Abī Jadd are more complete than yours.' He replied: 'That is because he used to write them down.'[23]

---

[20] Al-Khaṭīb, *al-Taṭfīl*, vol 1, pg 126-7. Translation taken from *The Art of Party-Crashing*, pg 114-7.

[21] Abū Nuʿaym, *Ḥilyat al-Awliyāʾ*: Tarjumat Muʿāwiyah; Sunan al-Dārimī: Muqaddimah—Bāb man rakhaṣa fī kitābat al-ʿilm.

[22] *Al-muḥaddith al-fāṣil*, pg 371.

[23] Sunan al-Dārimī: Muqaddimah—Bāb man lam yara kitābat al-ḥadīth.

CHAPTER 6: ḤADĪTH PRESERVATION

Ḥadīth was written down in the time of the Companions, and even in the lifetime of the Prophet ﷺ. The Qur'ān is filled with the notions of reading (qirā'ah), writing, and the pen. The Prophet did stop his Companions from writing down his ḥadīth in the early days of Islam so that they would not muddle that with the Qur'ān. However, when the Qur'ānic style and its unique way of expression became more established, he allowed them to write down ḥadīth reports.

There is an abundance of evidence that prove the writing of ḥadīth in his lifetime. The Prophet sent letters and documents to neighboring kings and to his governors and workers. Many of these contain details of charity and the penal code (such as the rules of qiṣāṣ and blood money). Similarly, some of his sermons were written down. Abū Hurayrah reports the following:

BOOK OF LOST THINGS—CHAPTER: HOW LOST ITEMS IN MAKKAH ARE MADE KNOWN

Yaḥyā b. Mūsā reported to us: al-Walīd b. Muslim reported to us: Awzāʿī reported to us: Yaḥyā b. Abī Kathīr reported to me: Abū Salamah b. ʿAbd al-Raḥmān reported to me: Abū Hurayrah reported to me:

When God granted victory to His Prophet over the people of Makkah, he stood up among the people and, after praising God and glorifying Him, said: 'Surely, God had prevented the elephants from entering Makkah, and now has given authority to His Messenger and the believers over it. Fighting was previously forbidden for anyone before me and was made permissible for me for a part of the day, and it will not be allowed for anyone after me. Its game should not be chased, its thorny bushes should not be uprooted, and picking up its fallen things is not allowed except for one who makes public announcement for it. He whose relative is murdered has the option either to accept a compensation for it or to retaliate.'

ʿAbbās said, 'Except *idhkhir* (a type of grass), for we use it in our graves and houses?' The Prophet affirmed: 'Except *idhkhir*.' Abu Shāh of Yemen stood up and said, 'O Messenger of God, write it for me!' The Prophet ordered, 'Write it for Abu Shāh.'

صحيح البخاري - كتاب في اللقطة - باب كيف تعرف لقطة أهل مكة

حَدَّثَنَا يَحْيَى بْنُ مُوسَى: حَدَّثَنَا الْوَلِيدُ بْنُ مُسْلِمٍ: حَدَّثَنَا الْأَوْزَاعِيُّ قَالَ: حَدَّثَنِي يَحْيَى بْنُ أَبِي كَثِيرٍ قَالَ: حَدَّثَنِي أَبُو سَلَمَةَ بْنُ عَبْدِ الرَّحْمَنِ قَالَ: حَدَّثَنِي أَبُو هُرَيْرَةَ رَضِيَ اللهُ عَنْهُ قَالَ: لَمَّا فَتَحَ اللهُ عَلَى رَسُولِهِ صَلَّى اللهُ عَلَيْهِ وَسَلَّمَ مَكَّةَ، قَامَ فِي النَّاسِ، فَحَمِدَ اللهَ وَأَثْنَى عَلَيْهِ، ثُمَّ قَالَ: إِنَّ اللهَ حَبَسَ عَنْ مَكَّةَ الْفِيلَ وَسَلَّطَ عَلَيْهَا رَسُولَهُ وَالْمُؤْمِنِينَ، فَإِنَّهَا لَا تَحِلُّ لِأَحَدٍ كَانَ قَبْلِي، وَإِنَّهَا أُحِلَّتْ لِي سَاعَةً مِنْ نَهَارٍ، وَإِنَّهَا لَا تَحِلُّ لِأَحَدٍ بَعْدِي، فَلَا يُنَفَّرُ صَيْدُهَا، وَلَا يُخْتَلَى شَوْكُهَا، وَلَا تَحِلُّ سَاقِطَتُهَا إِلَّا لِمُنْشِدٍ، وَمَنْ قُتِلَ لَهُ قَتِيلٌ فَهُوَ بِخَيْرِ النَّظَرَيْنِ: إِمَّا أَنْ يُفْدَى وَإِمَّا أَنْ يُقِيدَ فَقَالَ الْعَبَّاسُ: إِلَّا الْإِذْخِرَ، فَإِنَّا نَجْعَلُهُ لِقُبُورِنَا وَبُيُوتِنَا. فَقَالَ رَسُولُ اللهِ صَلَّى اللهُ عَلَيْهِ وَسَلَّمَ: إِلَّا الْإِذْخِرَ فَقَامَ أَبُو شَاهٍ، رَجُلٌ مِنْ أَهْلِ الْيَمَنِ، فَقَالَ: اكْتُبُوا

Al-Walīd b. Muslim, a sub-narrator in the isnād asked Awzā'ī, 'What did he mean when he said, 'Write it for me'? He replied, 'This sermon which he had heard from the Prophet.'[24]

لِي يَا رَسُولَ اللهِ، فَقَالَ رَسُولُ اللهِ صَلَّى اللهُ عَلَيْهِ وَسَلَّمَ: اكْتُبُوا لِأَبِي شَاهٍ قُلْتُ لِلْأَوْزَاعِيِّ: مَا قَوْلُهُ: اكْتُبُوا لِي يَا رَسُولَ اللهِ، قَالَ: هَذِهِ الْخُطْبَةُ الَّتِي سَمِعَهَا مِنْ رَسُولِ اللهِ صَلَّى اللهُ عَلَيْهِ وَسَلَّمَ.

The Companions had personal compilations (*ṣaḥīfah*, plural *ṣuḥuf*) in which they wrote ḥadīth, and many of these continued to circulate in later generations.[25] Many of these were discovered and published, such as the ṣaḥīfah of Hammām b. Munabbih. Dhahabī writes in his biography that 'he was the author of that sound ṣaḥīfah which he wrote from the reports of Abū Hurayrah and consisted of 140 reports which Ma'mar (d. 153/770)[26] narrated from him. This was published numerous times, including the following editions:

- *Ṣaḥīfah Hammām b. Munabbih*. Edited by Dr. Muḥammad Ḥamīdullah. Damascus: Majallat al-Majma' al-'Arabī. 1373.
- *Ṣaḥīfah Hammām b. Munabbih*. Paris: Islamic Center of Paris. 1399.
- *Ṣaḥīfah Hammām b. Munabbih 'an Abī Hurayrah*. Edited by Dr. Rif'at Fawzī 'Abd al-Muṭṭalib. Cairo: Maktabah al-Khānjī. 1406/1985.
- *Al-Ṣaḥīfah al-Ṣaḥīḥah: Ṣaḥīfah Hammām b. Munabbih*. Edited by 'Alī Ḥasan al-Ḥalabī. Beirut: al-Maktab al-Islāmī. 1407/1986.

---

[24] Ṣaḥīḥ Bukhārī: Kitāb al-'ilm—Bāb kitābat al-'ilm; Kitāb fī al-luqaṭah—Bāb kayfa tu'arrafu luqaṭatu ahl Makkah; Kitāb al-diyāt—Bāb man qutila lahū qatīl; Ṣaḥīḥ Muslim: Kitāb al-Ḥajj—Bāb taḥrīm Makkah wa ṣaydihā wa khalāhā wa shajarihā wa luqaṭatihā.

[25] Many Companions and Successors were known to have kept written compilations known as Ṣaḥīfah collections, which survived for many years but were mostly absorbed into later compilations. These early ad hoc collections, written on papyrus, parchment and early materials, followed no uniform pattern or methodology, and were primarily memory aids for their writers, containing skeletons of ḥadīth, often mixed with supplications and notes. The emphasis on this stage was mostly oral transmission. At least 50 Companions were known to have possessed such collections. —Dr. Jonathan AC Brown, *Hadith: Muhammad's Legacy in the Medieval and Modern World*.

[26] Ma'mar b. Rāshid was an early ḥadīth scholar from Baṣrah whose most famous student was 'Abd al-Razzāq al-Ṣan'ānī.

There was also a well-known ṣaḥīfah of ʿAlī b. Abī Ṭālib. Bukhārī relates through Shaʿbī from Abū Juḥayfah that he asked ʿAlī if he had any book. ʿAlī replied, 'No, except for Allah's Book, the understanding that is bestowed upon a Muslim individual, and this ṣaḥīfah.' He was asked, 'What is in this ṣaḥīfah?' ʿAlī replied, 'The rules of blood-money, ransom for captives, and the law that no Muslim is killed in retaliation for a disbeliever.'[27]

Al-Ṣaḥīfah al-Ṣādiqah was the personal collection of ʿAbdullah b. ʿAmr b. al-ʿĀṣ. Bukhārī relates through Wahb b. Munnabih from his brother that he heard Abū Hurayrah say: 'There was no one with more ḥadīth from the Prophet than I, except for ʿAbdullah b. ʿAmr, for he used to write, and I did not used to write.'[28] This work earned its name ('the Truthful Collection') because ʿAbdullah wrote these reports from the Prophet himself, and thus it was the most trustworthy reporting from him. This collection was so dear to ʿAbdullah that he used to say, 'Nothing from this world entices me except for the *Ṣādiqah* (the ṣaḥīfah I wrote from the Prophet ﷺ) and *Waḥṭ* (the land my father ʿAmr b. al-ʿĀṣ gave in charity)'.[29]

Saʿd b. ʿUbādah al-Anṣārī also had a ṣaḥīfah. Tirmidhī relates through Rabīʿah b. Abī ʿAbd al-Raḥmān from Suhayl from Abū Ṣāliḥ from his father from Abū Hurayrah, who said: 'The Prophet passed judgement based upon an oath along with a single witness.' Rabīʿah said: A son of Saʿd b. ʿUbādah said to me: 'We found in a book of Saʿd that the Prophet passed judgement based upon an oath along with a single witness.'[30]

ʿAbdullah b. Abī Awfā also possessed a ṣaḥīfah. Bukhārī relates through Mūsā b. ʿUqbah from Sālim Abī al-Naḍr that ʿAbdullah b. Abī Awfā wrote—which I read myself—that the Prophet ﷺ said: 'When you meet them, be steadfast.'[31]

---

[27] Ṣaḥīḥ Bukhārī: Kitāb al-ʿilm—Bāb kitābat al-ʿilm; Kitāb al-jihād wa al-sayr—Bāb fakkāk al-asīr.

[28] Ṣaḥīḥ Bukhārī: Kitāb al-ʿilm—Bāb kitābat al-ʿilm.

[29] Sunan al-Dārimī: Muqaddimah—Bāb man rakhaṣa fī kitābat al-ʿilm.

[30] Tirmidhī: Kitāb al-aḥkām ʿan rasūlillāh—Bāb mā jāʾa fī al-yamīn maʿa al-shāhid.

[31] Ṣaḥīḥ Bukhārī: Kitāb al-jihād wa al-sayr—Bāb al-ṣabr ʿinda al-qitāl. It is also found in fuller form in Ṣaḥīḥ Bukhārī: Kitāb al-jihād wa al-sayr—Bāb al-jannah taḥta bāriqah al-suyūf; Kitāb al-jihād wa al-sayr—Bāb kāna al-nabī idhā lam yuqātil awwala al-nahār akhkhara al-qitāl; Kitāb al-jihād wa al-sayr—Bāb lā

In addition, there were written collections of Samurah b. Jundub[32], Abū Rāfiʿ the client of the Prophet,[33] Abū Hurayrah,[34] Abū Mūsā al-Ashʿarī,[35] and Jābir b. ʿAbdullah. As for Jābir's ṣaḥīfah, Maʿmar relates that Qatādah once asked Saʿīd b. Abī ʿUrūbah to hold the Qurʾān open while he reviewed sūrah al-Baqarah. After recited the sūrah without a single mistake, Qatādah commented, 'I have memorized Jābir's ṣaḥīfah even more firmly than I memorized sūrah al-Baqarah, for it used to be recited to him.'[36]

In the generation of the Followers (tābiʿūn), many individuals became known for ḥadīth such as ʿAlqamah, Aswad, ʿUbaydah b. ʿAmr al-Salmānī, Masrūq, Ibrāhīm al-Nakhaʿī, ʿĀmir al-Shaʿbī, Saʿīd b. Jubayr, Saʿīd b, al-Musayyab, ʿUrwah b. al-Zubayr, ʿUbaydullah b. ʿAbdullah b. ʿUtbah b. Masʿūd, Ḥasan al-Baṣrī, Muḥammad b. Sīrīn, Mujāhid b. Jabr, Rajāʾ b. Ḥaywah, ʿAṭāʾ b. Abī Rabāḥ, Nāfiʿ the freed slave of Ibn ʿUmar, Ayyūb al-Sakhtiyānī, Ḥumayd al-Ṭawīl, and Hishām b. ʿUrwah b. al-Zubayr.

Among the junior Followers, there were six individuals who comprised a bulk of the circulating ḥadīth isnāds: Ibn Shihāb al-Zuhrī of Madīnah (d. 124/742), ʿAmr b. Dīnār of Makkah (d. 126/744),[37] Qatādah b. Diʿāmah al-Sadūsī

---

tamannaw liqā al-ʿaduww; Kitāb al-tamannī—Bāb karāhiyah tamannī liqā al-ʿaduww; Ṣaḥīḥ Muslim: Kitāb al-jihād wa al-sayr—Bāb karāhah tamannī liqā al-ʿaduww.

Basically, this ḥadīth is related through a letter from ʿAbdullah b. Abī Awfā to ʿUmar b. ʿUbaydullah, which Sālim the secretary of ʿUmar happened to read. Ibn Ḥajar comments that this proves the validity of mukātabah (written correspondence) as a form of ḥadīth transmission, because Sālim had not heard this ḥadīth from ʿAbdullah but read it in his letter. Nawawī goes even further to say that the majority of scholars of all disciplines affirmed the validity of mukātabah and ijāzah (permission), and the fact that both Bukhārī and Muslim related this ḥadīth lends support to that.

The full ḥadīth reveals that the Prophet in one of his battles delayed the march of his army until the sun declined and delivered the following address before marching out: *O people! Do not actively seek to face the enemy (in battle) but ask God to save you, and if you do face the enemy, then be steadfast. Know that Paradise lies under the shades of swords! O Allah! Revealer of the Book, Mover of clouds, and Vanquisher of the confederates, defeat them and bestow victory upon us.*

[32] Ibn Ḥajar, *Tahdhīb al-tahdhīb*, vol 4, pg 236.

[33] Al-Khaṭīb, *al-Kifāyah fī ʿilm al-riwāyah*, pg 330.

[34] Ibn ʿAbd al-Barr, *Jāmiʿ bayān al-ʿilm wa faḍlihī*, vol 1, pg 324.

[35] Manuscript: Maktabah Shahīd ʿAlī, Turkey. See Dr. Ṣubḥī al-Sāmurāʾī's introduction to al-Ṭībī's *al-Khulāṣah fī uṣūl al-ḥadīth*.

[36] Ibn Saʿd, *Ṭabaqāt*, vol 7, pg 229.

[37] Great Makkan scholar who inherited the position of the muftī of the Ḥaram after ʿAṭāʾ b. Abī Rabāḥ (d. 115/733). His greatest student was the muḥaddith of Makkah Sufyān b. ʿUyaynah.

of Baṣrah (d. 117/735),[38] Yaḥyā b. Abī Kathīr (d. 129/747) of Baṣrah,[39] Abū Isḥāq al-Sabī'ī (d. 127/745) of Kūfah,[40] and Sulaymān b. Mahrān al-A'mash of Kūfah (d. 148/765).[41]

Many individuals began to travel widely to pursue ḥadīth, beginning with the Companions. This phenomenon only strengthened with time. Jābir traveled for one month on his mount to hear one single ḥadīth. He traveled to Jerusalem to hear ḥadīth from Abū al-Dardā'. Makḥūl traveled to Egypt, Syria, Iraq, and Arabia to hear ḥadīth. Sa'īd b. al-Musayyab (d. 94/715).[42] They used to travel continuously day and night just to hear a few, or even a single, ḥadīth. Eventually, this became a widespread practice. The best work documenting these travels is al-Khaṭīb al-Baghdādī's *al-Riḥlah fī ṭalab al-ḥadīth.*

A manifestation of the diligence in preserving ḥadīth was the practice of reviewing ḥadīth with others after hearing them from a teacher. 'Aṭā' relates: We used to hear ḥadīth from Jābir, and after we left, we would review them with

---

[38] Being blind since the age of four, he was an authority in four sciences: tafsīr, history, fiqh and ḥadīth. Once he read Sūrah al-Baqarah to a student who was holding a mushaf, without a single mistake, and told his student, "I heard all the ḥadīth of Jābir from his Ṣaḥīfah once and knew them as well as I know this sūrah." According to one estimation that consisted of 400 ḥadīth. Qatādah came to learn from Sa'īd b al-Musayyab the senior Follower of Madīnah, and after 4 days, Sa'īd pushed his chest and said, 'O blind one, leave me, for you have taken all my ḥadīth and not left any!' Qatādah was the teacher of Abū Ḥanīfah, Sufyān al-al-Thawrī and Sufyān b. 'Uyaynah and others. He died of the plaque in Wāsiṭ.

[39] He was a pious scholar of Baṣrah who was considered by Shu'bah and Imām Aḥmad to be more knowledgeable than Zuhrī. Ibn Ḥibbān reports that whenever he attended a funeral, he would not eat or speak for some time. He had witnessed Anas b. Malik praying in the Ḥaram. He spent ten years seeking knowledge in Madīnah and used to say, 'Knowledge cannot be attained with bodily comfort.'

[40] Born 34/35, he met many Companions but narrated ḥadīth from senior Successors. 'Alī of Madīnah counted 300 teachers of his. He was known for extensive worship, completing the Qur'ān every three days. He was the most knowledgeable person in the reports and jurisprudence of 'Alī and Ibn Mas'ūd, so much so that it was said, 'Sitting with Abū Isḥāq was like sitting with 'Alī.' He even remembered a khuṭbah of 'Alī from his childhood. He became blind in later life and suffered from weaker memory but was still deemed reliable with rare mistakes.

[41] Client of the Asad clan, he was a leading scholar of Kūfah in knowledge, practice, piety, and worship. He was a proficient expert and had broad-ranging knowledge. He became blind in later life. He was cheerful with his Qur'ān students and slightly harsh with the ḥadīth students, with many interesting anecdotes related from him in this regard. Sufyān b. 'Uyaynah said: 'A'mash was the most knowledge of people in Qur'ān, ḥadīth and fiqh.' Wakī' said: 'A'mash has not missed the opening takbīr of the prayer in over seventy years.' Yaḥyā al-Qaṭṭān used to say: 'He was a supreme scholar of Islam.'

[42] Son-in-law of Abū Hurayrah who was deemed by Imām Aḥmad and others as the single greatest figure among the generation of the Followers.

one another. We found that Abū al-Zubayr was the best of us in preserving ḥadīth.[43]

ʿAbd al-Malik b. ʿAbd al-ʿAzīz al-Mājishūn relates from Ibrāhīm b. Saʾd: I asked my father Saʾd b. Ibrāhīm: 'Why has Zuhrī surpassed you?' He replied: 'Zuhrī used to enter the classes from the front rows and never from behind. He used to discuss lessons with students, not ignoring even the youngest or oldest student, or anyone in between. Afterwards, he would knock on the doors of the people of Madīnah, not leaving anyone behind, young or old, including men, women and children, and even the ladies within their tents.[44]

Formal Documentation of Ḥadīth

ʿUmar b. ʿAbd al-ʿAzīz wrote to his governor in Madīnah Abū Bakr b. Ḥazm, as previously mentioned, asking him to begin writing ḥadīth as he feared the decline of scholarship and learning.

Ibn Shihāb al-Zuhrī played an unprecedented role in spreading ḥadīth with meticulous preservation of chains and texts, and complete mastery over knowledge. His written collections survived in the libraries of the Umayyad rulers. Maʿmar b. Rāshid reported that when al-Walīd was killed, many books containing Zuhrī's ḥadīth reports were brought out from his libraries and transported over many animals due to their volume.[45] In this manner, Zuhrī laid the path for those who followed him in the second Hijrī century.

Those who were most prominent in authoring works of ḥadīth included the following: Abū Muḥammad ʿAbd al-Malik b. ʿAbd al-ʿAzīz b. Jurayj of Makkah (d. 150/767),[46] Muḥammad b. Isḥāq of Madīnah (d. 150/767), Maʿmar b. Rāshid of Yemen (d. 153/770),[47] Saʿīd b. Abī ʿUrūbah of Baṣrah (d. 156/772), Abū ʿAmr ʿAbd al-Raḥmān al-Awzāʿī of Syria (d. 157/774),[48] Muḥammad b. ʿAbd al-

[43] *Al-Jāmiʿ li akhlāq al-rāwī*, vol 1, pg 238.

[44] *Al-muḥaddith al-fāṣil*, pg 360-1.

[45] Ibn ʿAsākir, *Tarīkh Damishq:* biography of Maʿmar. Ibn Saʿd, *Ṭabaqāt*, vol 2, pg 389.

[46] Better known as Ibn Jurayj, from his Byzantine grandfather Georgios, he was a great scholar who studied with ʿAṭāʾ b. Abī Rabāḥ for 18 years, and also with ʿAmr b. Dīnār, Mujāhid, and others. His students included the historian al-Wāqidī and Sufyān b. ʿUyaynah.

[47] Persian-origin ḥadīth expert of Baṣrah who settled in Ṣanʿāʾ, Yemen.

[48] ʿAbd al-Raḥmān Awzāʿī was a great jurist of the Levant (born in Syria, settled in present-day Lebanon) and founder of a legal school that did not ultimately survive.

Raḥmān b. Abī Dhi'b of Madīnah (d. 158/775),[49] Rabī' b. Ṣabīḥ of Baṣrah (d. 160/777),[50] Shu'bah b. al-Ḥajjāj of Baṣrah (d. 160/777),[51] Sufyān al-Thawrī of Kūfah (d. 161/778), Layth b. Sa'd of Egypt (d. 175/791),[52] Ḥammād b. Salamah of Baṣrah (d. 167/783),[53] Imām Mālik b. Anas of Madīnah (d. 179/795), 'Abdullah b. al-Mubārak of Khurāsān (d. 181/797),[54] Hushaym b. Bashīr of Wāsiṭ (d. 188), Jarīr b. 'Abd al-Ḥamīd of Rayy (d. 188), 'Abdullah b. Wahb of Egypt (d. 197/813),[55] Sufyān b. 'Uyaynah of Makkah, Wakī' b. al-Jarrāḥ of Kūfah (d. 197/813),[56] and 'Abd al-Razzāq al-Ṣan'ānī of Yemen (d. 211/827).[57]

Those who followed them in the following generations included the great ḥadīth experts such as Imām Aḥmad b. Ḥanbal (d. 241/855), Ibn Abī Shaybah (d.

---

[49] Better known as Ibn Abī Dhi'b, he was a pious scholar of Madīnah considered to be on par with Imām Mālik and, according to Imām Aḥmad, even close to Sa'īd b. al-Musayyab in stature. Imām Shāfi'ī commented that he did not regret missing out on any teacher except for Layth b. Sa'd and Ibn Abī Dhi'b. His teachers included 'Ikrimah and Zuhrī (though he was not considered reliable in the ḥadīth of Zuhrī). He was extremely generous towards everyone, not criticizing anyone and allowing all to sit in his assemblies. Because of such associations, he was falsely accused of having Qadari beliefs. He was extremely devout, fasting on alternate days and praying during the night. His clothing and food were humble, and he survived for days on bread and oil. His student al-Wāqidī remarked that if he were told that the Day of Judgement were tomorrow, he would not have changed a thing. He used to memorize his ḥadīth, not relying on books. He was bold and did not fear advising rulers to their face, including Abū Jafar al-Manṣūr. He died in Kūfah.

[50] Ḥadīth expert of Baṣrah who related from Ḥasan al-Baṣrī, Ibn Sīrīn, 'Aṭā' b. Abī Rabāḥ. He was reportedly the first person to organize ḥadīth writing into chapter divisions. He participated in the courageous sea conquest of the Indian city of Bārbad under the general 'Abd al-Malik b. Shihāb al-Misma'ī during the reign of the 'Abbāssid ruler al-Mahdī (775—785). The victorious Muslim army was afflicted with scurvy, a disease that commonly afflicted poorly nourished sailors, causing 1,000 deaths in their ranks, including that of Rabī'.

[51] Shu'bah b. al-Ḥajjāj (d. 160/777) was a prominent ḥadīth scholar of Iraq who was one of the first to earn the title the "King of Ḥadīth" (*amīr al-mu'minīn fil ḥadīth*). When he died, Sufyān al-Thawrī remarked that ḥadīth itself had died.

[52] He was a great jurist and ḥadīth scholar of Egypt about whom Imām Shāfi'ī famously said: 'Layth was more knowledgeable than Mālik.'

[53] Muftī of Baṣrah and ḥadīth expert who was the teacher of Sībawayh.

[54] A noble scholar of ḥadīth and fiqh from the early generations, author of numerous beneficial works, known for great piety, worship, and courage. He died after returning from battle with the Byzantines in 181.

[55] Great Egyptian jurist who was a student of Imām Mālik and loyal proponent of his fiqh in Egypt and throughout the world.

[56] Wakī' b. al-Jarrāḥ was a renowned scholar of Iraq known for his great piety, prodigal memory, and aloofness from the rulers, who was a student of Abū Ḥanīfah and Sufyān al-Thawrī, and, later, the teacher of Shāfi'ī and Aḥmad b. Ḥanbal among others.

[57] Persian-origin ḥadīth expert who lived in Yemen and was a student of Ma'mar b. Rāshid (d. 153/770). He authored the famous Muṣannaf ḥadīth collection, and his students included Yaḥyā b. Ma'īn, Imām Aḥmad, and 'Alī al-Madīnī.

235/849),[58] Yaḥyā b. Maʿīn, ʿAlī b. al-Madīnī, and the authors of the six canonical ḥadīth works. These works are documented in detail in Shāh ʿAbd al-ʿAzīz al-Dehlawī's *Bustān al-muḥaddithīn*—which I had the honor of editing and translating into Arabic from Persian[59]—and Muḥammad b. Jaʿfar al-Kattānī's *al-Risālah al-mustaṭrifah,* among others.

[58] Abū Bakr ʿAbdullah b. Muḥammad b. Abī Shaybah was great ḥadīth scholar of Kūfah. He inherited the teaching position of ʿAbdullah b. Masʿūd in the masjid. After Ibn Masʿūd, it was occupied by ʿAlqamah, followed by Ibrāhīm, followed by Manṣūr, followed by Sufyān al-Thawrī, followed by Wakīʿ and then Ibn Abī Shaybah.

[59] London: Turath Publishing. 1428/2007.

PART 2: FOUNDATIONAL PRINCIPLES

The Meaning of Ṣaḥīḥ Ḥadīth

What is the true meaning of the ṣaḥīḥ (sound) ḥadīth? Experts of this discipline have used it for a variety of meanings, all of which have in common the idea of verifying the attribution of a report to its source.

What are the most notable of these meanings and usages?

Three Usages of Ṣaḥīḥ

There are three broad usages of the term ṣaḥīḥ. The first usage of ṣaḥīḥ is for a report attributed to the Prophet ﷺ which fulfills five conditions:

1. *Contiguous chain* (ittiṣāl): There must be clear continuity of the chain without any missing link or deception on the part of any narrator (tadlīs).
2. *Moral uprightness* (ʿadālah): Each narrator from the beginning to the end of the chain must be described as truthful in word and action, as known by the people of their era.
3. *Accuracy* (ḍabṭ): Each reporter must be accurate and precise in what they narrate, either through memory or through writing, and protected from any distortion, misrepresentation, gross mistakes, or negligence. Here, certain narrators distinguished themselves over others by the length of their companionship and fellowship with their teachers.
4. *Absence of contradictory elements* (shudhūdh): The reporter must not contradict another who is known to be stronger, either in number of corroborating chains or in description.
5. Being free of any *hidden weaknesses* (ʿillah): There must be reasonable certainty that the report does not contain any subtle weaknesses such as missing links while being apparently connected, being erroneously attributed to the Prophet, containing mistaken additions to the text, misrepresentation, distortion, mistaken substitutions, or their likes.

These conditions are specific to the Ṣaḥīḥ compilations of the two great experts Abū ʿAbdullah Muḥammad b. Ismāʿīl al-Bukhārī (d. 256/870)[1] and Abū al-Ḥusayn Muslim b. al-Ḥajjāj al-Qushayrī (d. 261/875).[2] Neither of them neglected a single one of these conditions—nor did they add others—for their reports except in their secondary corpus material (supporting narrations and chapter headings).

The second usage of ṣaḥīḥ is for those reports that are narrated by trustworthy individuals through chains that are overtly connected (without missing links), as well as for some reports of unknown individuals who were otherwise accepted by early experts and critics like Mālik, Shuʿbah and their likes.

This is the meaning of the term ṣaḥīḥ when used by the majority of early ḥadīth scholars like Imām Aḥmad b. Ḥanbal and his companions, Abū Dāwūd, and Tirmidhī—and even for Bukhārī and Muslim in their other works apart from their Ṣaḥīḥ compilations.

The third usage is for any report related by transmitters who have not been accused of lying, major mistakes, or gross negligence. This is the meaning of ṣaḥīḥ for reports exclusive to Ibn Khuzaymah, Ḥākim, Ibn Ḥibbān and others.[3]

---

[1] Compiled over 16 years through extensive research and travel and from over 1,000 teachers and from 600,000 narrations, the Ṣaḥīḥ of Muḥammad b. Ismāʿīl al-Bukhārī (d. 256/870) is the single-most authoritative ḥadīth collection in Sunni Islam, containing 9,082 ḥadīth (2,602 discounting repetitions) arranged in 106 books and 3,450 chapters. This collection stands out for the in-depth knowledge and insight it provides concerning ḥadīth. One thousand students listened to the collection from the Imām and transmitted it to posterity, though some figures put the number at 90,000.

[2] Containing 10,000 ḥadīth (3,030 without repetitions) and having took 15 years to complete, the Ṣaḥīḥ of Imām Muslim b. al-Ḥajjāj (d. 261/875) is considered the second most authoritative work (or ranked first by some) and described as better consolidated, with superior thematic arrangement, and easier to use than Bukhārī's work. However, it lacks Bukhārī's legal commentary and insights, as well as his use of reports from Companions and early scholars to supplement the primary material.

[3] As Dr. Akram often points out to his students, it is crucial to recognize the fluid usage of terminology, which is neither uniform nor universal but must be understood in each individual context. The term ṣaḥīḥ has been used in various ways by experts, but these are three basic usages based on degree of rigor, which will be referred to in tiers. The most rigorous use of ṣaḥīḥ is by Bukhārī and Muslim in their Ṣaḥīḥ compilations, followed by the less rigorous but still robust meaning as used by the early ḥadīth experts, and finally, the extremely lenient, and hence problematic, usage by later scholars such as Ḥākim, Ibn Ḥibbān and others. Dr. Akram sometimes adds a fourth category, even more problematic, that represents the authentication of reports by contemporary ḥadīth scholars like Aḥmad Muḥammad Shākir (d. 1958), Nāṣir al-Dīn al-Albānī (d. 1999) and Shuʿayb al-Arnaʾūṭ (d. 2016).

Why have you not included the Muwaṭṭa' in the first category? For two simple reasons: first, because the Muwaṭṭa' is a more complex work that can belong to multiple categories;[4] and second, everything that it contains from the first category of ṣaḥīḥ reports is already found in the Ṣaḥīḥayn collections.

Two-Tiered Usage of Ṣaḥīḥ for Bukhārī and Muslim

Why do you believe that Bukhārī and Muslim exhaustively compiled all primary-tier ṣaḥīḥ reports, not missing any report? Is it not established that they did leave out many ṣaḥīḥ reports? I stand by what I believe: Bukhārī and Muslim did not leave out any first-tier ṣaḥīḥ report in their Ṣaḥīḥayn and deliberately excluded second-tier ṣaḥīḥ reports.[5]

Please provide an example of Bukhārī declaring a report as ṣaḥīḥ that is outside of his Ṣaḥīḥ work and does not fulfill the conditions of that work. Tirmidhī relates in the Book of the Call to Prayer, Chapter: [What has been related about the beginning of the call to prayer]:

BOOK OF PRAYER—CHAPTER: THE ORIGIN OF THE CALL TO PRAYER Sa'īd b. Yaḥyā b. Sa'īd al-Umawī related to us: my father related to us: Muḥammad b. Isḥāq related to us: from Muḥammad b. Ibrāhīm b. al-Ḥārith al-Taymī: from Muḥammad b. 'Abdullah b. Zayd: from his father: When we awoke, we went to the Prophet ﷺ to inform him of our dream. He said: ⟨Indeed this dream is true. So go	**جامع الترمذي - أبواب الصلاة عن رسول الله صلى الله عليه وسلم - باب ما جاء في بدء الأذان** حَدَّثَنَا سَعِيدُ بْنُ يَحْيَى بْنِ سَعِيدٍ الْأُمَوِيُّ، قَالَ: حَدَّثَنَا أَبِي، قَالَ: حَدَّثَنَا مُحَمَّدُ بْنُ إِسْحَاقَ، عَنْ مُحَمَّدِ بْنِ إِبْرَاهِيمَ التَّيْمِيِّ، عَنْ مُحَمَّدِ بْنِ عَبْدِ اللهِ بْنِ زَيْدٍ، عَنْ

[4] For instance, it can be, and is, considered a work on jurisprudence. It is also a book of ḥadīth, as well as a work of reports from early generations (āthār).

[5] Dr. Akram believes that the Ṣaḥīḥ of Bukhārī and Muslim were meant to exhaustively compile all first-tier ṣaḥīḥ reports in circulation, which was done quite successively. There is simply no ḥadīth in existence that can be claimed, as people like Ḥākim do, to fulfill their primary-tier conditions which they happened to miss out on. It is also crucial to understand the structure of these two works, which consist of a primary and secondary corpus. See footnote 16 in this chapter.

to Bilāl, for he has a better and louder voice than you. Convey to him what was said to you, so that he may call (to the prayer) with that.﴿

ʿAbdullah b. Zayd said: When ʿUmar b. al-Khaṭṭāb heard Bilāl calling to the prayer in this way, he rushed to the Prophet, dragging his lower garment, and said: Oh Messenger of God! By the One Who sent you with the truth, I dreamt the same as what he said.' The Prophet responded: ﴾'Praise God, for this confirms it even more.'﴿

Abū ʿĪsā (Tirmidhī) said: The ḥadīth of ʿAbdullah b. Zayd is ḥasan ṣaḥīḥ.[6]

أَبِيهِ، قَالَ: لَمَّا أَصْبَحْنَا أَتَيْنَا رَسُولَ اللهِ صَلَّى اللهُ عَلَيْهِ وَسَلَّمَ فَأَخْبَرْتُهُ بِالرُّؤْيَا، فَقَالَ: إِنَّ هَذِهِ لَرُؤْيَا حَقٍّ، فَقُمْ مَعَ بِلَالٍ فَإِنَّهُ أَنْدَى وَأَمَدُّ صَوْتًا مِنْكَ، فَأَلْقِ عَلَيْهِ مَا قِيلَ لَكَ، وَلْيُنَادِ بِذَلِكَ، قَالَ: فَلَمَّا سَمِعَ عُمَرُ بْنُ الْخَطَّابِ نِدَاءَ بِلَالٍ بِالصَّلَاةِ خَرَجَ إِلَى رَسُولِ اللهِ صَلَّى اللهُ عَلَيْهِ وَسَلَّمَ وَهُوَ يَجُرُّ إِزَارَهُ، وَهُوَ يَقُولُ: يَا رَسُولَ اللهِ، وَالَّذِي بَعَثَكَ بِالْحَقِّ لَقَدْ رَأَيْتُ مِثْلَ الَّذِي قَالَ، قَالَ: فَقَالَ رَسُولُ اللهِ صَلَّى اللهُ عَلَيْهِ وَسَلَّمَ: فَلِلَّهِ الْحَمْدُ، فَذَلِكَ أَثْبَتُ.

حَدِيثُ عَبْدِ اللهِ بْنِ زَيْدٍ حَدِيثٌ حَسَنٌ صَحِيحٌ.

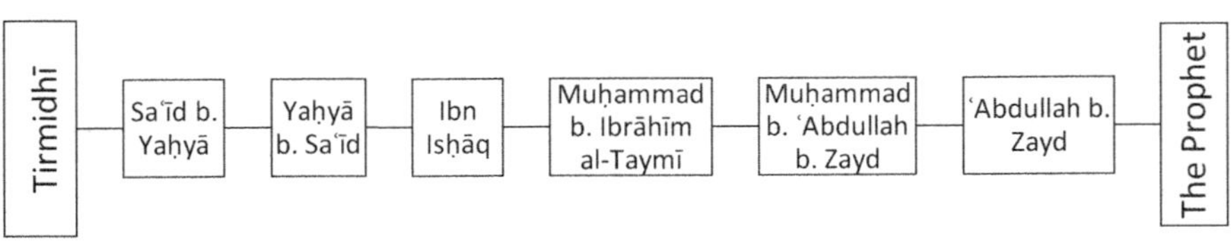

[6] Tirmidhī: Kitāb al-ṣalāh—Bāb mā jāʾa fī badʾ al-adhān. Abū Dāwūd relates the ḥadīth in greater detail in Kitāb al-ṣalāh—Bāb kayfa al-adhān.

Bayhaqī states in al-Sunan al-Kubrā: Tirmidhī states in Kitāb al-ʿIlal: I asked Muḥammad b. Ismāʿīl al-Bukhārī about this ḥadīth—i.e. the ḥadīth of Muḥammad b Ibrāhīm al-Taymī—and he said: 'In my view, it is a ṣaḥīḥ ḥadīth.'[7]

A large group of ḥadīth experts authenticated this report as ṣaḥīḥ. It was additionally related by Ibn Mājah, Ibn Khuzaymah, Dārimī, Aḥmad and others. Ibn Khuzaymah, after relating it, for instance, said: 'Among the reports of ʿAbdullah b. Zayd concerning the adhān, there is no sounder report than this one.'

The reason it was not related by Bukhārī or Muslim in their Ṣaḥīḥ compilations was due to Muḥammad b. Isḥāq (d. 150/767),[8] who is simply not on their conditions (for accepting reporters).

---

[7] *Al-Sunan al-Kubrā*, vol 3, pg 102.

[8] Abū Bakr Muḥammad b. Isḥāq b. Yasār b. Khiyār al-Aḥwal, better known as Ibn Isḥāq, is the famous historian of Madīnah and author of one of the earliest works on sīrah. He was controversial in ḥadīth circles and not considered strong or reliable. Bukhārī does not take from him at all, and Muslim only utilizes his reports as supporting evidence. There was personal animosity between him and Imām Mālik, his contemporary in Madīnah. The contrast between Mālik and Ibn Isḥāq reveals the very problem with Ibn Isḥāq and historians like Wāqidī. Ḥadīth experts such as Mālik were professional scholars who devoted their entire lives to studying and teaching in formal circles, researching ḥadīth reports, comparing information with their peers, and painstakingly authoring great works which were continually revised over time. The Muwaṭṭaʾ of Malik represents the epitome of ḥadīth scholarship and is the one of the most reliable and accurate ḥadīth works in our tradition to this day. Moreover, ḥadīth experts were concerned with practical matters and focused on learning and teaching the sunnah, in the tradition of the early Muslims.

Historians like Ibn Isḥāq, on the other hand, were more interested in collecting information and data about history, battles and other rare historical details, rather than sunnah. More akin to journalists than scholars, they worked by collecting information from wherever they could find it, including from the homes and descendants of Companions—many of these details passed down like personal family anecdotes and stories which are not known for accuracy. Not only did they receive information from non-scholars, but they also failed to critically analyze their information. As a result, many contradictory details are related in books of sīrah. The inclusion of Abū Mūsā al-Ashʿarī among the emigrants to Abyssinia in Ibn Isḥāq's sīrah is a glaring example of one such blunder. In contrast, the books of ḥadīth reveal that he was from Yemen and embraced Islam relatively late. For pre-Hijrah events, Ibn Isḥāq has little or no connected isnāds, while for post-Hijrah events, the matter is slightly better but not much more so. It is a mistake, therefore, to consider Ibn Isḥāq to be an expert on sīrah as opposed to ḥadīth scholars who are experts in their own field. *—This information comes from Shaykh Akram's classes on Tirmidhī.*

Give us an example of a ḥadīth authenticated by Imām Muslim which he did not include in his Ṣaḥīḥ. Muslim states in his Ṣaḥīḥ:[9]

BOOK OF PRAYER—CHAPTER: TASHAHHUD Saʿīd b. Manṣūr, Qutaybah b. Saʿīd, Abū Kāmil al-Jaḥdarī, and Muḥammad b. ʿAbd al-Malik al-Umawī—and the wording is from Abū Kāmil—related to us: Abū ʿAwānah related to us: from Qatādah: from Yūnus b. Jubayr: from Ḥiṭṭān b. ʿAbdullah al-Raqāshī:

I once prayed with Abū Mūsā al-Ashʿarī, and when he was sitting in the end of prayer, someone called out: 'Prayer has been made obligatory along with piety and charity!' When Abū Mūsā finished the prayer, he turned around and asked: 'Who among you said such a thing?' There was silence, and he asked again, only to be met with silence again. He then said, 'Maybe you said, Oh Ḥiṭṭān.' I replied: 'I did not, and I feared that you would think it was me.' Then a person came forward and confessed, saying: 'I only intended good.'

Abū Mūsā taught them: 'Don't you know what you have to say in your prayers? Verily the Messenger of God addressed us and explained to us all its aspects and taught us how to observe prayer.'

The Prophet said: *When you [intend to] pray, make your rows straight and appoint one person as your imām. When the imām recites the takbīr, you recite it, and when he completes al-*

صحيح مسلم - كتاب الصلاة - باب التشهد في الصلاة

حَدَّثَنَا سَعِيدُ بْنُ مَنْصُورٍ وَقُتَيْبَةُ بْنُ سَعِيدٍ وَأَبُو كَامِلٍ الْجَحْدَرِيُّ وَمُحَمَّدُ بْنُ عَبْدِ الْمَلِكِ الأُمَوِيُّ وَاللَّفْظُ لأَبِي كَامِلٍ قَالُوا: حَدَّثَنَا أَبُو عَوَانَةَ، عَنْ قَتَادَةَ، عَنْ يُونُسَ بْنِ جُبَيْرٍ، عَنْ حِطَّانَ بْنِ عَبْدِ اللهِ الرَّقَاشِيِّ قَالَ: صَلَّيْتُ مَعَ أَبِي مُوسَى الأَشْعَرِيِّ صَلاَةً، فَلَمَّا كَانَ عِنْدَ الْقَعْدَةِ قَالَ رَجُلٌ مِنَ الْقَوْمِ: أُقِرَّتِ الصَّلاَةُ بِالْبِرِّ وَالزَّكَاةِ. قَالَ: فَلَمَّا قَضَى أَبُو مُوسَى الصَّلاَةَ وَسَلَّمَ انْصَرَفَ، فَقَالَ: أَيُّكُمُ الْقَائِلُ كَلِمَةَ كَذَا وَكَذَا؟ قَالَ: فَأَرَمَّ الْقَوْمُ. ثُمَّ قَالَ: أَيُّكُمُ الْقَائِلُ كَلِمَةَ كَذَا وَكَذَا؟ فَأَرَمَّ الْقَوْمُ . فَقَالَ: لَعَلَّكَ يَا حِطَّانُ قُلْتَهَا. قَالَ: مَا قُلْتُهَا، وَلَقَدْ رَهِبْتُ أَنْ تَبْكَعَنِي بِهَا. فَقَالَ رَجُلٌ مِنَ الْقَوْمِ: أَنَا قُلْتُهَا، وَلَمْ أُرِدْ بِهَا إِلاَّ الْخَيْرَ.

[9] Muslims relates this ḥadīth at the end of his chapter on tashahhud, and so it represents secondary, supporting material for Muslim and not his primary corpus.

Fātiḥah, say: 'Āmīn,' for God would love you. And when he recites the takbīr and bows (rukū'), you also do the same. Know that the Imām bows before you and raises himself before you.

The Prophet continued: *The one is equivalent to the other. And when he says: 'sami'allāhu li man ḥamidah' ('God listens to him who praises Him'), you should say: 'Allāhumma rabbanā laka al-ḥamd' (Oh God, our Lord, to You is all praise'). God does listen to you indeed, for He has conveyed to us through the tongue of His Messenger that God listens to he who praises Him.*

And when the Imām recites the takbīr and prostrates, you should also recite the takbīr and prostrate, for the Imam prostrates before you and raises himself before you.

He then said: *The one is equivalent to the other. And when he sits (for tashahhud) the first words of every one amongst you should be:*

Al-taḥiyyātu al-ṭayyibātu al-ṣalawātu lillāhi, al-salāmu 'alayka ayyuha al-nabīyy wa raḥmatullāhi wa barakātuhu, al-salāmu 'alaynā wa 'alā 'ibādillāhi al-ṣāliḥīn, ash-hadu an lā ilāha illallāhu wa ash-hadu anna Muḥammadan 'abduhū wa rasūluhū.

('All services rendered by words, acts of worship and all good things are due to God. Peace be upon you, Oh Messenger, and God's mercy and blessings. Peace be upon us and upon the upright servants of God. I testify that there is no god but God, and I testify that Muḥammad is His servant and Messenger.)

فَقَالَ أَبُو مُوسَى: أَمَا تَعْلَمُونَ كَيْفَ تَقُولُونَ فِي صَلَاتِكُمْ؟ إِنَّ رَسُولَ اللهِ صَلَّى اللهُ عَلَيْهِ وَسَلَّمَ خَطَبَنَا فَبَيَّنَ لَنَا سُنَّتَنَا وَعَلَّمَنَا صَلَاتَنَا، فَقَالَ: إِذَا صَلَّيْتُمْ فَأَقِيمُوا صُفُوفَكُمْ، ثُمَّ لِيَؤُمَّكُمْ أَحَدُكُمْ فَإِذَا كَبَّرَ فَكَبِّرُوا. وَإِذْ قَالَ: غَيْرِ الْمَغْضُوبِ عَلَيْهِمْ وَلَا الضَّالِّينَ فَقُولُوا: آمِينَ، يُجِبْكُمُ اللهُ. فَإِذَا كَبَّرَ وَرَكَعَ فَكَبِّرُوا وَارْكَعُوا؛ فَإِنَّ الْإِمَامَ يَرْكَعُ قَبْلَكُمْ وَيَرْفَعُ قَبْلَكُمْ. فَقَالَ رَسُولُ اللهِ صَلَّى اللهُ عَلَيْهِ وَسَلَّمَ: فَتِلْكَ بِتِلْكَ. وَإِذَا قَالَ: سَمِعَ اللهُ لِمَنْ حَمِدَهُ، فَقُولُوا: اللَّهُمَّ رَبَّنَا لَكَ الْحَمْدُ، يَسْمَعِ اللهُ لَكُمْ فَإِنَّ اللهَ تَبَارَكَ وَتَعَالَى قَالَ عَلَى لِسَانِ نَبِيِّهِ صَلَّى اللهُ عَلَيْهِ وَسَلَّمَ: سَمِعَ اللهُ لِمَنْ حَمِدَهُ. وَإِذَا كَبَّرَ وَسَجَدَ فَكَبِّرُوا وَاسْجُدُوا فَإِنَّ الْإِمَامَ يَسْجُدُ قَبْلَكُمْ وَيَرْفَعُ قَبْلَكُمْ. فَقَالَ رَسُولُ اللهِ صَلَّى اللهُ عَلَيْهِ: فَتِلْكَ بِتِلْكَ. وَإِذَا كَانَ عِنْدَ الْقَعْدَةِ فَلْيَكُنْ مِنْ أَوَّلِ قَوْلِ أَحَدِكُمْ: التَّحِيَّاتُ الطَّيِّبَاتُ الصَّلَوَاتُ لِلهِ، السَّلَامُ عَلَيْكَ أَيُّهَا

النَّبِيُّ وَرَحْمَةُ اللهِ وَبَرَكَاتُهُ،
السَّلَامُ عَلَيْنَا وَعَلَى عِبَادِ اللهِ
الصَّالِحِينَ، أَشْهَدُ أَنْ لَا إِلَهَ إِلَّا
اللهُ وَأَشْهَدُ أَنَّ مُحَمَّدًا عَبْدُهُ
وَرَسُولُهُ.

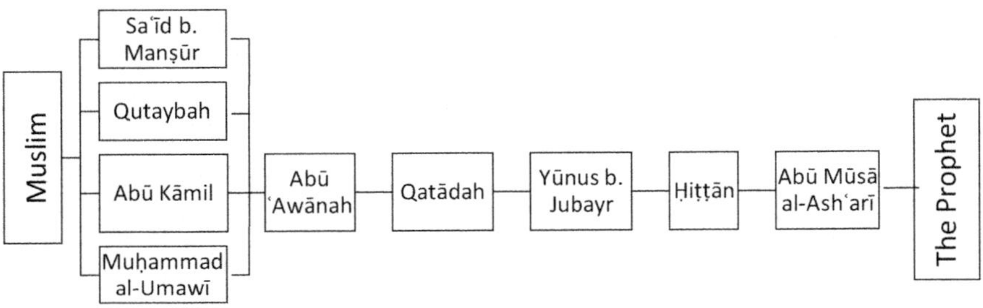

After relating this report, Muslim shares additional isnāds for the ḥadīth:

Abū Bakr b. Abī Shaybah related to us: Abū Usāmah related to us: Sa'īd b. Abī 'Arūbah related to us . . . And Abū Ghassān al-Misma'ī related to us: Mu'ādh b. Hishām related to us: my father related to us . . . And Isḥāq b. Ibrāhīm related to us: Jarīr related to us: from Sulaymān al-Taymī . . . And all of these relate from Qatādah with the same isnād.

In the ḥadīth transmitted by Jarīr from Sulaymān from Qatādah, there is the addition: *When he (the imām) recites, be silent*. And the words: *Verily God conveyed to us through the tongue of His*

حَدَّثَنَا أَبُو بَكْرِ بْنُ أَبِي شَيْبَةَ،
حَدَّثَنَا أَبُو أُسَامَةَ، حَدَّثَنَا سَعِيدُ
بْنُ أَبِي عَرُوبَةَ، ح وحَدَّثَنَا أَبُو
غَسَّانَ الْمِسْمَعِيُّ، حَدَّثَنَا مُعَاذُ
بْنُ هِشَامٍ، حَدَّثَنَا أَبِي، ح
وحَدَّثَنَا إِسْحَاقُ بْنُ إِبْرَاهِيمَ
أَخْبَرَنَا جَرِيرٌ، عَنْ سُلَيْمَانَ
التَّيْمِيِّ، كُلُّ هَؤُلَاءِ عَنْ قَتَادَةَ،
فِي هَذَا الإِسْنَادِ بِمِثْلِهِ وفِي
حَدِيثِ جَرِيرٍ، عَنْ سُلَيْمَانَ،
عَنْ قَتَادَةَ مِنَ الزِّيَادَةِ: وإذا

Prophet that: 'God listens to he who praises Him' are not found in any version except the report of Abū Kāmil from Abū ʿAwānah.

Abū Isḥāq (a student of Imam Muslim) said: Abū Bakr the son of Abū Naḍr's sister critically discussed this ḥadīth. Imam Muslim asked him: Whom can you find who is more accurate than Sulaymān? Abū Bakr replied to him: What about the hadith narrated by Abū Hurayrah (*when he recites, be silent*)?[10] Muslim replied: That ḥadīth is ṣaḥīḥ in my estimation. Abū Bakr then asked: Then, why have you not included it in your compilation? Muslim replied: I have not included in this work every ḥadīth which I deem authentic, but only such ḥadīth reports upon which there is agreement.[11]

قَرَأ فَأَنْصِتُوا ولَيْسَ فِي حَدِيثِ أَحَدٍ مِنهُمْ فَإِنَّ اللهَ قالَ عَلى لِسانِ نَبِيِّهِ: «سَمِعَ اللهُ لِمَنْ حَمِدَهُ» إلّا فِي رِوايَةِ أَبِي كامِلٍ، وحْدَهُ عَنْ أَبِي عَوانَةَ

قالَ أَبُو إِسْحاقَ: قالَ أَبُو بَكْرٍ: ابْنُ أُخْتِ أَبِي النَّضْرِ فِي هَذا الحَدِيثِ. فَقالَ مُسْلِمٌ: تُرِيدُ أَحْفَظَ مِن سُلَيْمانَ؟ فَقالَ لَهُ أَبُو بَكْرٍ: فَحَدِيثُ أَبِي هُرَيْرَةَ؟ فَقالَ: هُوَ صَحِيحٌ يَعْنِي وإذا قَرَأ فَأَنْصِتُوا فَقالَ: هُوَ عِنْدِي صَحِيحٌ فَقالَ: لِمَ لِمَ تَضَعْهُ ها هُنا؟ قالَ: لَيْسَ كُلُّ شَيْءٍ عِنْدِي صَحِيحٍ وضَعْتُهُ ها هُنا إِنَّما وضَعْتُ ها هُنا ما أَجْمَعُوا عَلَيْهِ

[10] This reference is to the ḥadīth of Abū Hurayrah, which was related by the four Sunan works and Musnad Aḥmad through Muḥammad b. ʿAjlān: from: Zayd b. Aslam: from Abū Ṣāliḥ: from Abū Hurayrah: which contains the same additional wording. See forthcoming discussion on next page.

[11] Ṣaḥīḥ Muslim: Kitāb al-ṣalāh—Bāb al-tashahhud fī al-ṣalāh.

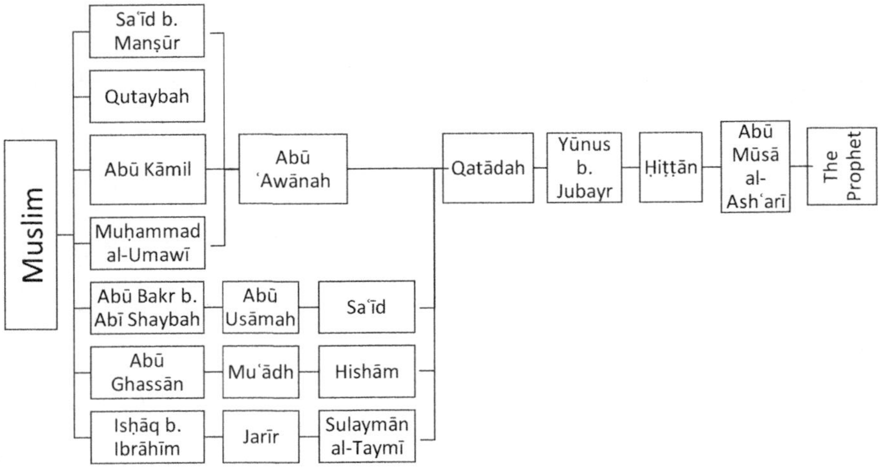

From this, we learn that Muslim deemed the ḥadīth of Abū Hurayrah ṣaḥīḥ but did not include it in his book. That ḥadīth is related by Abū Dāwūd:

BOOK OF PRAYER—CHAPTER: THE IMĀM PRAYING WHILE SEATED Sulaymān b. Ḥarb and Muslim b. Ibrāhīm related to us by way of meaning: from Wahb: from Muṣʿab b. Muḥammad: from Abū Ṣāliḥ: from Abū Hurayrah:

The Prophet ﷺ said: ❴*The imām of prayer is appointed to be followed, so when he says takbīr, say takbīr, and do not do so before him. When he bows, bow down, and do not do so before him. When he says: 'samiʿ allāhu li man ḥamidah' ('God listens to him who praises Him'), you should say: 'Allāhumma rabbanā laka al-ḥamd' (Oh God, our Lord, to You is all praise').*

Muslim [b. Ibrāhīm] said in his version of the report: '*Allāhumma rabbanā wa laka al-ḥamd' (Oh God, our Lord, and to You is all praise').*[12]

When the imām prostrates, you should prostrate, but do not prostrate before he does. When he prays standing, pray standing, and when he prays seated, all of you pray seated.❵

Muḥammad b. Ādam al-Miṣīṣī related to us: Abū Khālid related to us: from Ibn ʿAjlān: from Zayd b. Aslam: from Abū Ṣāliḥ: from Abū Hurayrah: that the Prophet ﷺ said: *Verily the imām is appointed to be followed . . .* He added the words: *When he recites, be silent.*

Abū Dāwūd commented: This addition (*When he recites, be silent*) is not sound, and

سنن أبي داود – كتاب الصلاة -

بابُ الإمامِ يُصَلِّي مِن قُعُودٍ

حَدَّثَنا سُلَيْمانُ بْنُ حَرْبٍ، ومُسْلِمُ بْنُ إبْراهِيمَ المَعْنى، عَنْ وُهَيْبٍ، عَنْ مُصْعَبِ بْنِ مُحَمَّدٍ، عَنْ أبِي صالِحٍ، عَنْ أبِي هُرَيْرَةَ، قالَ: قالَ رَسُولُ اللَّهِ ﷺ: «إنَّما جُعِلَ الإمامُ لِيُؤْتَمَّ بِهِ فَإذا كَبَّرَ فَكَبِّرُوا، ولا تُكَبِّرُوا حَتّى يُكَبِّرَ، وإذا رَكَعَ فارْكَعُوا ولا تَرْكَعُوا حَتّى يَرْكَعَ، وإذا قالَ: سَمِعَ اللَّهُ لِمَن حَمِدَهُ، فَقُولُوا: اللَّهُمَّ رَبَّنا لَكَ الحَمْدُ - قالَ مُسْلِمٌ: ولَكَ الحَمْدُ - وإذا سَجَدَ فاسْجُدُوا ولا تَسْجُدُوا حَتّى يَسْجُدَ، وإذا صَلّى قائِمًا فَصَلُّوا قِيامًا، وإذا صَلّى قاعِدًا فَصَلُّوا قُعُودًا أجْمَعُونَ»

قالَ أبُو داوُدَ: اللَّهُمَّ رَبَّنا لَكَ الحَمْدُ أفْهَمَنِي بَعْضُ أصْحابِنا عَنْ سُلَيْمانَ،

حَدَّثَنا مُحَمَّدُ بْنُ آدَمَ المِصِّيصِيُّ، حَدَّثَنا أبُو خالِدٍ، عَنِ ابْنِ عَجْلانَ، عَنْ زَيْدِ بْنِ أسْلَمَ، عَنْ أبِي صالِحٍ،

[12] Abū Dāwūd is noting the differences between his two teachers' narration of the report, the difference being a single letter: wāw. Sulaymān b. Ḥarb reported: *laka al-ḥamd,* while Muslim b. Ibrāhīm reported: *wa laka al-ḥamd.*

we consider the mistake to be from Abū Khālid.[13]

عَنْ أَبِي هُرَيْرَةَ، عَنِ النَّبِيِّ ﷺ، قَالَ: «إِنَّما جُعِلَ الإمامُ لِيُؤْتَمَّ بِهِ» بِهَذا الخَبَرِ زادَ «وإذا قَرَأَ فَأَنْصِتُوا»، قالَ أبو داوُدَ: «وهَذِهِ الزِّيادَةُ وإذا قَرَأَ فَأَنْصِتُوا لَيْسَتْ بِمَحْفُوظَةٍ الوَهْمُ عِنْدَنا مِن أَبِي خالِدٍ»

The expression 'upon which there is agreement' was used by Muslim in the context of comparing the two ḥadīth reports: that of Abū Mūsā al-Ashʿarī and Abū Hurayrah. He considered both reports to be ṣaḥīḥ. But the wording that was agreed upon was found in the report of Abū Mūsā and not in the report of Abū Hurayrah, and hence his inclusion of that.

Ibn Taymiyyah states: Muslim meant by his statement—'I have not included in this work every ḥadīth which I deem authentic, but only such ḥadīth reports upon which there is agreement'—that was agreed upon was the report of Abū Mūsā, and not that of Abū Hurayrah, and hence Muslim only reported the ḥadīth of Abū Mūsā and excluded that of Abū Hurayrah.[14]

More generally, the expression 'upon which there is agreement' refers to ṣaḥīḥ reports with conditions that are agreed upon by experts, which is the first of the three types of ṣaḥīḥ reports, which we have previously alluded to.[15]

---

[13] Abū Dāwūd: Kitāb al-ṣalāh—Bāb al-imām yuṣallī min quʿūd. Ibn Mājah also relates the same isnād, with the same addition in Kitāb iqāmat al-ṣalāh—Bāb idhā qaraʾa al-imām fa anṣitū. Scholars point out that in this ḥadīth of Abū Hurayrah, only Ibn ʿAjlān relates this addition (*When he recites, be silent*) whereas all other isnāds leave it out.

[14] *Majmūʿ*, vol 23, pg 317.

[15] Muslim is alluding to the fact that for his primary corpus, he intends to include highest-tier sound reports which are agreed upon by ḥadīth experts.

As Dr. Akram often points out, it is crucial to recognize the content-structure of works like Bukhārī and Muslim: they contain a primary corpus (termed *uṣūl*) which represents primary-tier ṣaḥīḥ reports only, and a secondary corpus which does not necessarily meet those criteria (usually representing second-tier ṣaḥīḥ reports or lesser than those) and is meant to augment and support the primary corpus.

Defect (ʿIllah) in Abū Hurayrah's Report

Although he did not include it in his Ṣaḥīḥ for specific reasons, Imām Muslim considered the ḥadīth of Abū Hurayrah with the addition (*'when he recites, be silent'*) to be ṣaḥīḥ, as did Imām Aḥmad and Ibn ʿAbd al-Barr. Ibn ʿAbd al-Barr says:

> Some of them considered Abū Khālid al-Aḥmar to be the sole reporter who has the addition, while others considered it to be Ibn ʿAjlān. And al-Nasāʾī does report the ḥadīth from other than Abū Khālid (which points to Ibn ʿAjlān as the source).[16]
>
> If someone were to object by saying that the addition (*When he recites, be silent*) only comes in the ḥadīth of Abū Hurayrah through Ibn ʿAjlān and in the ḥadīth of Abū Mūsā al-Ashʿarī through Jarīr from al-Taymī, we would respond by saying that those who opposed these two reporters were not greater in precision than them, so their additions here must be accepted. The likes of Imām Aḥmad b. Ḥanbal deemed this report ṣaḥīḥ, and that is all one needs to know due to his stature and knowledge in this field.[17]

Bukhārī's secondary corpus appears primarily in his chapter headings as muʿallaq (isnād-less) reports, while Muslim follows the classical ḥadīthist approach of starting with the soundest reports in each chapter (which would be his primary corpus) and following them up with supporting narrations referred to as *mutābaʿāt*. It would be a mistake to consider these reports at the ends of chapters to be part of Muslim's primary corpus, as many do.

It should be noted, as some scholars point out, that the ḥadīth of Abū Mūsā quoted above is part of Muslim's secondary corpus. In this chapter, Muslim relates three ḥadīth. The first ḥadīth is that of Abū Mūsā al-Ashʿarī and represents his primary corpus. It is then followed up with four supporting isnāds and versions for the same ḥadīth (known as *mutābaʿāt*). The second ḥadīth in the chapter is the report of Ibn ʿAbbās and represents a supporting ḥadīth (*shāhid*), which is followed by one additional follow-up isnād. The third and final ḥadīth is the report of Abū Mūsā al-Ashʿarī (the ḥadīth quoted above), which is also in a supporting capacity and further followed by two follow-up isnāds. See al-Hararī, *al-Kawkab al-wahhāj*, vol 7, pg 132.

[16] Al-Nasāʾī reports the ḥadīth from al-Jārūd b. Muʿādh from Abū Khālid from Ibn ʿAjlān, and follows up with another isnād from his teacher Muḥammad b. ʿAbdullah b. al-Mubārak from Muḥammad b. Saʿd al-Anṣārī from Ibn ʿAjlān in Kitāb al-iftitāḥ—Bāb taʾwīl qawluhū idhā quriʾa al-Qurʾānu fastamiʿū lahū. This points to Ibn ʿAjlān being the sole source of the addition in the ḥadīth of Abū Hurayrah.

[17] *Al-tamhīd*, Vol 11, pg 33-4.

Other experts disagreed, however, as Ibn Abī Ḥātim states: I heard my father (Abū Ḥātim al-Rāzī), when this report of Abū Khālid from Ibn ʿAjlān from Zayd b. Aslam from Abū Ṣāliḥ from Abū Hurayrah was mentioned, say the following: These words are not sound, for they are the mistakes of Ibn ʿAjlān. Khārijah b. Muṣʿab also reported this from Zayd b. Aslam, supporting Ibn ʿAjlān, but Khārijah is not a strong reporter.[18] Dāruquṭnī, when asked about this specific report with the addition, stated the following:

> This report of Muḥammad b. ʿAjlān was subject to many differences. Abū Khālid al-Aḥmar reported it Muḥammad b. ʿAjlān from Zayd b. Aslam from Abū Ṣāliḥ from Abū Hurayrah. Ismāʿīl b. Abān al-Ghanawī reported it from Ibn ʿAjlān from Zayd b. Aslam from Muṣʿab b. Shuraḥbīl from Abū Ṣāliḥ from Abū Hurayrah. Abū Saʾd al-Ṣāghānī reports it from Ibn ʿAjlān from his father from Abū Hurayrah. Muḥammad b. Saʾd al-Ash-halī reports it from Ibn ʿAjlān from Zayd b. Aslam. All of these isnāds contain the addition (*when he recites, be silent*).
>
> On the other hand, Layth reports from Ibn ʿAjlān from Abū al-Zinād from Aʿraj from Abū Hurayrah the same ḥadīth without the addition. Also, Yaḥyā b. al-ʿAlāʾ al-Rāzī reports it from Zayd b. Aslam from Abū Ṣāliḥ from Abū Hurayrah without the addition, and states: The addition (*when he recites, be silent*) is not soundly established in this report.[19]

In addition, ʿAbbās al-Dūrī relates: I heard Yaḥyā b. Maʿīn say about the report of Abū Khālid al-Aḥmar with the addition (*when he recites, be silent*): This addition has no weight, is not sound, and represents a mistake.[20] Bukhārī states in al-Kunā: It is not sound. Abū Dāwūd, as mentioned previously, said: This addition is not sound, and we consider the mistake to be from Abū Khālid. Al-Nasāʾī stated in Sunan al-Kubrā: We do not know of anyone else who supported Ibn ʿAjlān in reporting this addition. Bayhaqī in his Sunan said: It is a mistake on the part of Ibn ʿAjlān.' He also said in al-Maʿrifah: Experts agree that the

---

[18] *ʿIlal*, vol 2, 395-6.

[19] Dāruquṭnī, *ʿIlal*, vol 8, pg 186-7.

[20] *Tārīkh Ibn Maʿīn*, vol 3 pg 455.

addition is mistaken, including Yaḥyā b. Ma'īn, Abū Dāwūd, Abū Ḥātim al-Rāzī, Abū 'Alī, 'Alī b. 'Umar, and Abū 'Abdullah. Finally, he states: 'This report is known through Abū Khālid al-Aḥmar from Ibn 'Ajlān. Bukhārī states: This is not known among the ṣaḥīḥ reports of Abū Khālid. Aḥmad states: I see that he used to commit tadlīs (deception). Yaḥyā b. Ma'īn said: Abū Khālid was trustworthy (ṣadūq) but not a proof.[21]

The Hidden Defect in the Addition: *When he recites, be silent.*

The addition in this report ('*when he recites, be silent*') also has a subtle defect ('illah) which precluded Muslim's [full] inclusion in his Ṣaḥīḥ.[22] Sulaymān al-Taymī added in his report the words: (*when he recites, be silent*), which opposed what was reported by the other students of Qatādah: Hishām al-Dastuwā'ī, Sa'īd b. Abī 'Arūbah, Abū 'Awānah, and Ma'mar (whose isnād appear in Ṣaḥīḥ Muslim), as well as Shu'bah and Abān (whose isnād is reported by Abū 'Awānah), Hammām (reported in *Sharḥ ma'ānī al-āthār*), 'Adīyy b. Abī 'Umārah (reported by Dāruquṭnī), and Ḥammād b. Salamah, Ḥajjāj b. al-Ḥajjāj al-Bāhilī (reported in *Juz' al-qirā'ah khalf al-imām*).

After relating this report in his Sunan, Abū Dāwūd also confirms: 'The words: '*when the imām recites, be silent,*' are not sound and were only related by Sulaymān al-Taymī in this ḥadīth.'

Bazzār says in his Musnad: A group of Qatādah's students reported this ḥadīth through this isnād, but we know of no one except al-Taymī who reported the words: '*when the imām recites, be silent,*' except for one other report: Muḥammad b. Yaḥyā al-Qaṭ'ī related it to us: Sālim b. Nūḥ informed us: from 'Umar b. 'Āmir: from Qatādah: from Yūnus b. Jubayr: from Ḥiṭṭān: from Abū Mūsā: from the Prophet ﷺ the same ḥadīth related by Taymī.

The ḥadīth expert Ibn 'Ammār al-Shahīd said: We believe these words ('*When he recites, be silent*') are a mistake from al-Taymī and not sound. The

[21] Bayhaqī, *al-Qirā'ah khalf al-imām*, pg 131.

[22] To repeat, the faulty addition appears as a follow-up isnād at the end of a supporting report in the end of Muslim's chapter, and is clearly not part of Muslim's primary corpus.

expert students of Qatādah did not mention it, including Sa'īd (as reported by Muslim: Kitāb al-ṣalāh—Bāb al-tashahhud fī al-ṣalāh; al-Nasā'ī in Sunan al-Ṣughrā: Kitāb al-imāmah—Bāb mubādarat al-imām and Kitāb al-taṭbīq—Bāb qawulū rabbanā wa laka al-ḥamd; Ibn Mājah: Kitāb iqāmat al-ṣalāh wa al-sunnah fīhā—Bāb mā jā'a fī al-tashahhud), nor did Ma'mar (Muṣannaf 'Abd al-Razzāq 2:201 and Musnad Aḥmad 10:190), Abū 'Awānah (Muslim: Kitāb al-ṣalāh—Bāb al-tashahhud fī al-ṣalāh; Abū Dāwūd: Kitāb al-ṣalāh—Bāb al-tashahhud), or others (see 'ilal al-ḥadīth in Ṣaḥīḥ Muslim 82-6).

Dāruquṭnī in al-Sunan (1:330) states: Sufyān al-Thawrī reports from Sulaymān al-Taymī without the addition (*when he recites, be silent*), as did the following students from Qatādah: Hishām al-Dastuwā'ī, Sa'īd, Shu'bah, Hammām, Abū 'Awānah, Abān, 'Adīyy b. Abī 'Umārah. These were the reliable students of Qatādah.[23]

Dāruquṭnī states after being asked about the ḥadīth of Ḥiṭṭān from Abū Mūsā:

> Qatādah reports this ḥadīth, and his students differed over it. Sa'īd, Hishām, Abān, Abū 'Awānah, Ma'mar, and 'Adīyy relate from Qatādah from Yūnus from Ḥiṭṭān from Abū Mūsā with variant but related wordings.
>
> Sulaymān al-Taymī reports this isnād from Qatādah with the additional words: *and when he recites, be silent*. Mu'tamir, Jarīr b. 'Abd al-Ḥamīd, and Sufyān al-Thawrī relate this from Sulaymān. Mu'tamir, however, added the following words, which no one else mentioned: *ash-hadu an lā ilāha illa Allāh waḥdahū lā sharīka lahū.*
>
> Sālim b. Nūḥ al-'Aṭṭār reports from 'Umar b. 'Āmir and Sa'īd b. Abī 'Arūbah, both from Qatādah, through this same isnād: *And when the imām recites, be silent.*
>
> Shu'bah relates from Qatādah this isnād and does not explain the tashahhud in his report but only references 'the ḥadīth of tashahhud.'

---

[23] Dāruquṭnī, *al-Sunan*, Ḥadīth number 1250, vol 2, pg 121.

> Muthannā b. Sa'īd reports from Qatādah with an isnād that opposes all the others. He reports from Abū al-'Āliyah from Abū Mūsā, and mentions only the portion concerning tashahhud. This is a mistake on his part in relating from Abū al-'Āliyah.
>
> Ḥammād b. Salamah reports it from Azraq b. Qays from Ḥiṭṭān from Abū Mūsā as a mawqūf report (i.e. words of Abū Mūsā and not the Prophet).
>
> Bahz b. Asad and Naḍr b. Shumayl relate from Ḥammād this isnād and add: *When the Prophet ﷺ began the prayer, he raised his hands, and also when he bowed and lifted his head from rukū'*. But other than these two, the rest relate the report through Ḥammād as a mawqūf report.
>
> Maṭr al-Warrāq also relates this report from Zahdam al-Jarmī from Abū Mūsā as a mawqūf report.
>
> The correct version in these is what Sa'īd, Hishām and their likes relate from Qatādah. Sulaymān al-Taymī is reliable but he [mistakenly] added the words: *And when he recites, be silent.* Perhaps he was confused by the many differences among reliable reporters. Sālim b. Nūḥ was not strong. The correct version of the report of Azraq b. Qays from Ḥiṭṭān is what Ḥammād b. Salamah reported from Azraq as a mawqūf report. And Allah knows best.[24]

Dāruquṭnī states in *al-tatabu'*: Taymī opposed all the other students of Qatādah with this addition (*and when he recites, be silent*) . . . Only 'Umar b. 'Āmir supported him in relating this from Taymī, and 'Umar was not strong. Yaḥyā al-Qaṭṭān did not accept him. The agreement of the rest of the students of Qatādah against Taymī is evidence that he was mistaken.[25]

Bayhaqī states in al-Sunan al-Kubrā: Abū 'Abdullah the expert related to us: I heard the expert Abū 'Alī say: Jarīr in reporting from Taymī opposed all the other students of Qatādah in this ḥadīth. The correct version is the one reported by Hishām, Hammām, Sa'īd, Ma'mar, Abū 'Awānah, Ḥajjāj, and others—

---

[24] Dāruquṭnī, *al-'Ilal*, vol 7, pg 252-4.

[25] Dāruquṭnī, *al-ilzāmāt wa al-tatabbu'*, pg 170-1.

without this addition. Sālim b. Nawḥ relates from Ibn Abī ʿArūbah and ʿUmar b. ʿĀmir, both from Qatādah, and he was mistaken.[26]

Nawawī said: Know that this addition (*when he recites, be silent*) was differed over by experts. Bayhaqī relates in al-Sunan al-Kubrā from Abū Dāwūd al-Sijistānī that this addition is not sound. He reports similar views from Yaḥyā b. Maʿīn, Abū Ḥātim al-Rāzī, Dāruquṭnī, Abū ʿAlī of Nishapur (the teacher of Ḥākim). Bayhaqī states: I heard Abū ʿAlī say: This wording is not sound, because Taymī opposed all the other students of Qatādah in reporting it, and the agreement of these experts of ḥadīth in considering it weak takes precedence over the authentication of Muslim, especially since he does relate it with an explicit isnād.[27]

Abū Masʿūd of Damascus responds to Dāruquṭnī: Muslim only intended to relate the isnād of Taymī to highlight the differences in the ḥadīth from Qatādah, not to show that it was sound. His reporting of this isnād cannot be used to reject the large group of students who opposed Taymī.[28]

---

[26] Bayhaqī, *al-Sunan al-Kubrā* (ḥadīth number 2889), vol 2, pg 222.

[27] i.e. It is not part of his primary corpus but only as a follow-up isnād.

[28] Dāruquṭnī, *al-ilzāmāt wa al-tatabbuʿ*, pg 171.

Laxity of Second and Third Tier Ṣaḥīḥ

How have you included in the second use of ṣaḥīḥ some ḥadīth reports of unknown narrators? I have only included the reports of those unknown narrators who were accepted by the likes of Mālik and Shuʿbah. Tirmidhī states in the Book of Purity (Kitāb al-Ṭahārah), Chapter: [What Has Been Related About Sea Water That It is Pure]:

BOOK OF PURITY FROM THE MESSENGER—CHAPTER: THE WATER OF THE SEA IS PURE

Qutaybah narrated to us from Mālik . . . And al-Anṣārī Isḥāq b. Mūsā also narrated to us: Maʿan narrated to us: Mālik narrated to us: from Ṣafwān b. Sulaym: from Saʿīd b. Salamah—of the family of Ibn al-Azraq—that al-Mughīrah b. Abū Burdah—and he was from the clan of ʿAbd al-Dār—informed him that he heard Abū Hurayrah say:

A man asked God's Messenger: 'O Messenger of God! We sail the seas, and we only carry a little water with us. If we use it for ablution, we would go thirsty. So shall we perform ablution from the water of the sea?' God's Messenger replied: ⟨*Its water is pure, and its dead are lawful.*⟩

Abū ʿĪsā (Tirmidhī) said: This ḥadīth is ḥasan ṣaḥīḥ.[29]

جامع الترمذي - أبواب الطهارة عن رسول الله صلى الله عليه وسلم - باب ما جاء في ماء البحر أنه طهور

حَدَّثَنَا قُتَيْبَةُ، عَنْ مَالِكٍ. (ح) وَحَدَّثَنَا الْأَنْصَارِيُّ إِسْحَاقُ بْنُ مُوسَى، قَالَ: حَدَّثَنَا مَعْنٌ، قَالَ: حَدَّثَنَا مَالِكٌ، عَنْ صَفْوَانَ بْنِ سُلَيْمٍ، عَنْ سَعِيدِ بْنِ سَلَمَةَ مِنْ آلِ ابْنِ الْأَزْرَقِ أَنَّ الْمُغِيرَةَ بْنَ أَبِي بُرْدَةَ وَهُوَ مِنْ بَنِي عَبْدِ الدَّارِ أَخْبَرَهُ أَنَّهُ سَمِعَ أَبَا هُرَيْرَةَ يَقُولُ: سَأَلَ رَجُلٌ رَسُولَ اللهِ صَلَّى اللهُ عَلَيْهِ وَسَلَّمَ فَقَالَ: يَا رَسُولَ اللهِ، إِنَّا نَرْكَبُ الْبَحْرَ وَنَحْمِلُ مَعَنَا الْقَلِيلَ مِنَ الْمَاءِ، فَإِنْ تَوَضَّأْنَا بِهِ عَطِشْنَا، أَفَنَتَوَضَّأُ مِنَ الْبَحْرِ؟ فَقَالَ رَسُولُ اللهِ صَلَّى اللهُ عَلَيْهِ وَسَلَّمَ: هُوَ الطَّهُورُ مَاؤُهُ، الْحِلُّ مَيْتَتُهُ.

هَذَا حَدِيثٌ حَسَنٌ صَحِيحٌ.

[29] Tirmidhī: Kitāb al-ṭahārah ʿan rasūlillāh—Bāb mā jāʾa fī māʾ al-baḥr annahu ṭahūr.

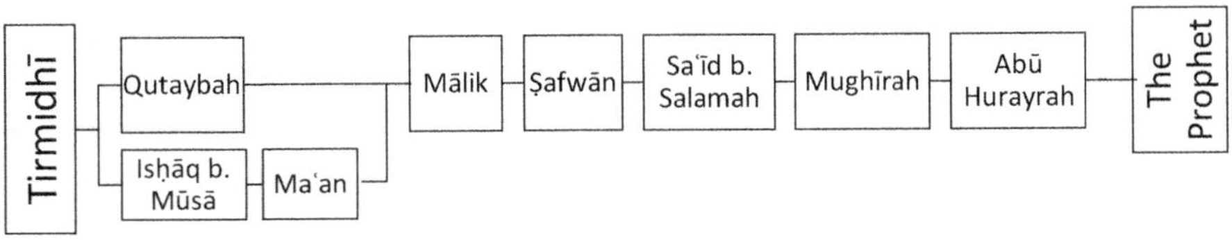

Sa'īd b. Salamah and al-Mughīrah b. Abī Burdah are both not very well-known. Ibn al-Madīnī said: 'Al-Mughīrah b. Abī Burdah was a man from the clan 'Abd al-Dār who heard ḥadīth from Abū Hurayrah, but the only report that he related from him is this one. Despite the relatively unknown status of some of its reporters, the ḥadīth was deemed ṣaḥīḥ because the likes of Malik reported it and relied upon it.'

Malik related this ḥadīth in the Muwaṭṭa', as did the authors of the Sunan,[30] Dārimī, and Ḥākim through Malik's isnād. Those others than Tirmidhī have also deemed it ṣaḥīḥ. Ibn 'Abd al-Barr says: Muḥammad b. 'Īsā Tirmidhī asked Bukhārī about it and he replied that it is a ṣaḥīḥ ḥadīth. Ḥākim also authenticated and related many supporting narrations. So this ḥadīth is ṣaḥīḥ and was acted upon by the jurists of the Muslim world. However, Bukhārī and Muslim did not relate it because it does not fulfill their conditions due to Sa'īd b. Salamah and Mughīrah b. Abī Burdah.

Sa'īd b. Salamah and al-Mughīrah b. Abū Burdah are both relatively unknown. Ibn al-Madīnī said: al-Mughīrah b. Abū Burdah was a man from the tribe of 'Abd al-Dār who heard ḥadīth from Abū Hurayrah, but he only heard this one ḥadīth. Despite that, they authenticated this ḥadīth notwithstanding the unknown status of some of its narrators, because it was a ḥadīth related and relied upon by Mālik.

Why do you say about the second type, 'overtly connected'? Because they authenticated ḥadīth of those who were known for tadlīs without fully investigating the reasons for that tadlīs, and examples of that are abundant in Tirmidhī and others.

---

[30] Among the six canonical ḥadīth texts, the four Sunan works are those of Tirmidhī, Abū Dāwūd, Nasā'ī and Ibn Mājah.

Why have you omitted all the conditions of authenticity in the third type? It is indeed as I have mentioned, and if you want to uncover the truth then look into those books for yourself and you will find them filled with ḥadīth of weak and even accused narrators.

Where are the reports of historians with respect to these three types of ṣaḥīḥ? They are in the third category, or even lesser than that, because they are filled with narrations that are disconnected at single or multiple levels, spuriously discovered, contradictory, extremely weak, and even fabricated, a fact which is not hidden from anyone who looks into them.

The Meaning of Ḥasan Ḥadīth

What is the true meaning of the ḥasan ḥadīth?

Experts of this discipline have used it in three meanings:

First, the compound term *ḥasan-ṣaḥīḥ*, utilized by Tirmidhī and others, was used for a report whose sources were known[1] and which fulfilled all the conditions of soundness (ṣaḥīḥ).

Second, the term *ḥasan* (without the *ṣaḥīḥ* qualifier) refers to a report whose sources are known and which fulfills all the conditions of soundness except for accuracy (ḍabṭ), which is compromised on the part of one or more narrator. Examples of this type are found abundantly in Tirmidhī's Sunan and among the supporting reports (mutābaʿāt) of the Ṣaḥīḥ of Bukhārī and Muslim (although others considered these supporting reports to be ṣaḥīḥ). When these reports have multiple paths of transmission which serve to remediate the compromised ḍabṭ and strengthen the overall ḥadīth, it is raised up and referred to as *ṣaḥīḥ li ghayrihī* (ṣaḥīḥ based on extrinsic factors).

Khaṭṭābī (d. 388/988)[2] states in *Maʿālim al-sunan*: 'Know that ḥadīth according to its experts are three types: ṣaḥīḥ, ḥasan and defective (saqīm). Ṣaḥīḥ is that which has a connected chain with upright narrators, while ḥasan is that whose sources are known and its reporters famous. Most ḥadīth consist of these (ṣaḥīḥ and ḥasan). These are the reports accepted by most scholars and used by most jurists. The book of Abū Dāwūd combines both of these types.'[3]

What Khaṭṭābī meant by 'most ḥadīth consist of these' was that most ḥadīth that exist are either ṣaḥīḥ or ḥasan. Also, his definition of ḥasan can also include many ṣaḥīḥ reports. Because of this, I have further divided these into ḥasan ṣaḥīḥ

---

[1] Its origins or sources (makhraj) being known implies that the report has traceable and connected isnāds to the source of the report, i.e. the Prophet.

[2] Abū Sulaymān Hamd b. Muḥammad al-Khaṭṭābī was a great Shāfiʿī scholar hailing from the Halmand province of present-day Afghanistan who wrote, among other works, Maʿālim al-Sunan as a commentary of the Sunan of Abū Dāwūd.

[3] *Maʿālim al-sunan*, vol 1, pg 2. Abū al-Faḍl al-ʿIrāqī (d. 806 AH) states: I have not found anyone who preceded Khaṭṭābī in this division, though the word ḥasan does appear among early scholars such as Shāfiʿī, Bukhārī and others. See *al-Taqyīd wa al-īḍāḥ sharḥ muqaddimah Ibn al-Ṣalāḥ*, pg 19.

and ḥasan. Ibn Daqīq al-ʿĪd comments on Khaṭṭābī's definition: This definition also fits ṣaḥīḥ reports which could be included within ḥasan.[4]

The third type is *ḥasan li ghayrihī* (ḥasan based on extrinsic factors) and is used for those reports which contain most conditions of ṣaḥīḥ apart from connected chains (ittiṣāl) or ḍabṭ and are collectively strengthened by the existence of multiple such reports. Tirmidhī states in al-ʿIlal: 'When we use '*ḥasan*' in our book for any ḥadīth, we mean that its isnād is ḥasan according to us: every ḥadīth that is reported by narrators who are not accused of lying, nor does it contradict stronger reports, and is reported through multiple isnāds. That is a ḥasan ḥadīth for us.'

This explanation removes so many difficulties concerning Tirmidhī's usages.

We find your classification imprecise and confounding basic fundamentals of sciences which do not suit your status. You should have divided ḥasan into ḥasan li dhātihī and ḥasan li ghayrihī, and into ḥasan ṣaḥīḥ and ḥasan ghayr ṣaḥīḥ. I have inclined towards this division in order to clarify and emphasize that the first type is not just ḥasan but a type of ṣaḥīḥ.

You said that the term 'ḥasan ṣaḥīḥ' is utilized by Tirmidhī and others. Who are the others? An example is what Tirmidhī states in the Book on Purity (Ṭahārah), Chapter: [What has been related about the one with excessive uterine bleeding that she can combine two prayers with one washing]:

[4] *Tadrīb al-rāwī*, vol 1, pg 166.

BOOK OF PURITY—CHAPTER: THE WOMAN WITH EXTRA-UTERINE BLEEDING COMBINING PRAYERS WITH ONE WASHING Muḥammad b. Bashshār related to me: Abū ʿĀmir al-ʿAwadī related to me: Zuhayr b. Muḥammad related to me: from ʿAbdullah b. Muḥammad b. ʿUqayl: from Ibrāhīm b. Muḥammad b. Ṭalḥah: from his uncle ʿImrān b. Ṭalḥah: from his mother Ḥamnah bint Jahsh, who said: I was suffering from excessive and severe bleeding, so I came to the Prophet to seek his advice. I found him in the house of my sister Zaynab bint Jaḥsh. I said, 'Messenger of Allah! I suffer from a case of severe and excessive blood flow. What do you order me to do for it, and does this prevent me from fasting and performing prayers?' He replied: 'Tie a cotton rag around yourself and the blood will go away.' I said, 'It is more than that.' He replied: 'Make it tight.' I said, 'It is more than that.' He said: 'Then use a cloth (to bind it).' I said, 'It is more than that. It flows too much.'

The Prophet then said: 'I will order you to do one of two things, whichever of them you do, it will be acceptable for you. You should know which of them you are able to do.' Then he said: 'This is only a blow from Shayṭān. Count your menses for six or seven days, which Allah knows,

جامع الترمذي - أبواب الطهارة عن رسول الله صلى الله عليه وسلم - باب في المستحاضة أنها تجمع بين الصلاتين بغسل واحد

حَدَّثَنَا مُحَمَّدُ بْنُ بَشَّارٍ، قَالَ: حَدَّثَنَا أَبُو عَامِرٍ الْعَقَدِيُّ، قَالَ: حَدَّثَنَا زُهَيْرُ بْنُ مُحَمَّدٍ، عَنْ عَبْدِ اللهِ بْنِ مُحَمَّدِ بْنِ عَقِيلٍ، عَنْ إِبْرَاهِيمَ بْنِ مُحَمَّدِ بْنِ، عَنْ عَمِّهِ عِمْرَانَ بْنِ طَلْحَةَ، عَنْ أُمِّهِ حَمْنَةَ بِنْتِ جَحْشٍ، قَالَتْ: كُنْتُ أُسْتَحَاضُ حَيْضَةً كَثِيرَةً شَدِيدَةً، فَأَتَيْتُ النَّبِيَّ صَلَّى اللهُ عَلَيْهِ وَسَلَّمَ أَسْتَفْتِيهِ وَأُخْبِرُهُ، فَوَجَدْتُهُ فِي بَيْتِ أُخْتِي زَيْنَبَ بِنْتِ جَحْشٍ فَقُلْتُ: يَا رَسُولَ اللهِ، إِنِّي أُسْتَحَاضُ حَيْضَةً كَثِيرَةً شَدِيدَةً، فَمَا تَأْمُرُنِي فِيهَا، قَدْ مَنَعَتْنِي الصِّيَامَ وَالصَّلَاةَ. قَالَ: أَنْعَتُ لَكِ الْكُرْسُفَ؛ فَإِنَّهُ يُذْهِبُ الدَّمَ قَالَتْ: هُوَ أَكْثَرُ مِنْ ذَلِكَ، قَالَ: فَتَلَجَّمِي، قَالَتْ: هُوَ أَكْثَرُ مِنْ ذَلِكَ، قَالَ: فَاتَّخِذِي ثَوْبًا، قَالَتْ: هُوَ أَكْثَرُ مِنْ ذَلِكَ، إِنَّمَا أَثُجُّ ثَجًّا، فَقَالَ النَّبِيُّ صَلَّى اللهُ عَلَيْهِ وَسَلَّمَ: سَآمُرُكِ بِأَمْرَيْنِ أَيَّهُمَا صَنَعْتِ أَجْزَأَ عَنْكِ، فَإِنْ قَوِيتِ عَلَيْهِمَا فَأَنْتِ أَعْلَمُ، فَقَالَ: إِنَّمَا هِيَ رَكْضَةٌ مِنَ الشَّيْطَانِ

then perform ghusl. When you see that you have become pure and clean, then perform prayer for twenty-three or twenty-four nights and their days. Perform prayers and fast, and that will be acceptable for you. Do this (if you can) just as (other) women who menstruate and become pure during their periods of menstruation and purity. If (not, and) you are able to delay Ẓuhr and hasten ʿAṣr then perform ghusl when you have become pure, and pray Ẓuhr and ʿAṣr together. Then delay Maghrib and hasten ʿIshāʾ, then perform ghusl and combine the two prayers. So do this (if you are able). Then perform ghusl with the dawn and pray. Do this, and fast if you are able to do so.' Then God's Messenger said: 'That is what is preferable to me of the two.'

Abū ʿĪsā (Tirmidhī) then states: This ḥadīth is ḥasan ṣaḥīḥ . . . I asked Muḥammad (i.e. Bukhārī) about this ḥadīth and he declared that it is ḥasan ṣaḥīḥ. And this is also what Aḥmad b. Ḥanbal said.[5]

فَتَحَيَّضِي سِتَّةَ أَيَّامٍ أَوْ سَبْعَةَ أَيَّامٍ فِي عِلْمِ اللهِ، ثُمَّ اغْتَسِلِي، فَإِذَا رَأَيْتِ أَنَّكِ قَدْ طَهُرْتِ وَاسْتَنْقَأْتِ فَصَلِّي أَرْبَعًا وَعِشْرِينَ لَيْلَةً أَوْ ثَلَاثًا وَعِشْرِينَ لَيْلَةً وَأَيَّامَهَا، وَصُومِي وَصَلِّي، فَإِنَّ ذَلِكِ يُجْزِئُكِ، وَكَذَلِكِ فَافْعَلِي، كَمَا تَحِيضُ النِّسَاءُ وَكَمَا يَطْهُرْنَ، لِمِيقَاتِ حَيْضِهِنَّ وَطُهْرِهِنَّ، فَإِنْ قَوِيتِ عَلَى أَنْ تُؤَخِّرِي الظُّهْرَ وَتُعَجِّلِي الْعَصْرَ ثُمَّ تَغْتَسِلِينَ حِينَ تَطْهُرِينَ، وَتُصَلِّينَ الظُّهْرَ وَالْعَصْرَ جَمِيعًا، ثُمَّ تُؤَخِّرِينَ الْمَغْرِبَ وَتُعَجِّلِينَ الْعِشَاءَ، ثُمَّ تَغْتَسِلِينَ، وَتَجْمَعِينَ بَيْنَ الصَّلَاتَيْنِ، فَافْعَلِي، وَتَغْتَسِلِينَ مَعَ الصُّبْحِ وَتُصَلِّينَ، وَكَذَلِكِ فَافْعَلِي، وَصُومِي إِنْ قَوِيتِ عَلَى ذَلِكَ، فَقَالَ رَسُولُ اللهِ صَلَّى اللهُ عَلَيْهِ وَسَلَّمَ: وَهُوَ أَعْجَبُ الْأَمْرَيْنِ إِلَيَّ.

هَذَا حَدِيثٌ حَسَنٌ صَحِيحٌ. وسَأَلْتُ مُحَمَّدًا عَنْ هَذَا الحَدِيثِ، فَقَالَ: هُوَ حَدِيثٌ حَسَنٌ .وهَكَذا قَالَ أَحْمَدُ بْنُ حَنْبَلٍ: هُوَ حَدِيثٌ حَسَنٌ صَحِيحٌ.

---

[5] Tirmidhī: Kitāb al-ṭahārah—Bāb mā jāʾa fī al-mustaḥāḍah annahā tajmaʿ bayna al-ṣalātayn bi ghuslin wāḥidin.

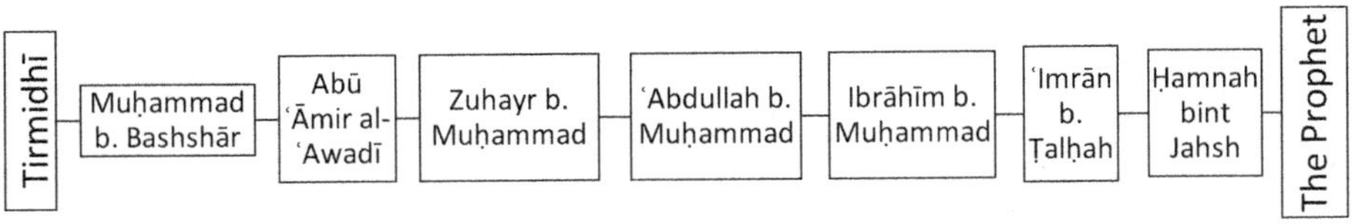

Why didn't Bukhārī and Muslim relate this ḥadīth when they and Aḥmad deemed it ṣaḥīḥ? I previously explained that Bukhārī and Muslim only intended to report primary-tier ṣaḥīḥ (the first type of ṣaḥīḥ) reports for their primary corpus (uṣūl). This ḥadīth is reported by ʿAbdullah b. Muḥammad b. ʿUqayl, and his ḍabṭ does not fulfill their conditions.

Can you provide another example of this type of report that Bukhārī and Muslim did not include in their work, while clarifying its problem? Tirmidhī relates the following:

BOOK OF PURITY—CHAPTER: CONCESSIONS IN THAT Qutaybah related to us: Abū al-Aḥwaṣ related to us: from Simāk b. Ḥarb: from ʿIkrimah: from Ibn ʿAbbās:

One of the wives of the Prophet performed ghusl with a bowl. God's Messenger wanted to perform ablution with it, so she said: 'O Messenger of God! Indeed I was ritually impure (junub).' So he said: {*Indeed, water never becomes ritually impure.*}

This ḥadīth is ḥasan ṣaḥīḥ.[6]

جامع الترمذي - أبواب الطهارة عن رسول الله صلى الله عليه وسلم - باب الرخصة في ذلك

حَدَّثَنَا قُتَيْبَةُ، قَالَ: حَدَّثَنَا أَبُو الْأَحْوَصِ، عَنْ سِمَاكِ بْنِ حَرْبٍ، عَنْ عِكْرِمَةَ، عَنِ ابْنِ عَبَّاسٍ، قَالَ: اغْتَسَلَ بَعْضُ أَزْوَاجِ النَّبِيِّ صَلَّى اللهُ عَلَيْهِ وَسَلَّمَ فِي جَفْنَةٍ، فَأَرَادَ رَسُولُ اللهِ صَلَّى اللهُ عَلَيْهِ وَسَلَّمَ أَنْ يَتَوَضَّأَ مِنْهُ، فَقَالَتْ: يَا رَسُولَ اللهِ، إِنِّي كُنْتُ جُنُبًا، فَقَالَ: إِنَّ الْمَاءَ لَا يُجْنِبُ.

هَذَا حَدِيثٌ حَسَنٌ صَحِيحٌ.

[6] Tirmidhī: Kitāb al-ṭahārah—Bāb al-rukhṣah fī dhālik. It is also related by the authors of the other Sunan works.

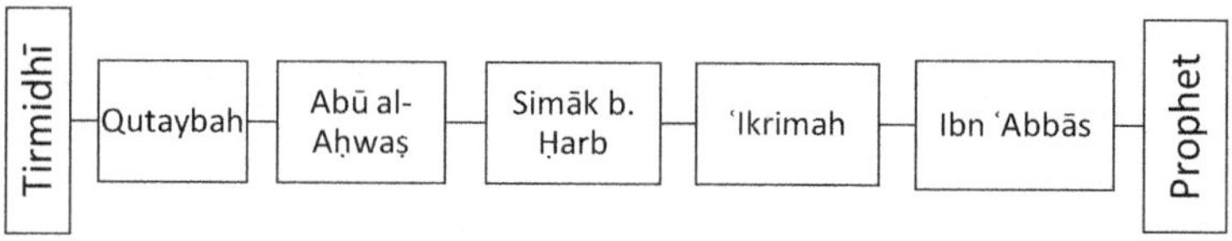

This ḥadīth was also related by Aḥmad, Abū Dāwūd, Nasā'ī, Ibn Mājah, and Dāruquṭnī. It was authenticated by Ibn Khuzaymah. Ḥākim related it through the isnād of Sufyān al-Thawrī and Shu'bah from Simāk b. Ḥarb, and said: 'This is a ṣaḥīḥ ḥadīth on the topic of purity, which Bukhārī and Muslim did not report, though there is no defect associated with it, as agreed by Dhahabī.' Ibn Ḥajar states in his *Fatḥ*: 'Many people found a defect in Simāk b. Ḥarb that he used to be prone to talqīn,[7] but Shu'bah accepted his report and related it from him, because he was known to accept only ṣaḥīḥ reports from his teachers.'[8]

Bukhārī only utilized Simāk for supporting material. Muslim accepted him but did not accept 'Ikrimah. But the ḥadīth of Simāk from 'Ikrimah is not like that. Ya'qūb b. Shaybah said: His narration from 'Ikrimah specifically is problematic. In reporting from other than 'Ikrimah, he is acceptable but not among the most proficient. Those who heard from Simāk earlier on, such as Shu'bah and Sufyān, their reports from him are sound and fully acceptable. Ibn al-Madīnī is reported to have said: Simāk's reporting from 'Ikrimah is problematic, for Sufyān and Shu'bah relate from him from 'Ikrimah [from Ibn 'Abbās], while others relate from him from Ibn 'Abbās directly.

Can you provide an example of the second type (ḥasan)? Tirmidhī relates the following:

BOOK OF PURITY—CHAPTER: WASHING THE FINGERS Ibrāhīm b. Sa'īd al-Jawharī related to us: Sa'd b. 'Abd al-Ḥamīd b. Ja'far related to us: 'Abd al-Raḥmān b. Abī al-Zinād

جامع الترمذي - أبواب الطهارة عن رسول الله صلى الله عليه وسلم - باب في تخليل الأصابع

[7] Talqīn refers to teachers accepting the hints of others in relating ḥadīth (whether pertaining to information about the isnād or other details), which was a common phenomenon in older age and was considered a form of unintentional negligence that compromised accuracy.

[8] *Fatḥ al-bārī*, vol 1, pg 300.

related to us: from Mūsā b. ʿUqbah: from Ṣāliḥ the freed slave of al-Tawʾamah: from Ibn ʿAbbās:

The Prophet ﷺ stated: {*When you perform ablution, wash between the fingers of your hands and feet.*}

This ḥadīth is ḥasan gharīb.[9]

حَدَّثَنَا إِبْرَاهِيمُ بْنُ سَعِيدٍ الْجَوْهَرِيُّ، قَالَ: حَدَّثَنَا سَعْدُ بْنُ عَبْدِ الْحَمِيدِ بْنِ جَعْفَرٍ، قَالَ: حَدَّثَنَا عَبْدُ الرَّحْمَنِ بْنُ أَبِي الزِّنَادِ، عَنْ مُوسَى بْنِ عُقْبَةَ، عَنْ صَالِحٍ مَوْلَى التَّوْأَمَةِ، عَنِ ابْنِ عَبَّاسٍ، أَنَّ رَسُولَ اللهِ صَلَّى اللهُ عَلَيْهِ وَسَلَّمَ قَالَ: إِذَا تَوَضَّأْتَ فَخَلِّلْ بَيْنَ أَصَابِعِ يَدَيْكَ وَرِجْلَيْكَ.

هَذَا حَدِيثٌ حَسَنٌ غَرِيبٌ.

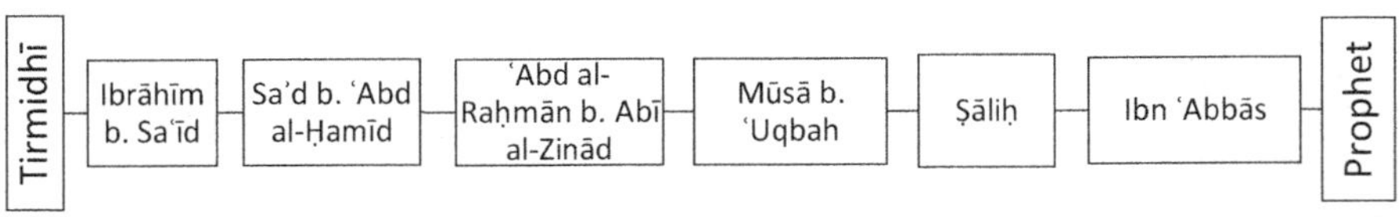

Tirmidhī states: 'I asked Muḥammad about this ḥadīth and he replied: It is a ḥasan ḥadīth. Mūsā b. ʿUqbah heard from Ṣāliḥ much earlier on, and Imām Aḥmad used to say: Whoever heard from Ṣāliḥ early on, his reports are ḥasan. As for those who heard from him late, it appeared that he weakened their reports.'[10] So this report does not reach the level of ṣaḥīḥ, and Bukhārī deemed it ḥasan. Another example is what Tirmidhī related:

BOOK OF PURITY—CHAPTER: RUNNING THE FINGERS THROUGH THE BEARD Yaḥyā b. Mūsā related to us: ʿAbd al-Razzāq related to us:

جامع الترمذي - أبواب الطهارة عن رسول الله صلى الله عليه وسلم - باب ما جاء في تخليل اللحية

[9] Tirmidhī: Kitāb al-ṭahārah—Bāb fī takhlīl al-aṣābiʿ.

[10] *Al-ʿIlal al-kabīr*, vol 1, pg 34.

from Isrāʾīl: from ʿĀmir b. Shaqīq: From Abū Wāʾil: from ʿUthmān:

The Prophet ﷺ ran his fingers through his beard.

This ḥadīth is ḥasan ṣaḥīḥ.[11]

حَدَّثَنَا يَحْيَى بْنُ مُوسَى، قَالَ: حَدَّثَنَا عَبْدُ الرَّزَّاقِ، عَنْ إِسْرَائِيلَ، عَنْ عَامِرِ بْنِ شَقِيقٍ، عَنْ أَبِي وَائِلٍ، عَنْ عُثْمَانَ بْنِ عَفَّانَ، أَنَّ النَّبِيَّ صَلَّى اللهُ عَلَيْهِ وَسَلَّمَ كَانَ يُخَلِّلُ لِحْيَتَهُ.

هَذَا حَدِيثٌ حَسَنٌ صَحِيحٌ.

Muḥammad [b. Ismāʿīl al-Bukhārī] said: The soundest report on running the fingers through the beard is that of ʿUthmān. I said to him: People have criticized this ḥadīth. He replied: It is ḥasan.[12]

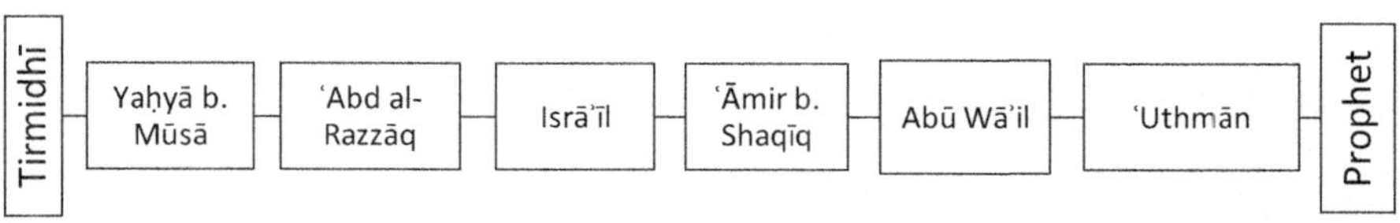

[11] Sunan al-Tirmidhī: Kitāb al-ṭahārah—Bāb mā jāʾa fī takhlīl al-liḥyah.

[12] *Al-ʿIlal al-kabīr,* vol 1, pg 33.

Give us an example of ṣaḥīḥ li ghayrihī. Tirmidhī relates the following:

BOOK OF PURITY—CHAPTER: WHAT HAS BEEN REPORTED ABOUT SIWĀK Abū Kurayb related to us: ʿAbdah b. Sulaymān related to us: from Muḥammad b. ʿAmr: from Abū Salamah: from Abū Hurayrah:

The Prophet ﷺ said: ﴾*Had it not been too difficult for my ummah, I would have commanded the use of siwāk before each prayer.*﴿

Muḥammad b. Isḥāq also reported this ḥadīth from Muḥammad b. Ibrāhīm from Abū Salamah from Zayd b. Khālid from the Prophet ﷺ.

The ḥadīth reports of Abū Salamah from Abū Hurayrah and Zayd b. Khālid, both from the Prophet, are ṣaḥīḥ in my estimation, because they have been reported through multiple chains from Abū Hurayrah from the Prophet. The ḥadīth of Abū Hurayrah is deemed ṣaḥīḥ because it is reported through more than one isnād. Muḥammad [b. Ismāʿīl al-Bukhārī], however, believed that the ḥadīth of Abū

جامع الترمذي - أبواب الطهارة عن رسول الله صلى الله عليه وسلم - باب ما جاء في السواك

حَدَّثَنَا أَبُو كُرَيْبٍ، قَالَ: حَدَّثَنَا عَبْدَةُ بْنُ سُلَيْمَانَ، عَنْ مُحَمَّدِ بْنِ عَمْرٍو، عَنْ أَبِي سَلَمَةَ، عَنْ أَبِي هُرَيْرَةَ قَالَ: قَالَ رَسُولُ اللهِ صَلَّى اللهُ عَلَيْهِ وَسَلَّمَ: لَوْلَا أَنْ أَشُقَّ عَلَى أُمَّتِي لَأَمَرْتُهُمْ بِالسِّوَاكِ عِنْدَ كُلِّ صَلَاةٍ.

وَقَدْ رَوَى هَذَا الْحَدِيثَ مُحَمَّدُ بْنُ إِسْحَاقَ، عَنْ مُحَمَّدِ بْنِ إِبْرَاهِيمَ، عَنْ أَبِي سَلَمَةَ، عَنْ زَيْدِ بْنِ خَالِدٍ، عَنِ النَّبِيِّ صَلَّى اللهُ عَلَيْهِ وَسَلَّمَ.

وَحَدِيثُ أَبِي سَلَمَةَ، عَنْ أَبِي هُرَيْرَةَ، وَزَيْدِ بْنِ خَالِدٍ، عَنِ النَّبِيِّ صَلَّى اللهُ عَلَيْهِ وَسَلَّمَ كِلَاهُمَا عِنْدِي صَحِيحٌ؛ لِأَنَّهُ قَدْ رُوِيَ مِنْ غَيْرِ وَجْهٍ عَنْ أَبِي هُرَيْرَةَ، عَنِ النَّبِيِّ صَلَّى اللهُ عَلَيْهِ وَسَلَّمَ هَذَا الْحَدِيثُ.

وَحَدِيثُ أَبِي هُرَيْرَةَ إِنَّمَا صُحِّحَ؛ لِأَنَّهُ قَدْ رُوِيَ مِنْ غَيْرِ وَجْهٍ.

Salamah from Zayd b. Khālid was more sound.[13]

وَأَمَّا مُحَمَّدٌ فَزَعَمَ أَنَّ حَدِيثَ أَبِي سَلَمَةَ، عَنْ زَيْدِ بْنِ خَالِدٍ أَصَحُّ.

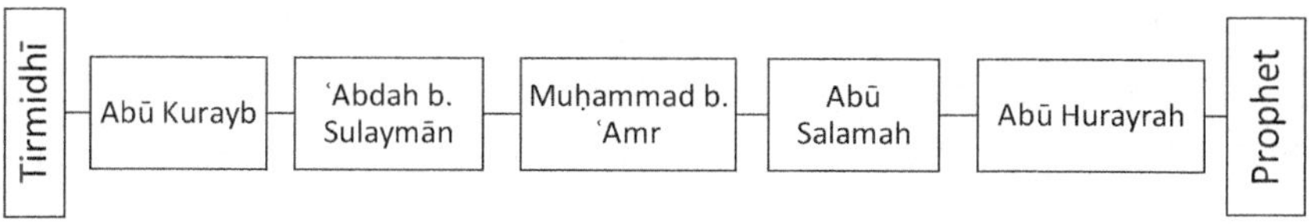

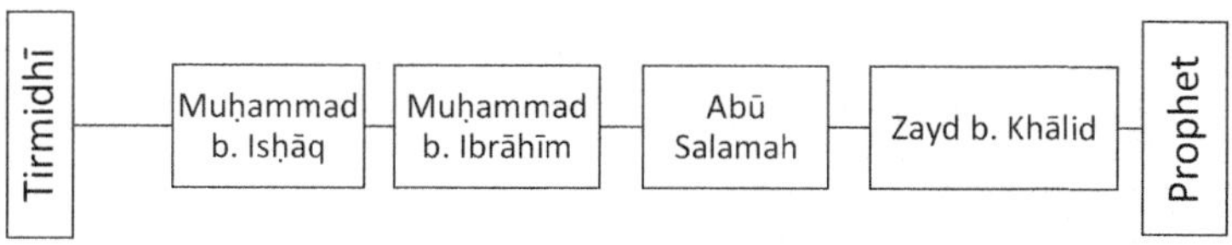

Give us an example of the third type. The book of Tirmidhī is filled with such examples, so there is no need to reproduce them here. However, there is a critical note that must be made: when, in a chapter, Tirmidhī deems a ḥadīth ḥasan due to multiple isnāds, and that ḥadīth is made up of multiple portions, he is referring only to that portion which is relevant to the chapter. Some people erroneously understood that when he does so, he is referring to the entire ḥadīth with all its portions as ḥasan. Further details on this are found in my forthcoming book, *Madkhal ilā Sunan al-Tirmidhī.*

[13] Tirmidhī: Kitāb al-ṭahārah—Bāb mā jā'a fī al-siwāk. It should be noted that this ḥadīth—*'Had it not been too difficult for my ummah, I would have commanded the use of siwāk before each prayer.'*— is a sound one related in Bukhārī, Muslim and the Muwaṭṭa' through A'raj through Abū Hurayrah. But here, the discussion is on the isnād of Abū Salamah from Abū Hurayra, and of Abū Salamah from Zayd b. Aslam, for the same ḥadīth. Keep in mind ḥadīth experts classified and discussed reports by isnāds, and every new isnād was considered a different ḥadīth.

The Meaning of Ḍaʿīf Ḥadīth

What is the meaning of ḍaʿīf ḥadīth? People have fallen into great errors from not fully comprehending the notion of daʿīf ḥadīth. There are some who categorically reject such reports while others embrace them fully treating them like ṣaḥīḥ and ḥasan ones. Yet others adopted a middle course, rejecting them only in matters of legal rulings while accepting them in non-legal matters like the virtues of specific deeds or general exhortations.

Which of these groups do you feel is inclined to the truth on the matter? Each of these approaches is partially correct and partially mistaken. But unfortunately, the matter has reached to an extent that these groups have pitted themselves against one other and hurled all sorts of accusations, ranging from benign to harsh.

But we always find you following this course of accusing others of mistakes while considering yourself alone as correct. I believe the correct position, based upon clear evidence, is the following:

The ḥadīth experts were clever scholars, highly proficient, and accurate in their craft. In that, they were qualitatively distinct from others. They chose to devote themselves to ḥadīth and never attributed to their Prophet ﷺ any report unless they verified its soundness and found in it the preconditions for authenticity (see chapter on ṣaḥīḥ ḥadīth). In the event that they could not verify the soundness of a report, they went on to treat it in a delicate and precise manner. If the report was ascertained to be a lie, for instance, they deemed it fabricated and false (mawḍūʿ). However, between sound and fabricated reports existed a vast arena which they termed daʿīf.

What was their stance concerning these daʿīf reports? The ḥadīth experts were the fairest and most just of people. Rather than treating these reports in a singular manner, they in fact turned to each individual report to study it carefully in order to classify it in a precise and academic manner.

Explain to us their unique classification that was fair and balanced, and free of extremes. They exerted their best efforts to studying the contents of the daʿīf reports and dividing them into various groups which ultimately fall under two broad categories: accepted (maqbūl) or rejected (mardūd).

Acceptable Daʿīf Reports

What were the accepted types of daʿīf reports? There are four categories:

The first are those daʿīf reports which were authenticated by Bukhārī and Muslim[1] and incorporated into their primary corpus.[2] These reports fulfilled the preconditions for being ṣaḥīḥ and also possessed many alternate routes of transmission, some of whose chains contained individuals who possessed an element of weakness which lowered their rank below that of primary-tier narrators. In other words, if a ḥadīth report was determined to be sound from other isnads, then Bukhārī or Muslim would sometimes relate the same report through an isnād which contained a weak transmitter. This is the practice of Bukhārī in particular, who, being extremely keen to derive many rulings from a single ḥadīth, on occasion feels the need to the relate the weaker isnād for additional benefits.[3]

Examples of such narrators are Ismāʿīl b. Abī Uways (d. 226/841)[4], who, were he to be alone in reporting a ḥadīth would render the report weak. However, when Ismāʿīl relates a ḥadīth which is also reported by reliable narrators such as ʿAbdullah b. Yūsuf al-Tinnīsī (d. 218/833)[5] or ʿAbdullah b. Maslamah al-Qaʿnabī (d. 221/836)[6], then Bukhārī occasionally utilizes Ismāʿīl's reports when the need arises.

Sometimes a ḥadīth is found in a well-known personal collection (ṣaḥīfah) of an author with sound verified isnads, while a weaker transmitter may happen to relate the same reports with a higher isnād. As an example, Muslim received the entire personal collection of Ḥafṣ b. Maysarah (d. 181/797)[7] with isnāds from

---

[1] Of course, these are not really daʿīf reports but ṣaḥīḥ, and they are classified here as the first category of daʿīf only as a matter of principle since their isnāds included weaker transmitters. See subsequent text for more elaboration.

[2] Keep in mind the content structure of Ṣaḥīḥ Bukhārī and Muslim, composed of primary and secondary corpus. See previous footnote 15 on page 45 for elaboration.

[3] In effect, this category refers to the use of isnāds of weaker transmitters for preexisting sound ḥadīth.

[4] Student and nephew of Imām Mālik who was a well-known ḥadīth scholar of Madīnah known to have issues with his accuracy.

[5] Great Syrian ḥadīth expert who settled in Egypt and was among the top students of Imām Mālik.

[6] One of the most renowned students of Mālik, known for his piety and worship. Both Tinnīsī and Qaʿnabī were top narrators of Mālik's Muwaṭṭa', and Bukhārī always prefers their reports over others.

[7] Reliable ḥadīth expert from Yemen who settled in Achelon in the Levant.

primary-tier reporters. However, this transmission happened to represent a low isnād (i.e. larger number of intermediary links). On the other hand, Suwayd b. Saʿīd al-Harawī (d. 240/854),[8] who was unanimously considered a weak reporter, related these with a higher isnād. Thus, Muslim sometimes relates these ḥadīth reports through Suwayd's isnād despite his status as a weak narrator. What justified this for Muslim was the fact that the ḥadīth was already deemed to be sound and pre-existed with isnāds from reliable and proficient reporters.

Sometimes the weak reporter is one whose reports could be used in less-complex matters, like the case of Fulayḥ b. Sulaymān (d. 168/784),[9] from whom Bukhārī relates occasionally in non-sophisticated issues that require less precision.[10]

In the end, you should know that Bukhārī and Muslim relate ḥadīth from weak reporters in their primary corpus only with two preconditions: that the weakness in the reporter be of a mild degree, and that the weak reporter be from their own teachers, about whom they were well-aware (i.e. whose conditions they could scrutinize properly).

The second category of accepted daʿīf reports are those which are related as supporting reports, i.e. secondary material. These represent reports that have one or more isnāds that fulfill the conditions of ṣaḥīḥ—which are used by Bukhārī and Muslim in their primary corpus—but then these ḥadīth are related through additional isnāds some of which contain reporters with a lower degree of accuracy (ḍabṭ).[11] This is rare in Ṣaḥīḥ Bukhārī but far more common in Ṣaḥīḥ Muslim.

The third type is the ḥadīth report that possesses an isnād which is not ṣaḥīḥ because it contains reporters with lower degrees of accuracy. This is the ḥadīth known as ḥasan (fair). When these ḥasan reports possess multiple similar isnads,

---

[8] Ḥadīth expert of Herat who settled in northern Iraq and related from Mālik and others.

[9] Early generation ḥadīth reporter of Madīnah who was deemed weak by most experts but considered acceptable by a few.

[10] Ibn Ḥajar responds to the question why Bukhārī relies on Fulayḥ the weak reporter: 'Bukhārī does not relate from him in the way that he relates from the likes of Mālik or Sufyān b. ʿUyaynah, but rather, he utilizes his reports mostly in the realm of virtues and heart-softeners.' See pg. 435, volume 1, *Fatḥ al-Bārī*.

[11] In essence, these represent weaker versions—that is, weaker transmissions—of sound ḥadīth reports. The difference from the first category is that these reports were not considered ṣaḥīḥ by Bukhārī or Muslim and only used in a supporting capacity and not in the primary corpus. This understanding was directly confirmed from the author.

they are then collectively raised to the level of ṣaḥīḥ (*ṣaḥīḥ li ghayrihī*). Similarly, if the precision is even lower on the part of some reporters and there exist multiple corroborating isnads, then they can be collectively raised to the level of ḥasan (*ḥasan li ghayrihī*). The fact is that the Ṣaḥīḥ collections of Bukhārī and Muslim do not contain any such reports, and anyone who claims otherwise is simply mistaken. Perhaps this resulted from confusing the first two types of weak reports (which are found in Bukhārī and Muslim) with the third.

The fourth type of potentially acceptable weak reports are the disconnected (mursal)[12] reports of senior Followers like Saʿīd b. al-Musayyab. A number of jurists including Imām Mālik and Abū Ḥanīfah deemed these reports ṣaḥīḥ. This is a respectable view.[13]

Unacceptable Daʿīf Reports

What then are the rejected daʿīf reports? They are also four types.

The first type of rejected weak reports are those with disconnected isnāds or those reported in an ambiguous manner (tadlīs)[14] by otherwise reliable reporters known for this practice. These reports are not considered extremely weak. Many people, therefore, have utilized them in non-legal matters relating to virtues and exhortations.

The second type are those reports mistakenly narrated by some as originating from the Prophet (known as 'marfūʿ') where in fact, ḥadīth experts have determined that they are reports of Companions (known as 'mawqūf'). These are potentially used in virtue.

The third type of rejected weak reports are the anomalous (shādh) ḥadīth, which consist of ḥadīth of reliable reporters that conflict with reports of more reliable reporters or a larger group of such reporters.[15] These simply represent mistakes on the part of these narrators and are hence not allowed to be used in

---

[12] Mursal refers to a ḥadīth that is reported by a Follower directly from the Prophet without mention of the intermediaries.

[13] For more details, see chapter on "Principles of Ḥadīth in the Ḥanafī School."

[14] Tadlīs is a term used for a range of practices in ḥadīth transmission in which one either conceals his teachers or relates from them with ambiguous references. This can occur deliberately or mistakenly.

[15] A shādh narration is one that appears otherwise sound but conflicts with stronger narrations.

any way, not even as supporting evidence. Unfortunately, many have erroneously used them in such a fashion, conveying an ignorance of the science of ḥadīth. Mistakes and errors can never be used to support anything at all.

The fourth category of rejected weak ḥadīth are the munkar reports,[16] which are ḥadīth of weak reporters that conflict with those of more reliable ones, or whose contents conflict with the meanings of the Qur'ān, the established sunnah, self-evident realities or clear reason. This category also includes ḥadīth reports of those who made frequent mistakes. This is the worst classification of da'īf ḥadīth reports and is extremely close to fabricated reports.

Use of Weak Reports in Virtues

The right approach on the issue of the use of weak reports is that there is no difference in their usage in rulings versus virtues, though many scholars accepted the use of certain weak reports in matters pertaining to virtues. If the matter were restricted to this, it would potentially be acceptable. Unfortunately, though, it has exceeded that and led many people to accept mistaken, extremely weak and even fabricated reports wholesale. Historically, reports were fabricated concerning the virtues of the Qur'ān, many good deeds entailing reward, and evil deeds meriting punishment. The motive for some of these fabricators was to encourage individuals to do good deeds and pay more attention to the Qur'ān. Some even did so expecting to be rewarded for that, which represents pure ignorance of God's religion. If only they had not done that and realized that the Qur'ān and sound ḥadīth reports of the Prophet ﷺ are sufficient for us concerning the virtues of deeds.

I feel it appropriate to include the insightful words of Aḥmad Muḥammad Shākir:

> I feel that exposing the weakness of reports is binding in every situation, because not doing so could lead people to consider these reports sound, especially when it comes to scholars of ḥadīth whose words are trusted. There is no real difference between virtues of deeds and rulings when it

[16] A munkar narration, like the anomalous one, conflicts with stronger evidences, but contains deeper, less benign, contradictions with often negative connotations or meanings.

comes to the principle of avoiding weak reports. Rather, on every matter, there is no proper evidence for anyone except what has been soundly transmitted from the Prophet ﷺ in terms of ṣaḥīḥ and ḥasan reports.

As for the statements of Aḥmad b. Ḥanbal, Ibn Mahdī, and Ibn al-Mubārak: 'When we report on matters pertaining to virtues, we are more lenient', they were referring to—as I consider accurate, and God knows best—accepting ḥasan reports which are less than ṣaḥīḥ, since in that time they did not clearly distinguish ṣaḥīḥ and ḥasan reports in their terminology. Early ḥadīth scholars only distinguished reports into sound (ṣaḥīḥ) and weak (ḍaʿīf).[17]

On this, Shaykh Yūsuf al-Qaraḍāwī also beautifully commented:

The ḥadīth on heart softeners, exhortations and warnings—although they do not contain any formal rulings concerning permissible (ḥalāl) or forbidden (ḥarām) matters—they surely do contain something else: they serve to establish significance and consequence, even if early experts did not pay this much heed. What this does is *alter the critical balance* of values that the All-Wise Legislator assigned to specific responsibilities and deeds. Every action, whether commanded or forbidden, has a particular value or price in the eyes of the Divine Legislator. It is simply not allowed for us to transgress those limits and balances set by God to elevate some matters beyond what was intended or lower others.[18]

---

[17] *Al-Bāʿith al-ḥathīth*, vol 1, pg 209.

[18] *Kayfa nataʿāmal maʿa al-sunnah al-nabawiyyah*, pg. 96

Shādh and Munkar Ḥadīth

What are shādh and munkar reports? Know that there are shādh and munkar reports, as well as shādh and munkar views. As a result of not recognizing the distinction between these, many people have fallen into confusion and muddled ideas.

What are shādh/munkar reports? People have defined shādh differently, but perhaps the best definition is that of Imām Shāfiʿī:

> A shādh report is not that a trustworthy reporter relates a ḥadīth that others did not, but it is when a group of trustworthy individuals narrate a ḥadīth in one wording while a single trustworthy person relates contrary to that wording, for he is deemed to have 'separated' (*shadhdha*) from the group.[1]

Here, the shādh report is the anomalous one, while its opposite is termed 'protected' (maḥfūẓ).

As for munkar, scholars also differed in defining it, but the widespread meaning is when a weak reporter relates something that opposes trustworthy reporters, or those who are stronger than them. Its opposite is termed 'well-known' (maʿrūf).

What are shādh/munkar views? A shādh view would be one that opposes another with stronger evidence—and there is no consideration for numbers here but only the strength of evidence. A munkar view would be one that opposes the innate nature that God created within human beings (fiṭrah) or sound intellect. Again, there is no consideration for numbers here, and even if, for example, most of humanity were to agree on something that clashes with the fiṭrah or ʿaql, it would not cease to be considered munkar. The notion of shādh and munkar can apply to both statements and actions.

Which category does fiqh and theology fall into? It falls into the second, that of views.

---

[1] Al-Khaṭīb, *al-Kifāyah fī ʿilm al-riwāyah, pg 144.*

What is the problem with compounding the two categories? We find so many people of theology and jurisprudence criticize other views as contradicting the majority, and they use the notion of numbers to accuse others, while forgetting that opposing large numbers does not detract from a view in any way, for views are built upon evidence. If numbers were a determining factor in preferring certain views, Abū Ḥanīfah would never have chosen the end of the timing of Ẓuhr prayer to be when shadows are double the length of objects, when in fact the majority of jurists everywhere, including his own companions Abū Yūsuf and Muḥammad b. al-Ḥasan al-Shaybānī, preferred the view that its time ends when shadows equal the length of objects. We even find Imām Malik, Awzāʾī, Shāfiʿī, and others adopt opinions that most other jurists did not share. There were so many issues which theologians, jurists and philosophers held solitary views on, which were never deemed shādh.

What do jurists mean when they deem an opinion as shādh? It would depend upon the context. Sometimes, for instance, they are referring to a shādh report, as in when Abū Ḥanīfah has two views attributed to him, and one of them is widely transmitted from him while the other one is rarely transmitted and becomes shādh (as a report). At other times, they meant by this expression that a certain view was shādh, i.e. based upon faulty evidence.

An Example of Shādh Reports in a Single Ḥadīth

Bukhārī relates the following ṣaḥīḥ ḥadīth:

BOOK OF ABLUTION—CHAPTER: IMPURITIES THAT BEFALL BUTTER AND WATER

Ismāʿīl related to us: Mālik related to me: from Ibn Shihāb al-Zuhrī: from ʿUbaydullah b. ʿAbdullah: from Ibn ʿAbbās: from Maymūnah, who said: The Prophet ﷺ was asked about a mouse that fell into clarified butter. He replied: ⟨*Remove it along with what*

صحيح البخاري - كتاب الوضوء - باب ما يقع من النجاسات في السمن والماء

حَدَّثَنَا إِسْمَاعِيلُ قَالَ: حَدَّثَنِي مَالِكٌ، عَنِ ابْنِ شِهَابٍ، عَنْ عُبَيْدِ اللهِ بْنِ عَبْدِ اللهِ، عَنِ ابْنِ عَبَّاسٍ، عَنْ مَيْمُونَةَ :

is around it, and then use the rest of the butter.} [2]

أَنَّ رَسُولَ اللهِ صَلَّى اللهُ عَلَيْهِ وَسَلَّمَ سُئِلَ عَنْ فَأْرَةٍ سَقَطَتْ فِي سَمْنٍ، فَقَالَ: أَلْقُوهَا وَمَا حَوْلَهَا، فَاطْرَحُوهُ وَكُلُوا سَمْنَكُمْ.

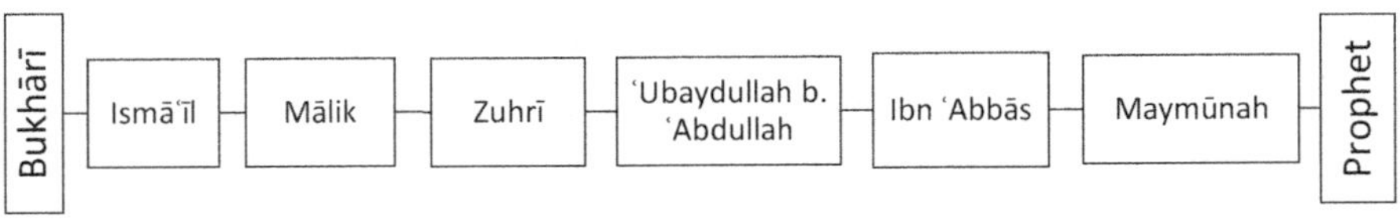

Mistake of Ma'mar

On the other hand, Abū Dāwūd and Aḥmad both relate the following through the isnād of 'Abd al-Razzāq (the version below is from Abū Dāwūd):

BOOK OF FOOD—CHAPTER: A MOUSE FALLING INTO BUTTER 'Abd al-Razzāq related to us: Ma'mar related to us: from Zuhrī: from Sa'īd b. al-Musayyab: from Abū Hurayrah: The Prophet ﷺ said: {*When a mouse falls into clarified butter, if it is solid, throw the mouse and what is around it away, but if it is in a liquid state, do not go near it.*} [3]

سنن أبي داود - كتاب الأطعمة - باب في الفارة تقع في السمن

حَدَّثَنَا أَحْمَدُ بْنُ صَالِحٍ، وَالْحَسَنُ بْنُ عَلِيٍّ وَاللَّفْظُ لِلْحَسَنِ قَالاَ: نَا عَبْدُ الرَّزَّاقِ، أَنَا مَعْمَرٌ، عَنِ الزُّهْرِيِّ، عَنْ سَعِيدِ بْنِ الْمُسَيِّبِ، عَنْ أَبِي هُرَيْرَةَ قَالَ: قَالَ رَسُولُ اللهِ صَلَّى اللهُ عَلَيْهِ وَسَلَّمَ: إِذَا وَقَعَتِ الْفَأْرَةُ فِي السَّمْنِ فَإِنْ كَانَ جَامِدًا فَأَلْقُوهَا وَمَا حَوْلَهَا، وَإِنْ كَانَ مَائِعًا فَلَا تَقْرَبُوهُ

---

[2] Ṣaḥīḥ Bukhārī: Kitāb al-wuḍū'—Bāb mā yaqa'u min al-najāsāt fī al-samn wa al-mā'.

[3] Abū Dāwūd: Kitāb al-Aṭ'imah—Bāb fī al-far'ah taqa'u fī al-samn; Musnad Aḥmad: Musnad Abī Hurayrah.

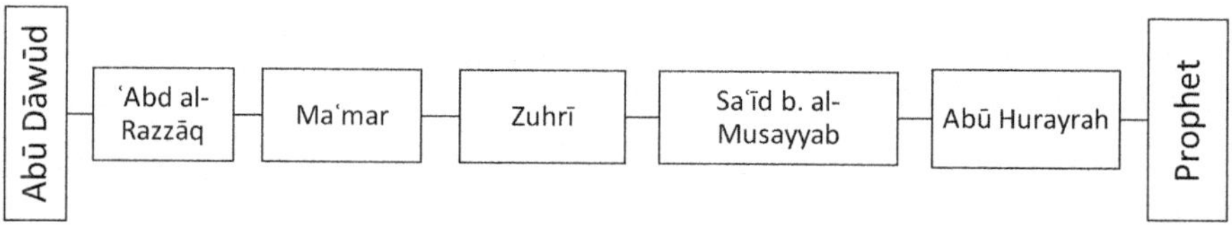

Maʿmar here opposed the other reporters of this tradition from Zuhrī: Malik, Sufyān b. ʿUyaynah, and Yūnus b. Yazīd (their isnāds appear in Bukhārī), Awzāʿī (isnād in Musnad Aḥmad), ʿAbd al-Raḥmān b. Isḥāq (al-Āḥād wa al-Mathānī of Ibn Abī ʿĀṣim), ʿUqayl b. Khālid (al-Ḍuʿafāʾ of ʿUqaylī). All of these students apart from Maʿmar relate from Zuhrī from ʿUbaydullah b. ʿAbdullah b. ʿUtbah b. Masʿūd from Ibn ʿAbbās from his aunt Maymūnah: After a mouse fell into clarified butter and died, the Prophet was asked, and he ﷺ responded: *Remove it and what is around it, and use the rest.*[4]

In essence, Maʿmar had opposed a large group in both the isnād and matn. Bukhārī comments after relating the ḥadīth through the isnād of Sufyān: 'It was mentioned to Sufyān that Maʿmar also relates the ḥadīth from Zuhrī from Saʿīd b. al-Musayyab from Abū Hurayrah. Sufyān replied: I heard this ḥadīth from Zuhrī many times, and I only heard him say that he received it from ʿUbaydullah from Ibn ʿAbbās from Maymūnah.'[5]

After relating the same report from Maʿn from Malik, Bukhārī relates the comment of Maʿn: 'Malik reported to us numerous times in this way: from Ibn ʿAbbās from Maymūnah.'[6]

Tirmidhī in al-ʿIlal quotes Bukhārī: The ḥadīth of Maʿmar from Zuhrī from Ibn al-Musayyab from Abū Hurayrah is a mistake which has no basis.[7]

Tirmidhī relates the same ḥadīth from Saʿīd b. ʿAbd al-Raḥmān al-Makhzūmī and Abū ʿAmmār, both from Sufyān, from Zuhrī from ʿUbaydullah from Ibn ʿAbbās from Maymūnah, and then adds the post-ḥadīth comments:

---

[4] The difference here is that the shādh report of Maʿmar adds into the ḥadīth text the qualification of distinguishing solid versus liquid butter. This likely represents a fiqh-based back-projection onto the ḥadīth.

[5] Bukhārī: Kitāb al-dhabāʾiḥ wa al-ṣayd—Bāb idhā waqaʿat al-farʾah fī al-samn al-jāmid aw al-dhāʾib.

[6] Ṣaḥīḥ Bukhārī: Kitāb al-wuḍūʾ—Bāb mā yaqaʿu min al-najāsāt fī al-samn wa al-māʾ. This ḥadīth is reported second in this chapter after the report of Ismāʿīl from Malik.

[7] *Al-ʿIlal al-kabīr*, Pg 298.

This ḥadīth is ḥasan ṣaḥīḥ. There are related reports on this from Abū Hurayrah.

This ḥadīth was related from Zuhrī from ʿUbaydullah from Ibn ʿAbbās, and this isnād does not mention Maymūnah. However, the ḥadīth of Ibn ʿAbbās from Maymūnah is sounder.

In addition, Maʿmar relates from Zuhrī from Saʿīd b. al-Musayyab from Abū Hurayrah. However, this particular report is not protected (ghayr maḥfūẓ).

I heard Muḥammad b. Ismāʿīl (Bukhārī) say: The ḥadīth of Maʿmar from Zuhrī from Saʿīd from Abū Hurayrah is a mistake which was made by Maʿmar, and the sound version is the ḥadīth of Zuhrī from ʿUbaydullah from Ibn ʿAbbās from Maymūnah.[8]

هَذَا حَدِيثٌ حَسَنٌ صَحِيحٌ. وَقَدْ رُوِيَ هَذَا الْحَدِيثُ عَنِ الزُّهْرِيِّ، عَنْ عُبَيْدِ اللهِ، عَنِ ابْنِ عَبَّاسٍ أَنَّ النَّبِيَّ صَلَّى اللهُ عَلَيْهِ وَسَلَّمَ سُئِلَ، وَلَمْ يَذْكُرُوا فِيهِ عَنْ مَيْمُونَةَ.

وَحَدِيثُ ابْنِ عَبَّاسٍ، عَنْ مَيْمُونَةَ أَصَحُّ. وَرَوَى مَعْمَرٌ عَنِ الزُّهْرِيِّ، عَنْ سَعِيدِ بْنِ الْمُسَيِّبِ، عَنْ أَبِي هُرَيْرَةَ، عَنِ النَّبِيِّ صَلَّى اللهُ عَلَيْهِ وَسَلَّمَ نَحْوَهُ، وَهُوَ حَدِيثٌ غَيْرُ مَحْفُوظٍ.

وَسَمِعْتُ مُحَمَّدَ بْنَ إِسْمَاعِيلَ يَقُولُ: وَحَدِيثُ مَعْمَرٍ، عَنِ الزُّهْرِيِّ، عَنْ سَعِيدِ بْنِ الْمُسَيِّبِ، عَنْ أَبِي هُرَيْرَةَ، عَنِ النَّبِيِّ صَلَّى اللهُ عَلَيْهِ وَسَلَّمَ، وَذَكَرَ فِيهِ أَنَّهُ سُئِلَ عَنْهُ، فَقَالَ: إِذَا كَانَ جَامِدًا فَأَلْقُوهَا وَمَا حَوْلَهَا وَإِنْ كَانَ مَائِعًا فَلَا تَقْرَبُوهُ. هَذَا خَطَأٌ، أَخْطَأَ فِيهِ مَعْمَرٌ، قَالَ: وَالصَّحِيحُ حَدِيثُ الزُّهْرِيِّ، عَنْعُبَيْدِ اللهِ، عَنِ ابْنِ عَبَّاسٍ، عَنْ مَيْمُونَةَ.

Mistakes from Students of Zuhrī and Mālik

Ibn Abī Ḥātim states:

[8] Tirmidhī: Kitāb al-Aṭʿimah—Bāb mā jāʾa fī al-farʾah tamūtu fī al-samn.

> I asked my father and Abū Zurʿah about the report of Qaʿnabī from Malik from Zuhrī from ʿUbaydullah from Ibn ʿAbbās that the Prophet was asked about the mouse . . . Abū Zurʿah replied: This report is in the Muwaṭṭaʾ of Malik from Zuhrī from ʿUbaydullah that the Prophet was asked about the mouse (as a mursal report). My father said that the correct report of Zuhrī is from ʿUbaydullah from Ibn ʿAbbās from Maymūnah from the Prophet.[9]

Dāruquṭnī, when asked about this report of Ibn ʿAbbās from Maymūnah in issue number 4007, stated the following:

> This is a report of Zuhrī, about which his students differed. Ibn ʿUyaynah reported it from Zuhrī from ʿUbaydullah from Ibn ʿAbbās from Maymūnah from the Prophet. Awzāʿī reported it from Zuhrī from ʿUbaydullah from Ibn ʿAbbās from the Prophet ﷺ.
>
> There were also differences from Mālik's students as follows:
>
> ʿAbd al-Raḥmān b. Mahdī, Ibrāhīm, ʿAbdullah b. Nāfiʿ, Ismāʿīl b. Abī Uways, Isḥāq b. ʿĪsā, and Maʿn b. ʿĪsā al-Ashjaʿī all reported it from Malik from Zuhrī from ʿUbaydullah from Ibn ʿAbbās from Maymūnah.
>
> Qaʿnabī, Shāfiʿī, and Muḥammad b. al-Qāsim al-Asadī reported it from Mālik from Zuhrī from ʿUbaydullah from Ibn ʿAbbās from the Prophet, without mentioning Maymūnah.
>
> Ibn Wahb reported it from Mālik from Zuhrī from ʿUbaydullah from the Prophet, without mentioning Ibn ʿAbbās.
>
> It was also reported from ʿAbd al-Malik b. al-Mājishūn from Mālik from Zuhrī from ʿUbaydullah from Ibn Masʿūd from the Prophet, but this is a mistake from its narrators.
>
> Isḥāq al-Anṣārī reported it from Maʿn from Mālik from Zuhrī from ʿUbaydullah from the Prophet as a mursal report. Also, Yūnus reported it from Zuhrī from ʿUbaydullah who said: It reached us

[9] Ibn Abī Ḥātim, *al-ʿIlal,* vol 4, pg 378.

that the Prophet . . . Also, Ibn Jurayj related it from Zuhrī from ʿUbaydullah as a mursal report.

ʿAbd al-Jabbār b. ʿUmar reported it from Zuhrī from Sālim from his father Ibn ʿUmar, and this was a clear mistake.

The correct report is from Zuhrī from ʿUbaydullah from Ibn ʿAbbās from Maymūnah.[10]

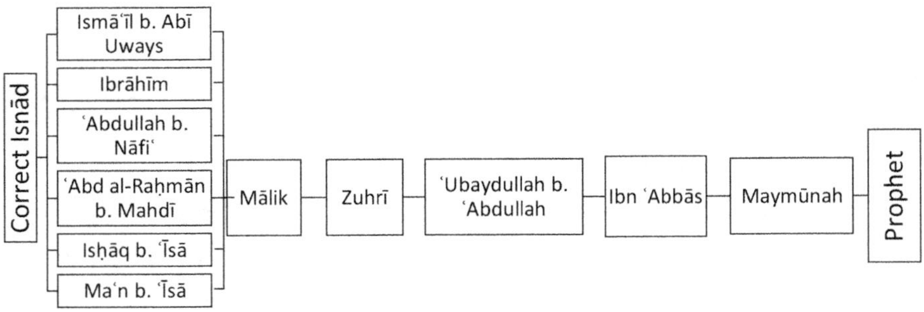

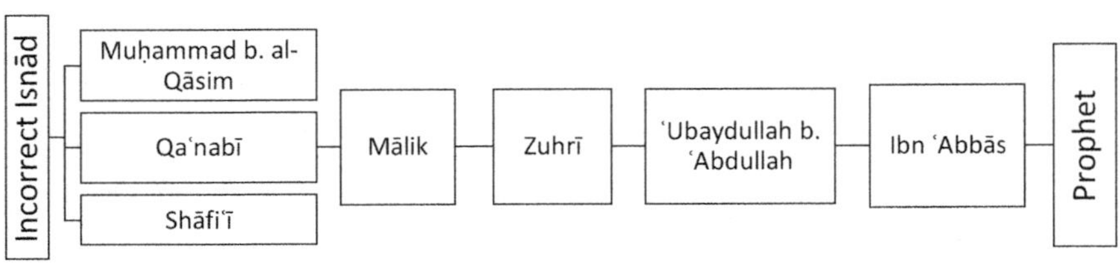

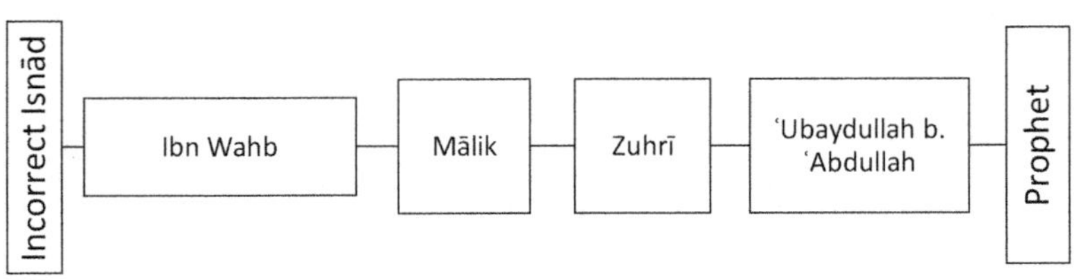

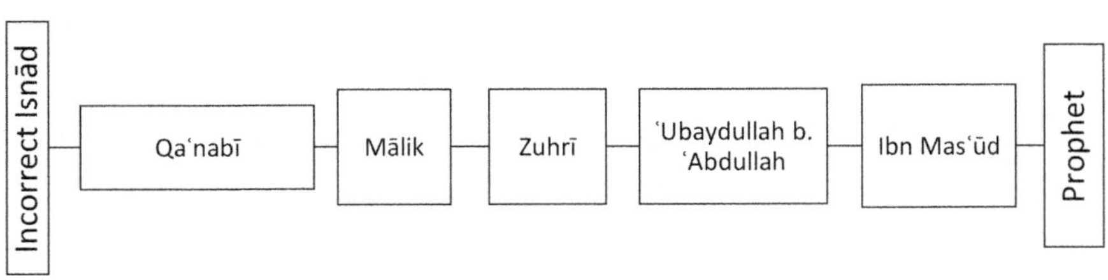

[10] Dāruquṭnī, *al-ʿIlal*, vol 15, pg 258-9.

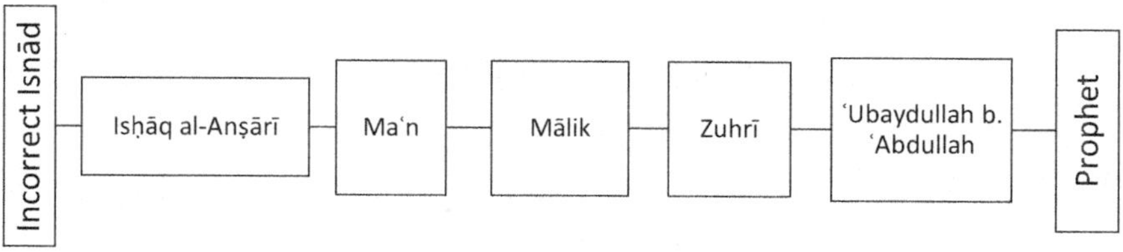

Dāruquṭnī, when asked about the report of Sa'īd b. al-Musayyab from Abū Hurayrah in issue 1357:

> Zuhrī reported it, and his students differed from him. Ma'mar related it from Zuhrī from Sa'īd from Abū Hurayrah, while all of Zuhrī's other students related it from Zuhrī from 'Ubaydullah from Ibn 'Abbās, and some added Maymūnah after Ibn 'Abbās.
>
> 'Abd al-Razzāq reports: 'Abd al-Raḥmān b. Būdhawayh reported to me: that Ma'mar used to mention the isnād from Zuhrī from 'Ubaydullah from Ibn 'Abbās as well was the isnād of Zuhrī from Sa'īd from Abū Hurayrah.[11]

Bazzār stated in his Musnad: 'We only know of Ma'mar who reported this ḥadīth from Zuhrī from Sa'īd from Abū Hurayrah, and he was opposed by all others in both isnād and matn.' Ibn 'Abd al-Barr stated: 'This is a strong contradiction in the isnād of Malik, and the correct version is that of Yaḥyā and those who followed him.' Ibn Ḥajar states in Fatḥ al-Bārī:

> The students of the Muwaṭṭa' reported this ḥadīth from Malik and differed over it. Some of them like Yaḥyā b. Yaḥyā related it from him like this (from Ibn 'Abbās from Maymūnah), while others like Qa'nabī reported it through Ibn 'Abbās without mentioning Maymūnah. Some of them like Ash-hab did not mention Ibn 'Abbās, and some of them like Yaḥyā b. Bukayr and Abū Muṣ'ab omitted both Ibn 'Abbās and Maymūnah.

[11] Dāruquṭnī, *al-'Ilal*, vol 7, pg 285-6.

No one [from Mālik's students] mentioned the words *'solid'*[12] in their report except for ʿAbd al-Raḥmān b. Mahdī. Abū Dāwūd al-Ṭayālisī[13] in his Musnad also relates it with these words through Sufyān b. ʿUyaynah from Zuhrī. However, Ḥumaydī and other expert students of Sufyān relate it without these words and considered its isnād, which included Ibn ʿAbbās and Maymūnah, to be strong, and that is correct.[14]

Mistake of ʿAbd al-Raḥmān b. Mahdī

Al-Nasāʾī states in his Sunan:

BOOK OF FARAʿ AND ʿATĪRAH[15]—CHAPTER: A MOUSE FALLING INTO BUTTER Yaʿqūb b. Ibrāhīm and Muḥammad b. Yaḥyā b. ʿAbdullah al-Naysābūrī both related to us: from ʿAbd al-Raḥmān: from Mālik: from Zuhrī: from ʿUbaydullah b. ʿAbdullah: from Ibn ʿAbbās: from Maymūnah: The Prophet was asked about a mouse that fell into *solid* clarified butter and said: ﴾*Take it out along with what is around it, and discard it.*﴿ [16]

سنن النسائي - كتاب الفرع والعتيرة - باب الفارة تقع في السمن

أَخْبَرَنَا يَعْقُوبُ بْنُ إِبْرَاهِيمَ الدَّوْرَقِيُّ، وَمُحَمَّدُ بْنُ يَحْيَى بْنِ عَبْدِ اللهِ النَّيْسَابُورِيُّ، عَنْ عَبْدِ الرَّحْمَنِ، عَنْ مَالِكٍ، عَنِ الزُّهْرِيِّ، عَنْ عُبَيْدِ اللهِ بْنِ عَبْدِ اللهِ، عَنِ ابْنِ عَبَّاسٍ، عَنْ مَيْمُونَةَ أَنَّ النَّبِيَّ صَلَّى اللهُ عَلَيْهِ وَسَلَّمَ سُئِلَ عَنْ فَأْرَةٍ وَقَعَتْ فِي سَمْنٍ جَامِدٍ، فَقَالَ: خُذُوهَا وَمَا حَوْلَهَا فَأَلْقُوهُ.

---

[12] The ḥadīth matn begins with: 'The Prophet was asked about a mouse that fell into *solid* clarified butter.'

[13] Abū Dāwūd al-Ṭayālisī (d. 203/819) was a Persian-origin ḥadīth expert of Baṣrah who authored a Musnad work, not to be confused with the more famous Abū Dāwūd, author of one of the Six Canonical Works.

[14] *Fatḥ*, vol 1, pg 344.

[15] Faraʿ was a pagan custom of offering the first offspring of livestock to their idols, while ʿatīrah was the practice of sacrificing a sheep in the month of Rajab.

[16] Nasāʾī, al-Sunan al-Kubrā: Kitāb al-faraʿ wa al-ʿatīrah—Bāb al-faʿrah taqaʿu fī al-samn.

All other of students of Mālik who related this isnād differed in this report and mentioned clarified butter without specifying *solid.* These included Ismāʿīl b. Abī Uways, Maʿn b. ʿĪsā, and ʿAbd al-ʿAzīz b. ʿAbdullah al-Uwaysī (whose reports appear in Ṣaḥīḥ Bukhārī); Khālid b. Makhlad and Zayd b. Yaḥyā (Sunan al-Dārimī); ʿAbdullah b. Wahb, Juwayriyah b. Asmāʾ and Saʿīd b. Abī Maryam (Sharḥ Mushkil al-Āthār); Saʿīd b. Dāwūd al-Zubayrī (Ṭabarānī, Muʿjam al-Awsaṭ); Yaḥyā b. Saʿīd al-Qaṭṭān (Dāruquṭnī, ʿIlal); Qaʿnabī (Ḥilyat al-Awliyāʾ); Ibrāhīm b. Tahmān (in his Mashyakhah); Ash-hab b. ʿAbd al-ʿAzīz (Ibn ʿAbd al-Barr, al-Tamhīd); ʿUbayd b. Ḥibbān (Tārīkh Dimishq); and Yaḥyā al-Laythī, Abū Muṣʿab, Ibn Ziyād and Muḥammad b. al-Ḥasan al-Shaybānī (Muwaṭṭaʾ).

All other students of Zuhrī also related it without the addition (*solid*) such as Sufyān b. ʿUyaynah and Yūnus b. Yazīd (Bukhārī); Maʿmar (Sunan Abī Dāwūd); and ʿAbd al-Raḥmān b. Isḥāq (al-Āḥād wa al-Mathānī, Ibn Abī ʿĀṣim).

Ibn Ḥajar states in al-Fatḥ: 'The word *solid* was not mentioned by anyone except ʿAbd al-Raḥmān b. Mahdī from Malik from Zuhrī, and by Abū Dāwūd al-Ṭayālisī through Sufyān b. ʿUyaynah from Zuhrī. However, Ḥumaydī and other expert students of Sufyān did not relate this addition.'[17]

---

[17] *Fatḥ al-bārī,* vol 1, pg 344.

If one were to ask the author, as I actually did, what the big deal is since the basic thrust of the ḥadīth is similar in all versions and the only additions have to do with near-single words (i.e. distinguishing *solid* butter), the answer lies in the careful and painstaking work of ḥadīth experts in meticulously researching and documenting primary ḥadīth evidence as accurately as possible. In the case of the '*solid butter*' qualification, this likely represents a juristic madhhab-based back projection onto ḥadīth texts that somehow unwittingly altered the primary ḥadīth text. Although there is little objection to the common-sense jurisprudence of reusing solid butter by discarding a dead mouse from the affected portions—and not applying this to liquid butter which would be discarded entirely—for jurists to base their views on this so-called ḥadīth which conveniently fits is not academically sound.

A related question would be this: if, in fact, the majority of ḥadīth reports are related by meaning, which is the predominant view of ḥadīth experts, then would not the minor '*solid* qualification' of this ḥadīth fit into that? Shaykh Akram responds that the qualification is not so minor, for ḥadīth experts indeed allowed the reporting of ḥadīth by meaning but only if it did not alter the meanings in any way. In this case, the meaning is altered to fit a jurisprudential view, which does not accurately convey what the Prophet actually said. When such potential alterations occur in the meanings and implications of ḥadīth, this warrants the full scrutiny and investigative skills of ḥadīth experts, as you can see in the above discussion.

Mursal Reports, Tadlīs, and Idrāj

There are a number of additional terms that are used in ḥadīth studies, particularly when it comes to discussions concerning ḥadīth defects, and they will be summarized here.

Irsāl

The Companions, especially junior ones, would readily learn ḥadīth from one another. At times, they would mention their intermediaries to the Prophet ﷺ, and, at other times, they would suffice themselves with quoting the Prophet ﷺ directly (a phenomenon known as *irsāl,* with such reports described as *mursal*). Irsāl is a form of disconnect in the chain. In later times, it became predominantly used for cases when Followers would quote the Prophet ﷺ without mentioning their intermediaries, i.e. the Companions. The truth is that irsāl is not specific to those cases but includes all forms of disconnection. Nawawī affirmed: 'The widespread view in fiqh and uṣūl is that all forms of broken links are considered mursal, and this was also espoused by Khaṭīb.'[1] Sakhāwī commented on this: 'He (Nawawī) equated overt irsāl with more subtle forms, and with tadlīs. Among those who equated it with ta'līq (isnād-less reports) was Abū Nu 'aym in al-Mustakhraj. Those who equated it with any disconnection (inqiṭā') included Bukhārī, Abū Zur'ah, Abū Ḥātim, Abū Dāwūd, Tirmidhī, and Dāruquṭnī.'[2]

Bukhārī and Muslim did not, as a rule, accept mursal reports, except in case of specific Companions when they were certain of their veracity. Most Mālikī and Ḥanafī jurists, on the other hand, generally accepted such reports. Imām Shāfi'ī adopted an intermediate approach in accepting mursal reports from senior Followers only. These various views are spelled out in detail in primary texts.

---

[1] Suyūṭī, *Tadrīb al-rāwī,* vol 1, pg 219.

[2] *Sharḥ al-taqrīb wa al-taysīr,* pg 101-2.

Mursal Reports of Companions

The correct position on the matter of the mursal reports of Companions is that that they are accepted in sunnah practices and rulings, but not in the realm of Prophetic biography, battles and tafsīr. The difference between the two is that sunnah refers to uninterrupted practices that are transmitted from generation to generation—and the Companions would never practice them unless they verified their precedence from the Prophet—while sīrah and tafsīr is related to information that comes from reports, not practices, and these could potentially be transmitted without verification, as they often were.[3]

On this, Imām Aḥmad said: 'Three matters often have no basis (isnād): tafsīr, wars, and battles.'[4] Ibn Taymiyyah stated the following:

> For those transmitted matters that are necessary in religion, God has designated certain evidences that allow us to determine what is sound from what is not. It is also well-known that much of what is transmitted in tafsīr is similar to what is transmitted in battles [in being based on weak evidence]. For this reason, Imām Aḥmad said: 'Three matters often have no basis (isnād): tafsīr, wars, and battles.' They are often reported without any proper source (i.e. isnād), for the majority of these reports are mursal reports of individuals such as ʿUrwah b. al-Zubayr, Shaʿbī, Zuhrī, Mūsā b. ʿUqbah, Ibn Isḥāq, and those that followed them like Yaḥyā b. Saʿīd al-Umawī, Walīd b. Muslim, and Wāqidī.
>
> The most informed people on maghāzī (Prophetic events and battles) were the people of Madīnah, then those of Syria, and then

[3] Shaykh Akram points out here that actions and practices are more protected than mere information that does not affect one's actions like some tafsīr and sīrah details. He usually lists various reasons. One, since deeds are positive acts, generally a person performs an action when they are more certain of it, as opposed to thoughts and ideas. Two, since actions are public and visible, and often congregational, they are more likely to be corrected by other Companions when problematic or deficient. Three, actions and sunnah practices mostly arose for the Companions through active discussions and learning from the Prophet and from one another. For these reasons and others, taking sunnah from the actual and normative practices of Companions and early Muslims is safer and sounder than accepting all their reports on details of sīrah and theoretical tafsīr.

[4] Ibn Taymiyyah, *al-Muqaddimah fī uṣūl al-tafsīr,* pg 22.

Iraq. The people of Madīnah were the most knowledgeable because these events took place among them. The people of Syria followed next because they were known fighters and people of jihād, because of which they possessed a familiarity with these events more than others. For this reason, Syrians held the book of Abū Isḥāq al-Fazārī (d. 183/805)[5] in high regard and considered his teacher Awzāʾī[6] to be the most informed of all scholars in this field.

The most learned people in tafsīr are those of Makkah, because they were the companions of Ibn ʿAbbās, such as Mujāhid, ʿAṭāʾ b. Abī Rabāḥ, ʿIkrimah his freed slave, Ṭāwūs, Abū Shaʿthāʾ, Saʿīd b. Jubayr and others. Then, there are the people of Kūfah, who were companions of Ibn Masʿūd, and the scholars of tafsīr in Madīnah like Zayd b. Aslam from whom Mālik, as well as his son ʿAbd al-Raḥmān, learned tafsīr. And from ʿAbd al-Raḥmān, ʿAbdullah b. Wahb learned tafsīr.[7]

In this discussion, Ibn Taymiyyah further discusses mursal reports and their rulings (which can be consulted by the reader).

To give a practical example on mursal reports, historians relate a report from Qurād Abū Nūḥ, which Tirmidhī also relates as follows:

BOOK OF VIRTUES—CHAPTER: THE BEGINNINGS OF THE PROPHETHOOD OF THE PROPHET Al-Faḍl b. Sahl Abū al-ʿAbbās al-Aʿraj al-Baghdādī reported to us: ʿAbd al-Raḥmān b. Ghazwān (Qurād) reported to us: Yūnus b. Abī Isḥāq related to us: from Abū Bakr b. Abī Mūsā al-Ashʿarī: from his father:

﴾Abū Ṭālib departed to Syria, and the Prophet went with him along with some older men from Quraysh. When they came to the

[5] Abū Isḥāq Muḥammad b. Ibrāhīm al-Ḥārith was an Iraqi scholar and historian, descendant of the north Arabian tribe of Fazārah, who was a student of Awzāʾī and legal adviser on war-related issues to Hārūn al-Rashīd. He served in the front-lines of battles and authored Kitāb al-siyar on legal issues pertaining to war based upon the teachings of Awzāʾī.

[6] Abū ʿAmr ʿAbd al-Raḥmān al-Awzāʾī (d. 157/774) was a prominent jurist-scholar of the Levant, born in Damascus and buried near Beirut, founder of a legal school that did not survive.

[7] *Majmūʿ*, vol 13, pg 345-6.

place of a monk, they stopped and began setting up their camp. The monk came out to them. Before that time, they used to pass by him, and he would never come out nor pay them any heed.

While they were setting up their camp, the monk came into their midst until he came and took the hand of the Messenger of God. He then said to them: 'This is the leader of the worlds! This is the Messenger of the Lord of the worlds, who shall raise him as a mercy to the worlds!'

The elders of Quraish asked him: 'What do you know about this?' He replied: 'When you people approached from the desert, every single rock and tree fell down prostrating, and they do not prostrate except for a Prophet. And I can recognize him by the seal of the Prophethood which is below his shoulder blade, like an apple.'

Then he went back to prepare some food for them. When he brought it to them, the Prophet was out tending to the camels. He asked them to bring him. When the Prophet came, there was a cloud over him that was shading him. When he came close to the people, he found that they had beaten him to the shade of a tree. When he sat down, the shade of the tree inclined towards him. The monk said: 'Look at the shade of the tree inclining towards him.'

He stood over them and advised them not to take the Prophet to Rome, because if the Romans were to see him, they would recognize him by his description and kill him. The monk turned around and saw seven people who had just come from Rome. He asked them: 'Why have you come?' They replied: 'We came because this Prophet is going to appear during this month, and there isn't a road left except that people have been sent to it. We have been informed about him, and we have been sent to this road of yours.'

The monk asked them: 'Is there anyone better than you behind you?' They said: 'We only have news of him from this road of yours.' He said: 'Do you think that if there were a matter that God wished to bring about, could there be anyone who could turn it away?' They replied: 'No.'

So they gave him their pledge and stayed with him. And he said: 'I ask you by God, which of you is his guardian?' They replied: 'Abū Ṭālib.' Thus, he kept adjuring him until Abū Ṭālib returned him back to Makkah, and sent Abū Bakr and Bilāl with him. And the monk gave him provisions of a type of bread and olive oil.}

This ḥadīth is ḥasan gharīb, and we only know it through this isnād.[8]

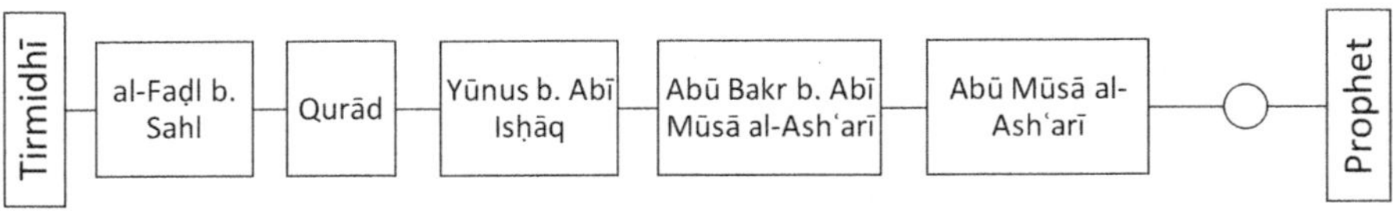

This account is a mursal report from Abū Mūsā al-Ash'arī, for he did not witness it. Scholars have discussed this report critically at length. Dhahabī, for instance, states the following:

> Qurād, whose name was 'Abd al-Raḥmān b. Ghazwān, was the sole reporter of this ḥadīth. He was reliable (thiqah), upon whom Bukhārī and Nasā'ī relied. Many individuals heard the ḥadīth from Qurād, and Tirmidhī deemed it ḥasan.
>
> However, it is a ḥadīth that is extremely unsound (munkar). Where was Abū Bakr? He was about ten years old, for he was two and a half years younger than the Prophet. And where was Bilāl during this time? Abū Bakr did not purchase his freedom until after Prophethood, and he was not even born during this time. Also, if there was a cloud shading him, how could the shade of the tree incline towards him if he were already shaded? The shade of the

[8] Tirmidhī: Kitāb al-manāqib—Bāb mā jā'a fī bad' nubuwwat al-nabī. Bazzār relates the ḥadīth with the exact same isnād in his Musnad (from al-Faḍl b. Sahl from Qurād . . .) and comments: 'This ḥadīth was reported from Abū Bakr only by Yūnus, and from Yūnus only by Qurād.' Ibn Abī Shaybah in his Muṣannaf reports the same ḥadīth from Qurād directly. Ḥākim relates the ḥadīth from two intermediaries to Qurād and comments that the ḥadīth is sound on the conditions of Bukhārī and Muslim.

cloud would obscure the shade of the tree under it. The Prophet never mentioned Abū Ṭālib in his recounting the story of the monk, nor did the Quraysh or any of those elders. As these people were highly inclined to these types of stories, had it really occurred, it would have become famous among them. Moreover, the Prophet would already have had traces of prophethood in him and would not have rejected revelation when it came to him at that first moment in the cave of Ḥirā᾽ when he confessed to Khadījah that he feared losing his mind. He would never have gone to the tops of the mountains to consider throwing himself off. If Abū Ṭālib indeed felt this fear [for the Prophet's life] and returned him to Makkah, how did he later prepare himself to allow him to go to Syria to trade on behalf of Khadījah?[9]

The Phenomenon of Tadlīs

Tadlīs is a form of hiding defects, and it essentially means to be deceptive concerning the reality of something. In the context of ḥadīth, it means to obscure the identity of a reporter by diverting attention away from more well-known details. However, in ḥadīth it is mostly used in reference to the isnād: to relate from a teacher from whom one did not hear in a way that subtly conveys that one did, as in using expressions such as *qāla fulān* ('the teacher said . . ') or *ʿan fulān* ('on the authority of this teacher').

Tadlīs is actually quite common in ḥadīth reports. For practitioners of tadlīs, there could be one or more intermediaries to the teacher.

As an example, ʿAlī b. Khashram states: We were once with Sufyān b. ʿUyaynah, who said to us: 'Zuhrī said . . .' We asked him, 'Did Zuhrī relate this to you?' He was silent, and continued as before: 'Zuhrī said . . .' We asked once again, 'Did you hear this from Zuhrī?' He then answered, 'I did not hear it from Zuhrī, nor from his students. But it was reported to me from ʿAbd al-Razzāq from Maʿmar from Zuhrī.'[10]

---

[9] *Siyar*, vol 1, pg 58-9.
[10] Khaṭīb, *al-Kifāyah*, pg 359.

Most scholars disparaged tadlīs, and Shuʿbah was the harshest of them on this. It is reported from him that he said: 'Tadlīs is the brother of lying;' and, 'For me, falling into zinā (adultery) is better than tadlīs.'

The moderate approach here is to consider the chain disconnected when practitioners of tadlīs utilize vague wordings that do not explicitly convey audition or direct connection. However, when those same individuals use explicit words such as 'I heard;' 'he reported to us;' or 'he related to us,' then their reports are accepted and relied upon. The Ṣaḥīḥ of Bukhārī and Muslim as well as other reliable books contain many of these reports.

Tadlīs of Senior Reporters

Some of the most senior and reliable experts that engaged in tadlīs were Aʿmash and Qatādah, despite their stature in knowledge. Bukhārī and Muslim did not accept their muʿanʿan reports (those narrated by the vague connector *'an*, meaning 'on the authority of') except when they verified their audition.

On the other hand, Sufyān b. ʿUyaynah—as is widely known—did not generally engage in tadlīs except from trustworthy reporters. Therefore, experts did not consider his tadlīs to be problematic and did not pursue its verification.

Sufyān al-Thawrī did engage in tadlīs from weaker reporters but did so only rarely. These specific reports, however, were well-known, and so, scholars generally accepted his muʿanʿan reports unless there was specific evidence to the contrary for individual reports.

If one were to wonder what made individuals of the stature of Sufyān al-Thawrī and others engage in tadlīs, I would say that ḥadīth scholars being human teachers taught in a variety of ways and settings. Sometimes, they endeavored to diligently provide complete and accurate isnāds for their reports, while at other times they chose not to provide such isnads. At times, they chose to focus on a ḥadīth matn while overlooking the isnād, sometimes making mistakes as a result. These lapses are a problem only if they are frequent. If they are occasional and rare, as in the case of Sufyān al-Thawrī, then this is fully acceptable from him.

Fortunately, Bukhārī and Muslim did not include any of Sufyān's weaker reports in their Ṣaḥīḥ.[11]

Idrāj

Idrāj linguistically means to insert or add something, and in ḥadīth terminology it refers to when a reporter adds their own words to a Prophetic ḥadīth such that readers could mistakenly consider them to be the Prophet's words. The inserted portion of the report is termed *mudraj*. These additions can occur in the isnād or matn of a ḥadīth.

Historically, this phenomenon represents explanatory remarks on the part of Companions, Followers or reporters at other levels, such as their providing descriptions of specific terms or explaining certain names and titles that appear in the ḥadīth. Obviously, there is great benefit in these explanations and descriptions, and they deserve to be praised. However, many of those without expertise in ḥadīth began to consider these part of the ḥadīth texts, so experts were forced to clarify them.

An Example of Idrāj

An example appears in a report from Abū Dāwūd:

BOOK OF PRAYER—CHAPTER: TAHSAHHUD 'Abdullah b. Muḥammad al-Nufaylī reported to us: Zuhayr reported to us: al-Ḥasan b. Ḥurr reported to us: from al-Qāsim b. Mukhaymirah: 'Alqamah	سنن أبي داود- كتاب الصلاة - باب التشهد

[11] This represents one of the insights of Shaykh Akram, who emphasizes that the teaching context and intent of the teacher needs to be taken into consideration when viewing reports and views of scholars. Many ḥadīth reports are recorded in formal classroom settings, while others are often documented from less-formal settings such as scholarly discussions and ḥadīth reviews (mudhākarah). Bukhārī, the careful and diligent scholar that he was, for instance, reviewed many ḥadīth with the renowned Imām Aḥmad but did not report a single ḥadīth from him in his Ṣaḥīḥ simply because he had not received these reports from Imām Aḥmad in a proper setting and manner. Had he reported from him directly, Bukhārī's isnāds would have been extremely high, but he chose to forgo prestige in favor of academic integrity.

took hold of my hand and reported to me that ʿAbdullah b. Masʿūd took his hand, and the Prophet ﷺ took ʿAbdullah's hand and taught him the tashahhud of prayer.

He then mentioned [the well-known] supplication in the ḥadīth of Aʿmash on tashahhud, and then said:[12] *'When you say this, or have completed this, then you have completed the prayer. If you want to stand up, then stand, and if you want to remain sitting, then remain sitting.'*[13]

حَدَّثَنَا عَبْدُ اللهِ بْنُ مُحَمَّدٍ النُّفَيْلِيُّ، نَا زُهَيْرٌ، نَا الْحَسَنُ بْنُ الْحُرِّ، عَنِ الْقَاسِمِ بْنِ مُخَيْمِرَةَ، قَالَ: أَخَذَ عَلْقَمَةُ بِيَدِي فَحَدَّثَنِي أَنَّ عَبْدَ اللهِ بْنَ مَسْعُودٍ أَخَذَ بِيَدِهِ، وَأَنَّ رَسُولَ اللهِ صَلَّى اللهُ عَلَيْهِ وَسَلَّمَ أَخَذَ بِيَدِ عَبْدِ اللهِ فَعَلَّمَهُ التَّشَهُّدَ فِي الصَّلَاةِ، فَذَكَرَ مِثْلَ دُعَاءِ حَدِيثِ الْأَعْمَشِ: إِذَا قُلْتَ هَذَا، أَوْ قَضَيْتَ هَذَا فَقَدْ قَضَيْتَ صَلَاتَكَ، إِنْ شِئْتَ أَنْ تَقُومَ فَقُمْ، وَإِنْ شِئْتَ أَنْ تَقْعُدَ فَاقْعُدْ.

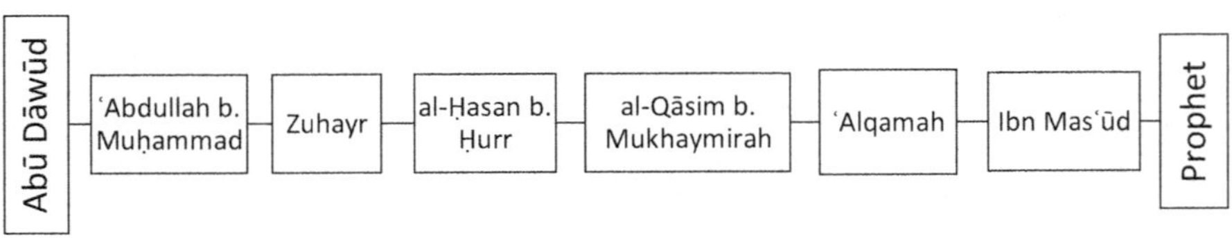

Mudraj Report with: 'When you say this, you have completed the prayer.'

Many others reported this ḥadīth from Zuhayr b. Muʿāwiyah, differing from him.

[12] Reference to the well-known ḥadīth on tashahhud, which goes through Aʿmash, related by Abū Dāwūd prior to this ḥadīth, as the first report in the chapter on tashahhud.

[13] Sunan Abī Dāwūd: Kitāb al-ṣalāh—Bāb al-tashahhud.

ʿAbd al-Raḥmān b. Thābit b. Thawbān differed from Zuhayr [as reported in Ṣaḥīḥ Ibn Ḥibbān] in reporting it from al-Ḥasan b. al-Ḥurr with this isnād and separating the words of the Prophet from the words of Ibn Masʿūd, as he stated at the end of the ḥadīth:

Ibn Masʿūd said: 'When you have completed this, you have completed the prayer; so if you wish, you may sit, or if you wish, you may leave.'[14]	قَالَ عَبْدُ اللهِ بْنُ مَسْعُودٍ: فَإِذَا فَرَغْتَ مِنْ هَذَا فَقَدْ فَرَغْتَ مِنْ صَلَاتِكَ، فَإِنْ شِئْتَ فَاثْبُتْ، وَإِنْ شِئْتَ فَانْصَرِفْ.

Ḥusayn b. ʿAlī al-Juʿfī (Musnad Aḥmad), Muḥammad b. ʿAjlān (Ṭabarānī, Muʿjam al-Kaʿbīr), and Muḥammad b. Aban (Sunan Dāruquṭnī), all report the same ḥadīth from al-Ḥasan b. al-Ḥurr and restrict themselves to the marfūʿ (Prophetic) portion and exclude the latter portion of the ḥadīth which is the statement of Ibn Masʿūd.

Shabābah b. Sawwār (Sunan Dāruquṭnī) relates it from Zuhayr, and, similar to the report of Ibn Thawbān, distinguishes between the words of the Prophet and Ibn Masʿūd.

Aḥmad b. Yūnus, Aḥmad b. ʿAbd al-Malik b. Wāqid al-Ḥarrānī, and Abū Bilāl al-Ashʿarī (Ṭabarānī, Muʿjam al-Kaʿbīr) report it from Zuhayr without the mudraj portion.

The students of Ibn Masʿūd all related his ḥadīth, and none of them mentioned the mudraj portion. These include Abū Wāʾil and ʿAbdullah b. Sakhbarah (whose reports appear in Bukhārī and Muslim), Abū al-Aḥwaṣ ʿAwf b. Mālik and Aswad b. Yazīd (Sunan Tirmidhī), and Abū ʿUbaydah b. ʿAbdullah b. Masʿūd (Sunan Ibn Mājah). Ibn Ḥibbān even went to the extent of designating a chapter in his Ṣaḥīḥ to clarify the matter: 'Chapter: Clarifying that the statement '*When you have said this, you have fulfilled your responsibility*' is a

[14] Ṣaḥīḥ Ibn Ḥibbān: Kitāb al-ṣalāh—Bāb ṣifat al-ṣalāh—dhikr al-bayān bianna qawluhū fa idhā qulta hādhā faqad qaḍayta mā ʿalayk.

statement of Ibn Mas'ūd and not that of the Prophet, which was added by Zuhayr to the report.' Dāruquṭnī stated in his Sunan:

BOOK OF PRAYER—CHAPTER: THE DESCRIPTION OF TASHAHHUD AND ITS OBLIGATIONS Zuhayr b. Mu'āwiyah reported it from al-Ḥasan b. al-Ḥurr and added words to the end of the report: '*When you say this, or have com pleted this, then you have completed the prayer. If you want to stand up, then stand, and if you want to remain sitting, then remain sitting.*' Some of the reporters from Zuhayr added these words to the ḥadīth and connected them to the Prophet. Shabābah then separated them and clarified them as words of Ibn Mas'ūd. This is more likely to be correct than considering it to be part of the ḥadīth of the Prophet because Ibn Thawbān reported the ḥadīth like this from al-Ḥasan b. al-Ḥurr and made the statement from Ibn Mas'ūd. Also, [this is supported by] the agreement of Ḥusayn al-Ju'fī, Muḥammad b. 'Ajlān, and Muḥammad b. Abān in reporting it from al-Ḥasan b. al-Ḥurr without the extra portion, and the agreement of all who report the tashahhud from 'Alqamah and others from Ibn Mas'ūd like that. And God knows best.[15]

سنن الدارقطني- كتاب الصلاة - باب صفة التشهد ووجوبه

وَرَوَاهُ زُهَيْرُ بْنُ مُعَاوِيَةَ، عَنِ الْحَسَنِ بْنِ الْحُرِّ فَزَادَ فِي آخِرِهِ كَلَامًا، وَهُوَ قَوْلُهُ إِذَا قُلْتَ هَذَا - أَوْ فَعَلْتَ هَذَا - فَقَدْ قَضَيْتَ صَلَاتَكَ، فَإِنْ شِئْتَ أَنْ تَقُومَ فَقُمْ، وَإِنْ شِئْتَ أَنْ تَقْعُدَ فَاقْعُدْ وَأَدْرَجَهُ بَعْضُهُمْ عَنْ زُهَيْرٍ فِي الْحَدِيثِ وَوَصَلَهُ بِكَلَامِ النَّبِيِّ صَلَّى اللهُ عَلَيْهِ وَسَلَّمَ، وَفَصَلَهُ شَبَابَةُ، عَنْ زُهَيْرٍ، وَجَعَلَهُ مِنْ كَلَامِ ابْنِ مَسْعُودٍ، وَقَوْلُهُ أَشْبَهُ بِالصَّوَابِ مِنْ قَوْلِ مَنْ أَدْرَجَهُ فِي حَدِيثِ النَّبِيِّ صَلَّى اللهُ عَلَيْهِ وَسَلَّمَ لِأَنَّ ابْنَ ثَوْبَانَ رَوَاهُ عَنِ الْحَسَنِ بْنِ الْحُرِّ كَذَلِكَ، وَجَعَلَ آخِرَهُ مِنْ قَوْلِ ابْنِ مَسْعُودٍ، وَلِاتِّفَاقِ حُسَيْنٍ الْجُعْفِيِّ وَابْنِ عَجْلَانَ وَمُحَمَّدِ بْنِ أَبَانَ فِي رِوَايَتِهِمْ عَنِ الْحَسَنِ بْنِ الْحُرِّ عَلَى تَرْكِ ذِكْرِهِ فِي آخِرِ الْحَدِيثِ، مَعَ اتِّفَاقِ كُلِّ مَنْ رَوَى التَّشَهُّدَ عَنْ عَلْقَمَةَ وَعَنْ غَيْرِهِ عَنْ

[15] Sunan al-Dāruquṭnī: Kitāb al-ṣalāh—Bāb ṣifat al-tashahhud wa wujūbihī.

عَبْدِ اللهِ بْنِ مَسْعُودٍ عَلَى ذَلِكَ وَاللهُ أَعْلَمُ.

Dāruquṭnī was asked about the ḥadīth of tashahhud from ʿAlqamah from Ibn Masʿūd in issue number 766 of *al-ʿIlal*:

> Zayd b. Abī Unaysah, ʿUfayr b. Maʿdān, and Saʿīd b. Abī ʿArūbah report it from Ḥammād from Ibrāhīm from ʿAlqamah from ʿAbdullah as a marfūʿ ḥadīth.
>
> Sufyān al-al-Thawrī, Ḥamzah al-Zayyāt, Ibrāhīm al-Ṣāʾigh, and Abū Ḥanīfah differed from them by reporting it from Ḥammād from Abū Wāʾil from ʿAbdullah. It was also said to be reported from Hishām al-Dustuwāʾī and Zayd b. Abī Unaysah, both from Ḥammād from Abū Wāʾil. Perhaps Ḥammād related it from both.
>
> Abū Ḥamzah Maymūn also reported it from Ibrāhīm from ʿAlqamah from ʿAbdullah as a marfūʿ report. From Abū Ḥamzah, Ṣaghdī b. Sinān and Abū Maʿshar al-Barāʾ Yūsuf b. Yazīd reported it.
>
> Ḥuṣayn b. ʿAbd al-Raḥmān reported it from Ibrāhīm from ʿAlqamah from ʿAbdullah as a mawqūf report (statement of Ibn Masʿūd). Yazīd b. Abī Ziyād reported it from Ibrāhīm from ʿAlqamah from Aswad from ʿAbdullah as a mawqūf report also. Aʿmash related it, as Zāʾidah reported from him, from Ibrāhīm from Aswad from ʿAbdullah.
>
> The isnād that is most likely to be correct in all of these is the report of Abū Wāʾil [from ʿAbdullah].
>
> Al-Ḥasan b. al-Ḥurr reported it from al-Qāsim b. Mukhaymirah from ʿAlqamah from ʿAbdullah. From al-Ḥasan, the following reported it: Muḥammad b. ʿAjlān, Ḥusayn b. ʿAlī al-Juʿfī, Zuhayr b. Muʿāwiyah, and ʿAbd al-Raḥmān b. Thābit b. Thawbān. From these, Ibn ʿAjlān and Ḥusayn al-Juʿfī agreed in their wording. As for Zuhayr, he added some words at the end of the report, which some of those reporting from him inserted into the ḥadīth: *'When you have fulfilled this, or have completed this, then you have completed the prayer. If you want to stand up, then stand.'*

Shabābah b. Sawwār reported it from Zuhayr and distinguished these words in his report by specifying that they were from Ibn Masʿūd. Similarly, Ibn Thawbān reported it from al-Ḥasan b. al-Ḥurr and also distinguished the Prophet's words from Ibn Masʿūd's. And this is correct.[16]

Ibn al-Ṣalāḥ stated:

Its famous example includes what we related about tashahhud from Abū Khaythamah Zuhayr b. Muʿāwiyah from al-Ḥasan b. al-Ḥurr from al-Qāsim b. Mukhaymirah from ʿAlqamah from ʿAbdullah b. Masʿūd: that the Prophet taught him the tashahhud in prayer . . . This is how Abū Khaythamah reported it from al-Ḥasan b. al-Ḥurr, adding to the ḥadīth those words: '*when you have said this . . .*'

These are surely the words of Ibn Masʿūd and not the words of the Prophet. Evidence for this include the fact that the trustworthy and pious one ʿAbd al-Raḥmān b. Thābit b. Thawbān reported this ḥadīth from al-Ḥasan b. al-Ḥurr and mentioned this clarification. Also, both Ḥusayn al-Juʿfī and Ibn ʿAjlān both reported the ḥadīth from al-Ḥasan b. al-Ḥurr without the extra words, as did all those who related the tashahhud from ʿAlqamah and others from Ibn Masʿūd. Shabābah related it from Abū Khaythamah and also distinguished the words.[17]

[16] Dāruquṭnī, *al-ʿIlal*, vol 5, pg 125-8.
[17] *Muqaddimah Ibn al-Ṣalāḥ*, pg 96.

Stance of Bukhārī and Muslim on Mursal and Mawqūf Reports

What was the stance of Bukhārī and Muslim on disputed reports that were mursal and mawqūf? Their position was to investigate disputed reports and come to a conclusion about each. If they determined such reports to be fully and properly connected to the Prophet, they would include them. If they determined reports to be disconnected (mursal) or statements of Companions (mawqūf), they did not include them. If they could not conclude decisively, they deemed them irreconcilable (muḍṭarib) and left them out. They were both independent scholars, who sometimes agreed or disagreed on specific reports.

Some people claim that Bukhārī and Muslim considered every disputed report with respect to the issue of mursal or mawqūf as defective and left them out. This is a view of those who are ignorant of these two works. In fact, I do not even rule out the possibility that others would go even further to claim that Bukhārī and Muslim rejected all narrators who were subject to any differences regarding their reliability and acceptance. *Please provide us with example of reports which were subject to these types of disputes and were still included by Bukhārī and Muslim*. Very well, there are so many examples, but I will share a few.

A Disputed-Origin Ḥadīth Report in Bukhārī and Muslim

Muslim relates the following:

BOOK OF MOSQUES AND PLACES OF PRAYER—CHAPTER: THE DISLIKE OF IKTHIṢĀR (PLACING HANDS ON WAIST) IN PRAYER Al-Ḥakam b. Mūsā al-Qanṭarī reported to me: ʿAbdullah b. al-Mubārak reported to us . . . And Abū Bakr b. Abī Shaybah

صحيح مسلم - كتاب المساجد ومواضع الصلاة - باب كراهة الاختصار فِي الصلاة

وَحَدَّثَنِي الْحَكَمُ بْنُ مُوسَى الْقَنْطَرِيُّ، حَدَّثَنَا عَبْدُ اللهِ بْنُ الْمُبَارَكِ (ح) قَالَ:

reported to us: Abū Khālid[1] and Abū Usāmah[2] reported to us: All of these related from Hishām: from Muḥammad (Ibn Sīrīn): from Abū Hurayrah: {The Prophet ﷺ forbade praying with one's hands on one's waist.} [3]

وَحَدَّثَنَا أَبُو بَكْرِ بْنُ أَبِي شَيْبَةَ، حَدَّثَنَا أَبُو خَالِدٍ، وَأَبُو أُسَامَةَ، جَمِيعًا عَنْ هِشَامٍ، عَنْ مُحَمَّدٍ، عَنْ أَبِي هُرَيْرَةَ عَنِ النَّبِيِّ صَلَّى اللهُ عَلَيْهِ وَسَلَّمَ أَنَّهُ نَهَى أَنْ يُصَلِّيَ الرَّجُلُ مُخْتَصِرًا. وَفِي رِوَايَةِ أَبِي بَكْرٍ قَالَ : نَهَى رَسُولُ اللهِ صَلَّى اللهُ عَلَيْهِ وَسَلَّمَ.

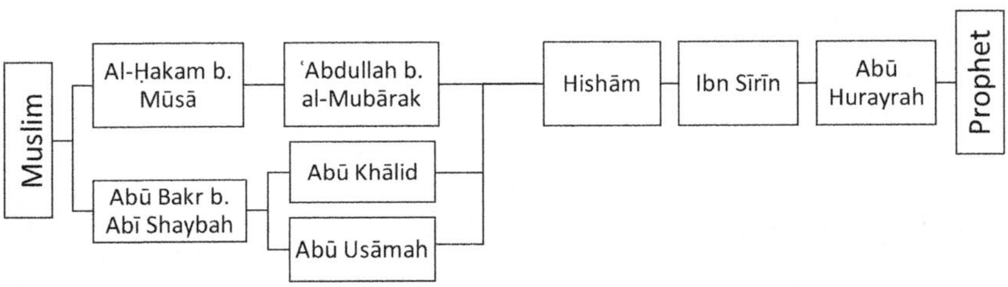

Bukhārī consecutively relates the following two ḥadīth:

BOOK OF ACTIONS IN PRAYER—CHAPTER: FORBIDDANCE OF KHASR (PLACING HANDS ON WAIST) IN PRAYER Abū al-Nuʿmān reported to us: Ḥammād reported to us: from Ayyūb: from Muḥammad: from Abū Hurayrah: {We were forbidden from praying with ours hands on our waists.}

صحيح البخاري - كتاب العمل في الصلاة - باب الخصر في الصلاة

حَدَّثَنَا أَبُو النُّعْمَانِ: حَدَّثَنَا حَمَّادٌ، عَنْ أَيُّوبَ، عَنْ مُحَمَّدٍ، عَنْ أَبِي هُرَيْرَةَ رَضِيَ اللهُ عَنْهُ قَالَ: نُهِيَ عَنِ الْخَصْرِ فِي الصَّلَاةِ وَقَالَ هِشَامٌ وَأَبُو هِلَالٍ، عَنِ ابْنِ سِيرِينَ، عَنْ

---

[1] Sulaymān b. Ḥayyān al-Aḥmar al-Jaʿfarī (d. 189-90 AH).

[2] Ḥammād b. Usāmah b. Zayd (d. 200-201 AH)

[3] Ṣaḥīḥ Muslim: Kitāb al-masājid wa mawāḍiʿ al-ṣalāh—Bāb karāhah al-ikhtiṣār fī al-ṣalāh.

أَبِي هُرَيْرَةَ، عَنِ النَّبِيِّ صَلَّى اللهُ عَلَيْهِ وَسَلَّمَ.

And Hishām and Abū Hilāl reported it from Ibn Sīrīn from Abū Hurayrah from the Prophet.

حَدَّثَنَا عَمْرُو بْنُ عَلِيٍّ: حَدَّثَنَا يَحْيَى: حَدَّثَنَا هِشَامٌ: حَدَّثَنَا مُحَمَّدٌ، عَنْ أَبِي هُرَيْرَةَ رَضِيَ اللهُ عَنْهُ قَالَ: نُهِيَ أَنْ يُصَلِّيَ الرَّجُلُ مُخْتَصِرًا.

ʿAmr b. ʿAlī reported to us: Yaḥyā reported to us: Hishām reported to us: Muḥammad reported to us: from Abū Hurayrah: It was forbidden for a person to pray with the hands at the hips.[4]

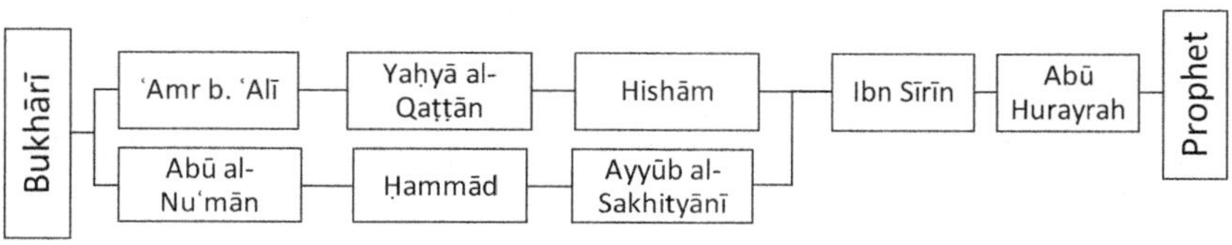

Dāruquṭnī was asked about this ḥadīth in issue number 1827:

Hishām b. Ḥassān reported it, and his students differed in reporting from him.

Zāʾidah b. Qudāmah, Abū Jaʿfar al-Rāzī, Muḥammad b. Salamah, ʿAbd al-Wahhab al-Thaqafī, Jarīr b. ʿAbd al-Ḥamīd, Jaʿfar al-Aḥmar, and ʿAlī b. ʿĀṣim all relate from Hishām from Muḥammad from Abū Hurayrah from the Prophet [explicitly]. However, ʿAlī b. ʿĀṣim related it from both Khālid al-Ḥadhdhāʾ and Hishām and made it explicitly marfūʿ.

Sufyān al-Thawrī, Yaḥyā al-Qaṭṭān, Jaʿfar b. Ghiyāth, Asbāṭ b. Muḥammad, Yazīd b. Hārūn, and Ḥammād b. Zayd all reported it from Hishām from Ibn Sīrīn from Abū Hurayrah, with the wording '*it was forbidden*' (*nuhiya*), not making it explicitly marfūʿ.

[4] Ṣaḥīḥ Bukhārī: Kitāb al-ʿamal fī al-ṣalāh—Bāb al-khaṣr fī al-ṣalāh.

Ayyūb al-Sakhtiyānī and Ash'ath b. 'Abd al-Malik also reported it likewise. The report of Asbāṭ from Hishām contains the wording: '*We were prohibited*' *(nuhīnā)* which is akin to being explicitly marfū'.

Qatādah also relates it, while his students differed among themselves in relating from him.

Abū Ja'far al-Rāzī reports from Qatādah from Ibn Sīrīn from Abū Hurayrah from the Prophet, as reported by 'Āṣim b. Sayf al-Baḥrānī who reported it like that from Abū Ja'far.

Mihrān b. Abī 'Umar, Khalaf b. al-Walīd, and Abū al-Naḍr differed by reporting it from Abū Ja'far al-Rāzī from Hishām b. Ḥassān, whose differences were mentioned above.

Sa'īd b. Abī 'Arūbah reported it from Qatādah as a mursal report (Qatādah from the Prophet), differing from 'Āṣim b. Sayf's isnād.

'Imrān b. Khālid reported it from Ibn Sīrīn from Abū Hurayrah from the Prophet.

Previously we clarified that Ibn Sīrīn's piety and caution drove him, depending upon his state of teaching, to make some reports explicitly marfū', other ones marfū' only by way of indirect allusion, and some reports to refrain from making them marfū' at all and choosing to stop at the level of mawqūf (statements of Companions).[5]

[5] As Shaykh Akram explains, Ibn Sīrīn's piety and fear of misattribution caused him to be over-cautious, and so, mawqūf reports of an individual such as him are not necessarily so. It is a mistake by some to consider all such reports mawqūf, when they are disputed and variably reported as marfū' and mawqūf. Rather, the context and state of reporters is crucial to consider here.

A Disputed-Origin Ḥadīth Report in Bukhārī Alone

An example of such a report related by Bukhārī alone is as follows:

BOOK OF ADHĀN—CHAPTER: RAISING HANDS UPON STANDING FROM SECOND RAK'AH 'Ayyāsh reported to us: 'Abd al-A'lā reported to us: 'Ubaydullah reported to us: from Nāfi': from Ibn 'Umar:

Whenever Ibn 'Umar entered the prayer, he recited takbīr and raised his hands. And whenever he bowed, he would raise his hands. On saying: *sami'allāhu liman ḥamidahū,* he would raise his hands. Upon standing up after the second rak'ah, he would raise his hands.

Ibn 'Umar used to attribute that to the Prophet ﷺ. Ḥammād b. Salamah reported it from Ayyūb from Nāfi' from Ibn 'Umar from the Prophet ﷺ. And Ibn Ṭahmān reported it from Ayyūb from Mūsā b. 'Aqabah in condensed form.[6]

صحيح البخاري - كتاب الأذان - باب رفع اليدين إذا قام من الركعتين

حَدَّثَنَا عَيَّاشٌ قَالَ: حَدَّثَنَا عَبْدُ الْأَعْلَى قَالَ: حَدَّثَنَا عُبَيْدُ اللهِ، عَنْ نَافِعٍ: أَنَّ ابْنَ عُمَرَ كَانَ إِذَا دَخَلَ فِي الصَّلَاةِ كَبَّرَ وَرَفَعَ يَدَيْهِ، وَإِذَا رَكَعَ رَفَعَ يَدَيْهِ، وَإِذَا قَالَ: سَمِعَ اللهُ لِمَنْ حَمِدَهُ. رَفَعَ يَدَيْهِ، وَإِذَا قَامَ مِنَ الرَّكْعَتَيْنِ رَفَعَ يَدَيْهِ، وَرَفَعَ ذَلِكَ ابْنُ عُمَرَ إِلَى نَبِيِّ اللهِ صَلَّى اللهُ عَلَيْهِ وَسَلَّمَ رَوَاهُ حَمَّادُ بْنُ سَلَمَةَ، عَنْ أَيُّوبَ، عَنْ نَافِعٍ، عَنِ ابْنِ عُمَرَ، عَنِ النَّبِيِّ صَلَّى اللهُ عَلَيْهِ وَسَلَّمَ. وَرَوَاهُ ابْنُ طَهْمَانَ، عَنْ أَيُّوبَ وَمُوسَى بْنِ عُقْبَةَ، مُخْتَصَرًا.

---

[6] Ṣaḥīḥ Bukhārī: Kitāb al-adhān—Bāb raf' al-yadayn idhā qāma min al-rak'atayn. Muslim does not include this report at all in his *Ṣaḥīḥ*, but he does include two other related reports: an undoubtedly Prophetic ḥadīth of Zuhrī from Sālim from Ibn 'Umar from the Prophet (which contains the addition of 'raising hands *to the level of his shoulders*') and another related report of the Companion Mālik b. al-Ḥuwayrith.

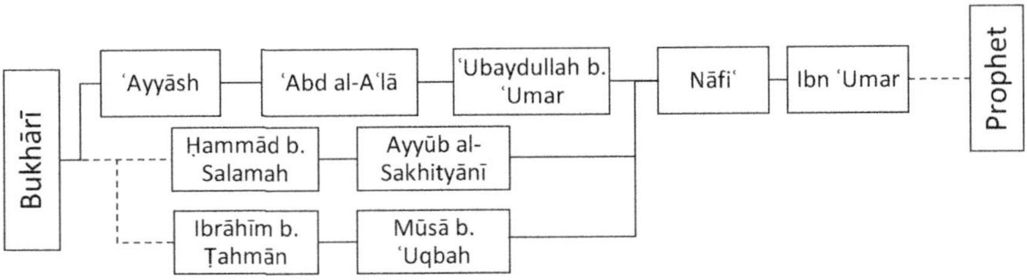

Dāruquṭnī was asked in issue number 2902 about the ḥadīth of Nāfiʿ from Ibn ʿUmar that the Prophet, when he stood for prayer, would raise his hands to the level of his shoulders:

> ʿUbaydullah b. ʿUmar reported this ḥadīth, and his students differed. Baqiyyah reported it from ʿUbaydullah from Nāfiʿ from Ibn ʿUmar that *the Prophet in the beginning of his prayer would raise his hands*—and they did not add anything more to the report.
>
> ʿAbd al-Aʿlā reported it from ʿUbaydullah from Nāfiʿ from Ibn ʿUmar from the Prophet, and mentioned the raising of the hands at the start of prayer, at rukūʿ, upon the statement: *samiʿallāhu liman ḥamidahū*, and upon rising from the second rakʿah.
>
> ʿAbd al-Wahāb al-Thaqafī supported him in relating it from ʿUbaydullah with this wording except for the attribution to the Prophet.
>
> Ismāʿīl b. ʿAyyāsh reported it from Mūsā b. ʿUqbah and ʿAbdullah [sic][7] b. ʿUmar from Nāfiʿ from Ibn ʿUmar that the Prophet raised his hands during the start of prayer, the rukūʿ, and sajdah. Ismāʿīl is weak in his reports from the people of Madīnah.
>
> Muḥammad b. Bashshār reported it from ʿUbaydullah from Nāfiʿ from Ibn ʿUmar as his action and not that of the Prophet, mentioning the raising of hands at the start, during rukūʿ, and during sajdah.
>
> The most correct report is that of ʿAbd al-Aʿlā.
>
> Imām Mālik reported if from Nāfiʿ, and there were many differences among his students.

[7] The text states ʿAbdullah b. ʿUmar, which is likely a mistake and possible refers to ʿUbaydullah b. ʿUmar, as per the editor Maḥfūẓ al-Raḥmān Salafī. See footnote 2, pg 13, vol 13.

Rizqullāh b. Mūsā reported it from Yaḥyā al-Qaṭṭān from Mālik from Nāfiʿ from Ibn ʿUmar from the Prophet, and mentioned raising hands during the start, and before and after rukūʿ. No other person supported him in this report.

What is sound from Mālik is what he reported in the Muwaṭṭaʾ from Nāfiʿ from Ibn ʿUmar as a mawqūf report, that he raised his hands at the start and when he raised his head from rukūʿ.

It is related from ʿAbdullah b. Nāfiʿ al-Ṣāʾigh, Khālid b. Makhlad, Isḥāq al-Juhanī, all from Mālik from Nāfiʿ from Ibn ʿUmar from the Prophet with the same words reported by Rizqullāh b. Mūsā from Yaḥyā al-Qaṭṭān, but this report is not sound from Mālik.

Dāwūd b. ʿAbdullah reported it from Nāfiʿ[8] from Ibn ʿUmar that the Prophet raised his hands at every rising and lowering. This report is mistakenly attributed to Mālik in two respects: its attribution to the Prophet and its wording.

It is reported from Ayyūb al-Sakhtiyānī and Mūsā b. ʿUqbah, both from Nāfiʿ from Ibn ʿUmar, with the following differences:

Ibrāhīm b. Ṭahmān reported from both of them and raised the report to the Prophet, mentioning raising hands at the start, and before and after rukūʿ. Ḥammād b. Salamah supported him in reporting it from Ayyūb.

It is also said to be reported from Hadiyyah from Ḥammād b. Zayd, but that is meant to refer to Ḥammād b. Salamah, and God knows best.

The correct isnād is from Ḥammād b. Zayd from Ayyūb from Nāfiʿ from Ibn ʿUmar as a mawqūf report. This is how Abū Ḍamrah reported it: from Mūsā b. ʿUqbah from Nāfiʿ from Ibn ʿUmar.

It is also reported from ʿUmar b. Muḥammad b. Zayd b. ʿAbdullah b. ʿUmar from Nāfiʿ from Ibn ʿUmar as a marfūʿ report.

Ismāʿīl b. Umayyah and Layth b. Saʿd reported it from Nāfiʿ from Ibn ʿUmar. The mawqūf version is most sound from Nāfiʿ.

[8] According to Maḥfūẓ al-Raḥmān Salafī, there is likely a missing link here, and the isnād should be: Dāwūd from Mālik from Nāfiʿ.

Zayd b. Wāqid reported it from Nāfiʿ from Ibn ʿUmar in a stranger wording: 'when he saw a man praying without raising his hands, he would stone him with pebbles.'

Muḥārib b. Dithār was also differed upon. ʿĀṣim b. Kulayb reported it from Muḥārib from Ibn ʿUmar and raised it to the Prophet: that when he stood [after] the two rakʿahs, would say takbīr and raise his hands.

Abū Isḥāq al-Shaybānī and al-Naḍr b. Muḥārib b. Dithār both related from Muḥārib from Ibn ʿUmar as a mawqūf report. Similarly, Muḥammad b. Zayd reported it from Ibn ʿUmar as a mawqūf report, mentioning raising hands at the opening, and before and after rukūʿ.

And it is reported from Ḥuṣayn from Mujāhid from Ibn ʿUmar that he did not raise his hands except in the beginning of prayer, and never did so after that. Abū Bakr b. ʿAyyāsh reported this from Ḥuṣayn, and this is a mistake either from Abū Bakr or from Ḥuṣayn.

The correct report from Ibn ʿUmar is as we mentioned above.[9]

---

[9] Dāruquṭnī, *al-ʿIlal*, vol 13, pg 13-6.

A Disputed-Origin Ḥadīth Report in Muslim Alone

An example of such a report related by Muslim alone is as follows:

BOOK OF PURITY—CHAPTER: TIME DURATION FOR WIPING OVER KHUFFAYN Isḥāq b. Ibrāhīm al-Ḥanẓalī reported to us: ʿAbd al-Razzāq reported to us: al-Thawrī reported to us: from ʿAmr b. Qays al-Milāʾī: from al-Ḥakam b. ʿUtaybah: from al-Qāsim b. Mukhaymirah: from Shurayḥ b. Hāniʾ: I came to ʿĀʾishah to ask her about wiping over the khuffayn. She replied: 'Go ask ʿAlī b. Abī Ṭālib, for he has traveled with the Prophet ﷺ.' We did ask him, and he replied: ⟨God's Messenger designated the limit as three days and nights for the traveler and one day and night for the resident.⟩ When Sufyān used to mention ʿAmr he would praise him.

صحيح مسلم - كتاب الطهارة - باب التوقيت في المسح على الخفين

وَحَدَّثَنَا إِسْحَاقُ بْنُ إِبْرَاهِيمَ الْحَنْظَلِيُّ ، أَخْبَرَنَا عَبْدُ الرَّزَّاقِ،أَخْبَرَنَا الثَّوْرِيُّ، عَنْ عَمْرِو بْنِ قَيْسٍ الْمُلَائِيِّ عَنِ الْحَكَمِ بْنِ عُتَيْبَةَ، عَنِ الْقَاسِمِ بْنِ مُخَيْمِرَةَ، عَنْ شُرَيْحِ بْنِ هَانِئٍ قَالَ: أَتَيْتُ عَائِشَةَ أَسْأَلُهَا عَنِ الْمَسْحِ عَلَى الْخُفَّيْنِ، فَقَالَتْ: عَلَيْكَ بِابْنِ أَبِي طَالِبٍ فَسَلْهُ، فَإِنَّهُ كَانَ يُسَافِرُ مَعَ رَسُولِ اللهِ صَلَّى اللهُ عَلَيْهِ وَسَلَّمَ، فَسَأَلْنَاهُ، فَقَالَ: جَعَلَ رَسُولُ اللهِ صَلَّى اللهُ عَلَيْهِ وَسَلَّمَ ثَلَاثَةَ أَيَّامٍ وَلَيَالِيَهُنَّ لِلْمُسَافِرِ، وَيَوْمًا وَلَيْلَةً لِلْمُقِيمِ، قَالَ: وَكَانَ سُفْيَانُ إِذَا ذَكَرَ عَمْرًا أَثْنَى عَلَيْهِ .

Isḥāq reported to us: Zakariyāʾ b. ʿAdī reported to us: from ʿUbaydullah b. ʿAmr: from Zayd b. Abī Unaysah: from al-Ḥakam: this same isnād.

وَحَدَّثَنَا إِسْحَاقُ، أَخْبَرَنَا زَكَرِيَّاءُ بْنُ عَدِيٍّ، عَنْ عُبَيْدِ اللهِ بْنِ عَمْرٍو، عَنْ زَيْدِ بْنِ أَبِي أُنَيْسَةَ، عَنِ الْحَكَمِ بِهَذَا الْإِسْنَادِ مِثْلَهُ

Zuhayr b. Ḥarb reported to me: Abū Muʿāwiyah reported to us: from Aʿmash: from al-Ḥakam: from al-Qāsim b. Mukhaymirah: from Shurayḥ b. Hāniʾ: I asked ʿĀʾishah about the matter of wiping. She

وَحَدَّثَنِي زُهَيْرُ بْنُ حَرْبٍ، حَدَّثَنَا أَبُو مُعَاوِيَةَ، عَنِ الْأَعْمَشِ، عَنِ الْحَكَمِ، عَنِ الْقَاسِمِ بْنِ مُخَيْمِرَةَ، عَنْ شُرَيْحِ بْنِ هَانِئٍ قَالَ: سَأَلْتُ عَائِشَةَ عَنِ الْمَسْحِ عَلَى الْخُفَّيْنِ، فَقَالَتِ: ائْتِ عَلِيًّا فَإِنَّهُ أَعْلَمُ بِذَلِكَ مِنِّي، فَأَتَيْتُ عَلِيًّا، فَذَكَرَ عَنِ النَّبِيِّ صَلَّى اللهُ عَلَيْهِ وَسَلَّمَ بِمِثْلِهِ .

replied: Go to ʿAlī, for he is more aware on this than me. I came to ʿAlī and he reported from the Prophet this same ḥadīth.[10]

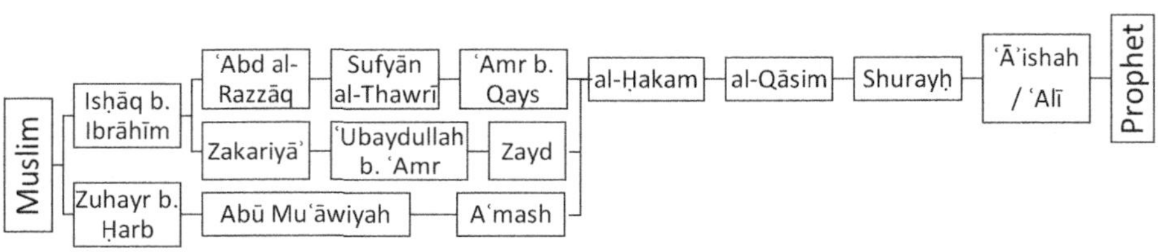

Dāruquṭnī in issue number 379 was asked about the ḥadīth of Shurayḥ b. Hāniʾ from ʿAlī b. Abī Ṭālib from the Prophet about the wiping over the khuffayn:

> It is a ḥadīth reported by al-Qāsim b. Mukhaymirah and al-Miqdām b. Shurayḥ, both from Shurayḥ b. Hāniʾ. Al-Ḥakam reported it from al-Qāsim, and his students differed. Those who reported it from al-Ḥakam were Amr b. Qays al-Mulāʾī, Zayd b. Abī Unaysah, ʿAbd al-Malik b. Ḥumayd b. Abī Ghaniyyah, Abū Khālid al-Dālānī, al-Qāsim b. al-Walīd al-Hamdānī, and Idrīs b. Yazīd al-Awdī.
>
> From Aʿmash there were differences. Abū Muʿāwiyah al-Ḍarīr and ʿAmr b. ʿAbd al-Ghaffār both reported it from Aʿmash from al-Ḥakam and raised it to the Prophet. On the other hand, Zāʾidah b. Qudāmah, ʿAlī b. Ghurāb, and Aḥmad b. Bashīr reported it from Aʿmash as a mawqūf report from ʿAlī, and not raised to the Prophet. It is also

[10] Ṣaḥīḥ Muslim: Kitāb al-ṭahārah—Bāb al-tawqīt fī al-masḥ ʿalā al-khuffayn. Bukhārī does not include this ḥadīth in his Ṣaḥīḥ at all.

reported from Azhar b. Sa'd al-Sammān from Ibn 'Awn from Sulaymān al-Taymī from A'mash as a mursal report which is also mawqūf.

Also, the son of 'Abd al-Raḥmān b. Abī Laylah, Muḥammad b. 'Ubaydullah al-'Arzamī, and Ḥajjāj b. Arṭāh reported it from al-Ḥakam as a marfū' report.

Al-Ajlaḥ, Mālik b. Mighwal, and Abū Ḥanīfah reported it from al-Ḥakam as a mawqūf report.

Shu'bah's reports were also subject to differences. Yaḥyā al-Qaṭṭān reported from him as a marfū' report, and Abū al-Walīd supported him in reporting from Abū Khalīfah from him. Ghundur was the one who reported it from Shu'bah and mentioned—then doubted—that Shu'bah had raised it to the Prophet, whereas the other students of Shu'bah reported it as a mawqūf report.

Layth b. Abī Sulaym reported it from al-Ḥakam but dropped al-Qāsim from the isnād. From Layth, his students differed. Shaybān reported it from Layth from al-Ḥakam from Shurayḥ from 'Alī from Bilāl. Mu'tamir reported it from Layth from al-Ḥakam and Ḥabīb, both from Shurayḥ from Bilāl without mentioning 'Alī. The mention of Bilāl in the report is mistake from Layth, because of the agreement of all other students of al-Ḥakam, as well as the agreement of the students of Shurayḥ, in not mentioning Bilāl.

Abū Isḥāq al-Sabī'ī reported the ḥadīth and his students differed from him.

Sufyān al-Thawrī reported it from Abū Isḥāq from al-Qāsim from Shurayḥ from 'Alī as a marfū' report to the Prophet. Ḥammād b. Shu'ayb supported him in relating it from Abū Isḥāq. Muḥammad b. Muṣ'ab al-Qarqasānī, who was not an expert, also supported him in reporting it from Mālik b. Mighwal, Isrā'īl, Zuhayr, and Abū 'Awānah, all from Abū Isḥāq as a marfū' report.

The students of Zuhayr and Isrā'īl differed from this by reporting it from them through Abū Isḥāq as a mawqūf report. Abū al-Aḥwaṣ Sallām b. Sulaym, Yūnus b. Abī Isḥāq, al-Ḥasan b. Ṣāliḥ, and Yazīd b. Abī Ziyād all reported it from Abū Isḥāq as a mawqūf report. Yazīd also heard it from al-Qāsim as a mawqūf report. Sufyān b. 'Uyaynah reported it from

Yazīd as a marfū' report, whereas all others reported it from Yazīd as mawqūf. Muḥammad b. Abān reported it from al-Ḥasan b. al-Ḥurr from al-Qāsim as a marfū' report whereas Zuhayr reported is as mawqūf.

'Abdah b. Abī Lubābah reported it from al-Qāsim from Shurayḥ from 'Alī as a mawqūf report. Al-Miqdām reported it from his father Shurayḥ from 'Alī, and his students differed. Sharīk reported it from Miqdām as a marfū' report, as did Shu'bah through the transmission of Abū Qatādah al-Ḥarrānī from him, whereas Mis'ar reported it from him as a mawqūf report.

'Abd al-Malik b. Abī Sulaymān reported it from the son of Shurayḥ, without naming him, from his father from 'Alī as a marfū' report. It is said that this son of Shurayḥ was Muḥammad, the brother of Miqdām, and God knows best.

'Abbās b. Dhurayḥ reported it from Shurayḥ from 'Alī as a mawqūf report.

The correct version is the marfū' report due to the agreement of the expert students of al-Ḥakam, who were previously mentioned, and God knows best.[11]

---

[11] Dāruquṭnī, *al-'Ilal*, vol 3, pg 230-5.

A Disputed Mursal Ḥadīth Report in Bukhārī and Muslim

The following ḥadīth appears in Bukhārī and Muslim. Muslim relates the following:

BOOK OF ĪMĀN—CHAPTER: CLARIFYING THE FAITH THROUGH WHICH ONE ENTERS PARADISE AND THE FACT THAT ONE WHO HOLDS ON TO THE COMMANDS ENTERS PARADISE Abū Bakr b. Isḥāq reported to me: ʿAffān reported to us: Wuhayb reported to us: Yaḥyā b. Saʿīd reported to us: from Abū Zurʿah: from Abū Hurayrah: A bedouin came to the Prophet and said: 'Messenger of God, tell me an action which I can do to enter Paradise.'

The Prophet ﷺ replied: ﴾Worship God without associating anyone alongside Him, establish the obligatory prayers, pay the obligatory zakāh, and fast Ramadan.﴿ The bedouin replied: 'By Him Whose Hands hold my life, I will not exceed this in any way, nor will I detract anything from it!' When he turned his back, the Prophet stated: ﴾Whoever is pleased to see a person of Paradise should look at him.﴿ [12]

صحيح مسلم - كتاب الإيمان - باب بيان الإيمان الذي يدخل به الجنة وأن من تمسك بما أمر به دخل الجنة

وَحَدَّثَنِي أَبُو بَكْرِ بْنُ إِسْحَاقَ ، حَدَّثَنَا عَفَّانُ ، حَدَّثَنَا وُهَيْبٌ ، حَدَّثَنَا يَحْيَى بْنُ سَعِيدٍ ، عَنْ أَبِي زُرْعَةَ ، عَنْ أَبِي هُرَيْرَةَ أَنَّ أَعْرَابِيًّا جَاءَ إِلَى رَسُولِ اللهِ صَلَّى اللهُ عَلَيْهِ وَسَلَّمَ فَقَالَ : يَا رَسُولَ اللهِ ، دُلَّنِي عَلَى عَمَلٍ إِذَا عَمِلْتُهُ دَخَلْتُ الْجَنَّةَ ، قَالَ : تَعْبُدُ اللهَ لَا تُشْرِكُ بِهِ شَيْئًا ، وَتُقِيمُ الصَّلَاةَ الْمَكْتُوبَةَ ، وَتُؤَدِّي الزَّكَاةَ الْمَفْرُوضَةَ ، وَتَصُومُ رَمَضَانَ ، قَالَ : وَالَّذِي نَفْسِي بِيَدِهِ لَا أَزِيدُ عَلَى هَذَا شَيْئًا أَبَدًا ، وَلَا أَنْقُصُ مِنْهُ ، فَلَمَّا وَلَّى قَالَ النَّبِيُّ صَلَّى اللهُ عَلَيْهِ وَسَلَّمَ : مَنْ سَرَّهُ أَنْ

[12] Ṣaḥīḥ Muslim: Kitāb al-īmān—Bāb bayān al-īmān alladhī yudkhalu bihi al-jannah wa anna man tamassaka bimā umira bihi dakhala al-jannah.

يَنْظُرَ إِلَى رَجُلٍ مِنْ أَهْلِ الْجَنَّةِ ،
فَلْيَنْظُرْ إِلَى هَذَا.

Bukhārī reported the same ḥadīth as follows:

BOOK OF ZAKĀH, CHAPTER: OBLIGATION OF ZAKĀH Muḥammad b. ʿAbd al-Rahim reported to me: ʿAffān b. Muslim reported to us: Wuhayb reported to us: from Yaḥyā b. Saʿīd: from Abū Zurʿah: from Abū Hurayrah: A bedouin came to the Prophet . . .

Musaddad[13] reported to us: from Yaḥyā: from Abū Ḥayyān: Abū Zurʿah reported to me: from the Prophet the same ḥadīth.

صحيح البخاري - كتاب الزكاة - باب وجوب الزكاة

حَدَّثَنِي مُحَمَّدُ بْنُ عَبْدِ الرَّحِيمِ: حَدَّثَنَا عَفَّانُ بْنُ مُسْلِمٍ: حَدَّثَنَا وُهَيْبٌ ، عَنْ يَحْيَى بْنِ سَعِيدِ بْنِ حَيَّانَ ، عَنْ أَبِي زُرْعَةَ ، عَنْ أَبِي هُرَيْرَةَ رَضِيَ اللهُ عَنْهُ: أَنَّ أَعْرَابِيًّا أَتَى النَّبِيَّ صَلَّى اللهُ عَلَيْهِ وَسَلَّمَ فَقَالَ . . .

حَدَّثَنَا مُسَدَّدٌ ، عَنْ يَحْيَى ، عَنْ أَبِي حَيَّانَ قَالَ: أَخْبَرَنِي أَبُو زُرْعَةَ ، عَنِ النَّبِيِّ صَلَّى اللهُ عَلَيْهِ وَسَلَّمَ: بِهَذَا

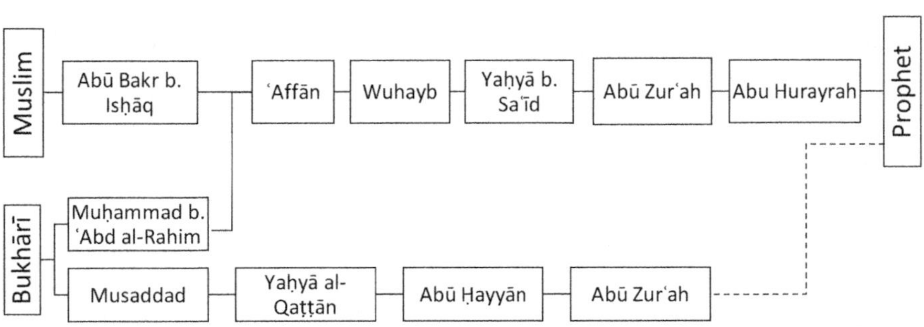

[13] Musaddad b. Musarhad (d. 228/843) was a great ḥadīth expert of Baṣrah who compiled a Musnad collection. Apart from Muslim and Ibn Mājah, the rest of the six authors of the ḥadīth canon related from him.

It was a point of contention whether this represented a mursal report or a fully connected one. Bukhārī mentioned both isnāds and chose the connected one as the correct one. Muslim also chose the connected report as the sound one, and did not even reference the mursal version in his Ṣaḥīḥ. Dāruquṭnī stated: Yaḥyā al-Qaṭṭān reported it but differed from Wuhayb in reporting from Abū Ḥayyān from Abū Zurʿah as a mursal report to the Prophet (Abū Zurʿah quoting the Prophet directly).[14]

Ibn Ḥajar responds to Dāruquṭnī in his introduction: 'Bukhārī reported the ḥadīth of Yaḥyā al-Qaṭṭān after the ḥadīth of Wuhayb, indicating that the defect [in the ḥadīth] was not major since Wuhayb was an expert, and hence, he related Wuhayb's ḥadīth first since it contained an addition. Also supporting its meaning is another report which both Bukhārī and Muslim accepted in Kitāb al-īmān through Jarīr and Ismāʿīl b. ʿUlayyah from Abū Ḥayyān. This report strengthens the report of Wuhayb.'[15]

A Disputed Mursal Ḥadīth Report in Bukhārī Alone

Bukhārī reports the following:

BOOK OF IʿTIKĀF—CHAPTER: IʿTIKĀF IN THE MIDDLE TEN DAYS OF RAMADAN ʿAbdullah b. Abī Shaybah reported to us: Abū Bakr reported to us: from Abū Ḥuṣayn: from Abū Ṣāliḥ: from Abū Hurayrah: ﴾The Prophet used to perform iʿtikāf for ten days each Ramadan, but in the year of his demise, he performed it for twenty days.﴿ [16]

صحيح البخاري - أبواب الاعتكاف - باب الاعتكاف في العشر الأوسط من رمضان

حَدَّثَنَا عَبْدُ اللهِ بْنُ أَبِي شَيْبَةَ : حَدَّثَنَا أَبُو بَكْرٍ، عَنْ أَبِي حَصِينٍ ، عَنْ أَبِي صَالِحٍ ، عَنْ أَبِي هُرَيْرَةَ رَضِيَ اللهُ عَنْهُ قَالَ : كَانَ النَّبِيُّ صَلَّى اللهُ عَلَيْهِ وَسَلَّمَ يَعْتَكِفُ فِي كُلِّ رَمَضَانٍ عَشَرَةَ أَيَّامٍ ، فَلَمَّا كَانَ الْعَامُ الَّذِي قُبِضَ فِيهِ اعْتَكَفَ عِشْرِينَ يَوْمًا.

---

[14] Dāruquṭnī, *al-Ilzāmāt,* pg 204.

[15] *Fath,* vol 1, pg 356.

[16] Ṣaḥīḥ Bukhārī: Kitāb al-iʿtikāf—Bāb al-iʿtikāf fī al-ʿashr al-awsaṭ min Ramaḍān.

Bukhārī also reported this ḥadīth from Khālid b. Yazīd from Abū Bakr with the same subsequent isnād.[17]

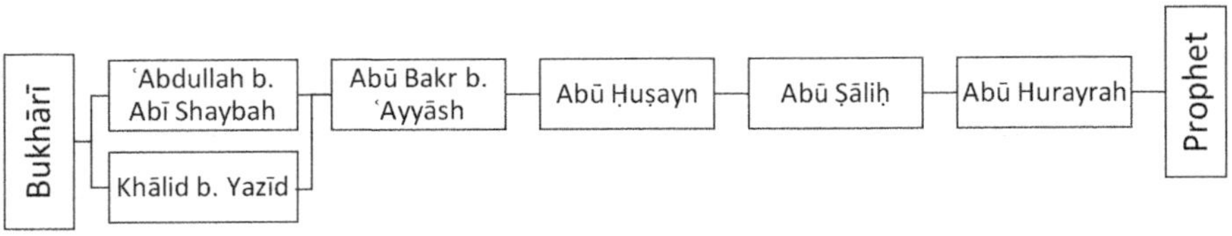

Muslims did not include this report in his Ṣaḥīḥ due to the dispute over whether it is mursal or connected. Ibn Abī Ḥātim states:

> I asked my father about the ḥadīth of Abū Bakr b. ʿAyyāsh from Abū Ḥuṣayn, and he said: The sound report is what al-Thawrī reported from Abū Ḥuṣayn from Abū Ṣāliḥ, who said: 'the Prophet used to perform iʿtikāf . . .' as a mursal report.[18]

He also states:

> I asked Abū Zurʿah about the report of ʿAbd al-Razzāq from Maʿmar from Zuhrī from ʿUrwah from ʿĀʾishah from the Prophet, as well as the report of Zuhrī from Saʿīd b. al-Musayyab from Abū Hurayrah from the Prophet, that he used to perform iʿtikāf in the last ten days of Ramadan until God reclaimed his soul. Abū Muḥammad has said: Some students of Zuhrī reported it from Zuhrī from Abū Salamah from Abū Hurayra from the Prophet, while Nāfiʿ b. Yazīd reported it from ʿUqayl from Zuhrī from ʿUrwah and Ibn al-Musayyab, both from ʿĀʾishah from the Prophet. Layth b. Saʿd reported it from Zuhrī from Ibn al-Musayyab, who said: The Prophet performed iʿtikāf in the first ten days, then the middle ten days . . .
>
> Abū Zurʿah replied: The correct report in my estimation is Zuhrī from ʿUrwah from ʿĀʾishah and Saʿīd b. al-Musayyab from the Prophet.
>
> I asked Abū Zurʿah: The wordings differ, as if they were two reports.

---

[17] Ṣaḥīḥ Bukhārī: Kitāb faḍāʾil al-Qurʾān—Bāb kāna Jibrīl yaʿriḍu al-Qurʾāna ʿalā al-nabī.
[18] Ibn Abī Ḥātim, *al-ʿIlal*, pg 594.

He replied: No, they are the same ḥadīth, although the wordings may differ.[19]

Bazzār comments after relating the ḥadīth in his Musnad in the section of the reports of Abū Hurayrah: We don't know of any isnād for the ḥadīth of Abū Hurayrah except for this one.[20] Dāruquṭnī was asked in issue number 1986 about this report and said:

> Abū Bakr b. ʿAyyāsh reported it, and his students differed. Muslim b. Sallām al-Hāshimī, ʿUthmān b. Abī Shaybah, Abū Hishām, and Sulaymān b. Dāwūd al-Shādhakūnī reported it from Abū Bakr from Aʿmash from Abū Ṣāliḥ from Abū Hurayrah. Sufyān b. Wakīʿ differed from them and reported it from Abū Bakr from Abū Ḥuṣayn from Sālim b. Abī al-Jaʿd from Abū Hurayrah. ʿUmar b. Mūsā al-Ḥādī, the uncle of Qudaymī, differed and reported it from Abū Bakr from Aʿmash from Abū Ṣāliḥ from Abū Hurayrah. The correct report is that of those who report it from Abū Ḥuṣayn from Abū Ṣāliḥ from Abū Hurayrah.[21]

A Disputed Mursal Ḥadīth Report in Muslim Alone

A disputed mursal report that is related by Muslim alone is as follows:

BOOK OF ĪMĀN—CHAPTER: ABOUT GOD'S WORDS {AND WARN YOU NEAREST KIN)	صحيح مسلم - كتاب الإيمان - باب فِي قوله تَعَالَى وأنذر عشيرتك الْأقربين
Muḥammad b. ʿAbdullah b. Numayr reported to us: Wakīʿ and Yūnus b. Bukayr reported to us: Hishām b. ʿUrwah reported to us: from his father: from ʿĀʾishah: When the verse And warn your nearest kin was revealed, the	حَدَّثَنَا مُحَمَّدُ بْنُ عَبْدِ اللهِ بْنِ نُمَيْرٍ، حَدَّثَنَا وَكِيعٌ، وَيُونُسُ بْنُ بُكَيْرٍ قَالَا: حَدَّثَنَا هِشَامُ بْنُ عُرْوَةَ ، عَنْ أَبِيهِ،

[19] Ibid, vol 3, pg 104-6.

[20] Musnad al-Bazzār: Musnad Abī Hurayrah—Abū Ḥuṣayn ʿan Abī Ṣāliḥ.

[21] Dāruquṭnī, *al-ʿIlal,* vol 10, pg 218.

عَنْ عَائِشَةَ قَالَتْ: لَمَّا نَزَلَتْ { وَأَنْذِرْ عَشِيرَتَكَ الأَقْرَبِينَ } قَامَ رَسُولُ اللهِ صَلَّى اللهُ عَلَيْهِ وَسَلَّمَ عَلَى الصَّفَا، فَقَالَ: يَا فَاطِمَةُ بِنْتَ مُحَمَّدٍ، يَا صَفِيَّةُ بِنْتَ عَبْدِ الْمُطَّلِبِ، يَا بَنِي عَبْدِ الْمُطَّلِبِ، لَا أَمْلِكُ لَكُمْ مِنَ اللهِ شَيْئًا، سَلُونِي مِنْ مَالِي مَا شِئْتُمْ.

Prophet stood upon mount Ṣafā and said: ﴾O Fāṭimah bint Muḥammad! O Ṣafiyyah bint ʿAbd al-Muṭṭalib! O Clan of ʿAbd al-Muṭṭalib! I cannot avail you against God in anyway, but you can ask me what you wish from my own wealth.﴿ [22]

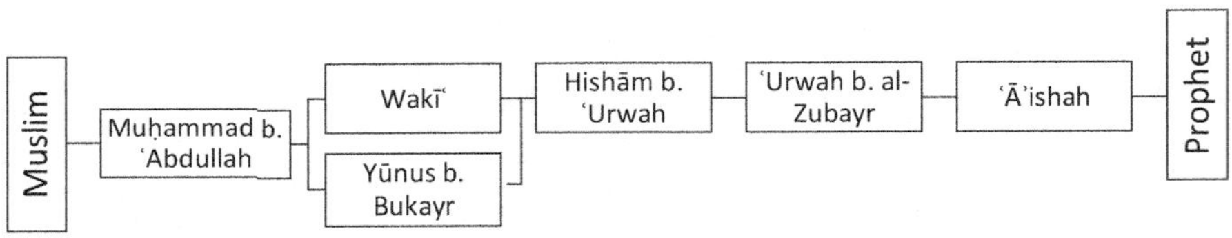

Tirmidhī comments after relating this same ḥadīth through his isnād:

هَذا حَدِيثٌ حَسَنٌ صَحِيحٌ وهَكَذا رَوى وكِيعٌ، وغَيْرُ واحِدٍ، عَنْ هِشامِ بْنِ عُرْوَةَ، عَنْ أَبِيهِ، عَنْ عائِشَةَ، نَحْوَ حَدِيثِ مُحَمَّدِ بْنِ عَبْدِ الرَّحْمَنِ الطُّفاوِيِّ، ورَوى بَعْضُهُمْ عَنْ هِشامِ بْنِ عُرْوَةَ، عَنْ أَبِيهِ، عَنِ النَّبِيِّ ﷺ مُرْسَلًا ولَمْ يَذْكُرْ فِيهِ عَنْ عائِشَةَ.

This ḥadīth is ḥasan ṣaḥīḥ. This is how Wakīʿ and others related it from Hishām b. ʿUrwah from his father from ʿĀʾishah, similar to the ḥadīth of Muḥammad b. ʿAbd al-Raḥmān al-Ṭufāwī. Others related from Hishām from his father from the Prophet ﷺ as a mursal report without mentioning ʿĀʾishah.[23]

[22] Ṣaḥīḥ Muslim: Kitāb al-īmān—Bāb fī qawlihi wa andhir ʿashīrataka al-aqarabīn.
[23] Tirmidhī: Kitāb al-tafsīr—Bāb wa min sūrah al-Shuʿarāʾ.

Dāruquṭnī states in issue number 3505:

> Hishām b. ʿUrwah reported it and his students differed from him. Wakīʿ b. Jarrāḥ, Muḥammad b. ʿAbd al-Raḥmān al-Ṭufāwī, and Abū Khālid al-Aḥmar reported it from Hishām from his father from ʿĀʾishah. Mālik b. Anas, Mufaḍḍal b. Faḍālah, and Muḥammad b. Kunāsah report it from Hishām from his father as a mursal report, which is more sound.[24]

After this, Dāruquṭnī relates his isnād through Wakīʿ, Muḥammad b. ʿAbd al-Raḥmān, and Abū Khālid from Hishām from his father from ʿĀʾishah as a connected report.[25]

[24] Dāruquṭnī, *al-ʿIlal,* vol 14, pg 163.

[25] Ibid.

Recital and Audition in Ḥadīth

What is the meaning of reading (qirā'ah) and audition (samā')? Qirā'ah refers to knowledge that comes through the medium of reading, whereas *samā'* refers to knowledge that is attained through hearing. This is not unlike one's sight, smell, or touch being a medium for attaining knowledge. Only when you actually taste a certain food can you claim that you have tasted it. If you have an illness that prevents you from tasting, you cannot claim in that case to have tasted anything. All these senses are sources as well as means to knowledge.

Knowing this allows you to understand that reading and hearing are two great means for attaining knowledge. They are never used in any other sense. When you say that you have read sūrah al-Baqarah or Ṣaḥīḥ al-Bukhārī, for instance, this means reading them with understanding and comprehension, and nothing else.

Is this understanding exclusive to the Arabic usage of 'reading' or can it apply to other languages? It applies, in fact, to all languages. When you ask someone, for example, if they have read grammar, or poetry, this refers to reading those subjects with comprehension. When you ask a person if they have read the poetry of Iqbal, Rumi, or Mutanabbī, it means reading them with understanding. When your mother asks, 'Don't you hear me?' it always refers to hearing with understanding.

What is their meaning in the Qur'ān? It is the same. They do not come in the Qur'ān in any other sense. There are many examples, including the following:

> *{When you recite the Qur'an, We place a hidden barrier between you and those who do not believe in the Hereafter; and We place a covering on their hearts so that they do not comprehend it, and We cause a heaviness in their ears; and when you mention your Lord, the Only True Lord, in the Qur'an, they turn their backs in aversion.}* [1]

> *{Had We revealed it to one of the non-Arabs and even if he had recited to them, they would still not have believed in it. Thus, have We caused this to*

[1] Qur'ān 17:45-6

penetrate the hearts of the culprits. They will not believe in it until they clearly see the grievous chastisement. But it comes upon them suddenly, seizing them unaware.﴿ [2]

﴾*And if any of those who associate others with God in His Divinity seeks asylum, grant him asylum that he may hear the Word of God, and then escort him to safety for they are a people who do not know.*﴿ [3]

What is their meaning in the words of the Prophet? His usage does not differ from that of the Qur'ān. For example, he stated the following:

﴾*If one recites the last two verses of Sūrah al-Baqarah at night, it is sufficient for him.*﴿ [4]

﴾*Do not make your houses as graveyards, for Satan runs away from the house in which Sūrah al-Baqarah is recited.*﴿ [5]

﴾*Recite the Qur'an, for on the Day of Resurrection it will come as an intercessor for those who recite It. Recite the two bright ones: al-Baqarah and Sūrah Āl 'Imrān, for on the Day of Resurrection they will come as two clouds or two shades, or two flocks of birds in ranks, pleading for those who recite them. Recite Sūrah al-Baqarah, for to take recourse to it is a blessing and to give it up is a cause of grief, and the magicians cannot confront it.*﴿ [6]

What is the incorrect meaning which you deny? Reading and audition stripped from the notion of knowledge and reduced to the idea of mere reciting with the tongue or listening with the ears without any comprehension or learning on one's part.[7]

---

[2] Qur'ān 26:198-202.

[3] Qur'ān 9:6.

[4] Ṣaḥīḥ Bukhārī: Kitāb faḍā'il al-Qur'ān—Bāb faḍl sūrah al-Baqarah.

[5] Ṣaḥīḥ Muslim: Kitāb ṣalāh al-musāfirīn wa qaṣrihā—Bāb istiḥbāb ṣalāh al-nāfilah fī baytihī.

[6] Ṣaḥīḥ Muslim: Kitāb ṣalāh al-musāfirīn wa qaṣrihā—Bāb faḍl qirā'āt al-Qur'ān.

[7] The traditional method of ḥadīth transmission was primarily two-fold: through audition (samā'), which consisted of passively hearing ḥadīth directly from the mouths of the teachers; or recital (qirā'ah),

This is a new usage, but there is no need to argue over terminology. You are right, and I am only contesting the usage of the terms of reading and audition, through all their related and derivative forms in the Qur᾿ān and Prophetic ḥadīth reports in this new way (reading and hearing without comprehension).

What do you say about the ḥadīth: 'I do not say that alif lām mīm is one letter, but each of them is one letter'? These are referring to the disjointed letters whose meanings are not known and show that reward is attained by reading something without knowledge behind it. This ḥadīth was reported by Tirmidhī from ʿAbdullah b. Masʿūd:

BOOK OF THE VIRTUES OF THE QUR᾿ĀN—CHAPTER: WHAT HAS BEEN REPORTED ABOUT RECITING A SINGLE LETTER OF THE QUR᾿ĀN

The Prophet ﷺ said: ﴾*Whoever reads one letter from God's Book will have one reward, each is multiplied by ten. And I do not say that alif lām mīm is one letter, but each of them is one letter.*﴿

جامع الترمذي - أبواب فضائل القرآن عن رسول الله صلى الله عليه وسلم - باب ما جاء فيمن قرأ حرفا من القرآن ماله من الأجر

حَدَّثَنَا مُحَمَّدُ بْنُ بَشَّارٍ ، قَالَ: حَدَّثَنَا أَبُو بَكْرٍ الْحَنَفِيُّ، قَالَ: حَدَّثَنَا الضَّحَّاكُ بْنُ عُثْمَانَ، عَنْ أَيُّوبَ بْنِ مُوسَى قَالَ: سَمِعْتُ مُحَمَّدَ بْنَ كَعْبٍ الْقُرَظِيَّ يَقُولُ: سَمِعْتُ عَبْدَ اللهِ بْنَ مَسْعُودٍ يَقُولُ: قَالَ رَسُولُ اللهِ صَلَّى اللهُ عَلَيْهِ وَسَلَّمَ: مَنْ قَرَأَ حَرْفًا مِنْ كِتَابِ اللهِ فَلَهُ بِهِ حَسَنَةٌ، وَالْحَسَنَةُ بِعَشْرِ أَمْثَالِهَا ، لَا أَقُولُ (الم) حَرْفٌ، وَلَكِنْ أَلِفٌ حَرْفٌ، وَلَامٌ حَرْفٌ، وَمِيمٌ حَرْفٌ.

This ḥadīth is related in more than one way from Ibn Masʿūd. Abū al-Aḥwaṣ reported it from Ibn Masʿūd. Some reporters raised it to the Prophet (as a marfūʿ report) while others stopped at Ibn Masʿūd (mawqūf report). This

in which the ḥadīth are actively read by the students to the teacher. Conversely, from the perspective of the student, either the student recites to the teacher (qirā᾿ah) or listens to others, or the teacher, reciting (samāʿ). Here Dr. Akram is pointing out that this is in fact a general methodology that extends to all knowledge. Either you read about something or hear it from someone. Instruction is either oral or written, coming from the teacher passively or being read to the teacher actively.

ḥadīth is ḥasan ṣaḥīḥ gharīb in this isnād.[8]	وَيُرْوَى هَذَا الْحَدِيثُ مِنْ غَيْرِ هَذَا الْوَجْهِ عَنِ ابْنِ مَسْعُودٍ، رَوَاهُ أَبُو الأَحْوَصِ، عَنِ ابْنِ مَسْعُودٍ، رَفَعَهُ بَعْضُهُمْ وَوَقَفَهُ بَعْضُهُمْ عَنِ ابْنِ مَسْعُودٍ. هَذَا حَدِيثٌ حَسَنٌ صَحِيحٌ غَرِيبٌ مِنْ هَذَا الْوَجْهِ

Actually, the Prophet and Companions—and even the rest of the Arabs—knew the meanings of these letters. Had that not been the case, they would have challenged the Qur'ān for being in a foreign tongue because of these meaningless letters. But the Arabs were known to use these letters in their customary speech. For this reason, scholars of every age endeavored to provide meanings for them.

So what then is the real meaning of qirā'ah? True *qirā'ah* is the reading of the Qur'ān in ṣalāh with comprehension, reflection and the intention to follow it. For ḥadīth, it would mean the same: to read ḥadīth with comprehension and the intent to act upon them. Similarly, audition is to listen with comprehension and acceptance. Ibn Taymiyyah says the following:

> The root meaning of the audition (samā') which was commanded by God is to listen to what the Prophet brought with comprehension and acceptance. For this reason, people are in four categories regarding the Prophetic message: those who reject him and avoid listening to him, those who hear his words but don't understand their meaning, those who understand but are not willing to accept, and those who listen to him with full understanding and willingness to accept.[9]
>
> The fourth type is what was commanded by God when He said the following in numerous verses:

---

[8] Tirmidhī: Kitāb faḍā'il al-Qur'ān—Bāb mā jā'a fī man qara'a ḥarfan min al-Qur'ān mā lahu min ajr.

[9] Ibn Taymiyyah, *Majmū'*, vol 8, pg 16.

{And when they hear what has been revealed to the Messenger you see that their eyes overflow with tears because of the truth that they recognize.} [10]

{Say: it was revealed to me that a band of jinn attentively listened to (the recitation of the Qur'ān) and then (went back to their people) and said: 'We have indeed heard a wonderful Qur'an which guides to the right way; so we have come to believe in it, and we will not associate aught with Our Lord in His Divinity.'} [11]

{And call to mind when We sent to you a party of the jinn that they may listen to the Qur'ān. When they reached the place, they said to one another: 'Be silent (and listen).' And when the recitation ended, they went back to their people as warners, saying: 'Our people, We have heard a scripture revealed after Mūsā, verifying the scriptures revealed before it; it guides to the Truth and to the Straight Way. Our people, respond to the call of him who calls you to God and believe in him.} [12]

{Tell them: 'Whether you believe in it, or do not believe,' but when it is recited to those who were given the knowledge before its revelation, they fall down upon their faces in prostration and say: 'Glory be to our Lord. Surely the promise of our Lord was bound to be fulfilled.'} [13]

{The true believers are those who, when God's name is mentioned, their hearts quake, and when His verses are recited to them their faith grows, and who put their trust in their Lord.} [14]

{And whenever a new sūrah is revealed some hypocrites ask the believers: 'Whose faith has increased because of this?' As for those who believe, it will certainly increase their faith, and they are joyful over that. But those whose hearts are affected with

---

[10] Qur'ān 5:83.

[11] Qur'ān 72:1.

[12] Qur'ān 46:29-31.

[13] Qur'ān 17:107-8.

[14] Qur'ān 8:2.

disease, every new sūrah added a fresh abomination to their abomination. They remain unbelievers till their death.} [15]

{*What We are sending down in the course of revealing the Qur'ān is a healing and a grace for those who have faith, but it adds only to the ruin of the wrong-doers.*} [16]

{*Had We revealed this as a non-Arabic Qur'ān they would have said: 'Why were its verses not clearly expounded? How strange, a non-Arabic scripture with an Arab audience!' Tell them: 'It is a guidance and a healing to the believers. But to those who do not believe, it serves as a plug in their ears and a covering over their eyes. It is as if they are being called from a place far away.*} [17]

{*This is a plain exposition for people, and a guidance and admonition for the God-fearing.*} [18] Here, plain exposition encompasses its understanding, guidance, and admonition.

{*These are the lights of discernment for people and guidance and mercy for those endowed with sure faith.*} [19]

{*Alif. Lām. Mīm. This is the Book of God: there is no doubt about it. It is guidance to Godfearing people.*} [20] [21]

[15] Qur'ān 9:124-5.
[16] Qur'ān 17:82.
[17] Qur'ān 41:44.
[18] Qur'ān 3:138.
[19] Qur'ān 45:20.
[20] Qur'ān 2:1-2.
[21] *Majmū'*, vol 13, pg 16.

The Meaning of Ijāzah

We see you requesting and welcoming Ijāzah from various teachers, both verbally and in writing. You seem to place them in a position of tremendous esteem and respect, even coveting them without end. Our question is: what is the value of these Ijāzahs that you have acquired and are proud of, being charmed by them in the same way people are normally allured by gold, silver, precious stones, and all other human passions? The full extent of their value rests upon comprehending the significance and meaning of the sanad.

Knowledge is Attained Through Two Ways

What is the sanad? Knowledge basically comes through either observation (naẓr) or transmission (khabr). If it happens to come from your own observation, i.e. from what you have developed or deduced yourself through the use of your own sense perception or intellect, then you only need to establish it and prove it through its evidences. If, however, you have received the knowledge from someone else who has in turn developed or deduced it himself, then in that case, you need to do two things: first, reference it back to its source, and then, establish its evidence.

When the source of the knowledge happens to be a prophet, however, then it is sufficient to reference one's intermediaries to the source. This referencing takes the place of both tasks and does not stand in need of further establishment of evidence.

Since it is apparent that the veracity of a report relies upon the intermediaries between yourself and the source—which is the origin of the report—then know that this religion is based only upon the Qurʾān and Sunnah.

Mass Transmission of the Qurʾān

Ever since God undertook the responsibility to preserve His Book in wording and meaning, it has continued to fill welcome ears in enjoyment and repeated by fragrant tongues disseminating its aroma. It has continued to fill the consciousness of submissive hearts seeking solace, and to fill human eyes with flowing tears. All of this has been taking place, without dispute, from the era of the Prophet to our days, generation after generation, century after century. For these reasons, in the matter of God's Book, there is no great need to mention one's intermediaries.

Transmission of Sunnah and Ḥadīth

The Companions received the practices of the Prophet and all of what was connected to him, including his noble speech, actions and tacit approvals. They preserved it in memory or through writing, and conveyed that to those who came after them in a trustworthy and earnest way. Then, generations of scholars came after them, transmitting from them reports of ḥadīth and other matters, all of that in writing as well as oral transmission. Then reports began to be narrated from these scholars, either through hearing from them directly, or through reading these reports to them along with mention of the intermediaries from the beginning to the ends of the chains of transmission.

Importance of Sanad/Isnād in Knowledge

In this process, audition (samāʿ) and recital (qirāʾah)[1] are the most noble and eminent means of receiving knowledge. It is also the most robust way of verifying reports and protecting them from distortions and errors. These intermediaries were called the *sanad* (literally 'support' or 'back'), because it is to them that reports are ascribed, upon them they stand, and with them they are verified. So, the statement, 'Mālik from Nāfiʿ from Ibn ʿUmar,' is a sanad that expresses that Mālik took this report from Nāfiʿ and that Nāfiʿ took it from Ibn ʿUmar. The process of mentioning the sanad became known as *isnād*.

We are convinced beyond doubt that this is the best academic way to verify reports or ḥadīth, but what is the advantage of the persistence of the sanad to Mālik after he included all his reports in the Muwaṭṭaʾ, and why don't scholars now refer to the Muwaṭṭaʾ directly? There are two basic reasons for that: First, each person who took the Muwaṭṭaʾ from Mālik differed slightly in the content of their reports and in the manner in which they took the Muwaṭṭaʾ from Mālik. Therefore, a

[1] See previous chapter.

need was felt to mention the specific narrators of Mālik in order to distinguish their reports.

Second, you must understand that knowledge is a human enterprise that is composed of three elements:

1. the possessor of knowledge, or teacher (known as *mu'allim*),
2. the seeker of knowledge, or student (*muta'allim*), and
3. that which is known, i.e. the subject matter (known as *ma'lūm*).

The subject matter is that which is known by this human being whom you benefit from. After you acquired it, it now becomes that which you know, and you in turn can relay it to others. Know that the teacher and student are both human beings, and that which is known (the subject) is also a human enterprise. Therefore, the transmission and inheritance of knowledge must necessarily be a human enterprise as well.

Where do books fall with respect to this? A book is simply the tracing, documentation, and capturing of that which is known, but it does not directly represent the subject matter. It is also essential for you to trace the subject that you acquired back to your teacher from whom the knowledge originated. God did not reveal books and scriptures by themselves but sent along with them prophets to teach and explain them to people.

We have understood the centrality of the human being in the path of knowledge, but what does that have to do with the Ijāzah?

Role of Ijāzah in Preserving Knowledge

Listening and reading are the two fundamental means to transmit knowledge as applied by all people and nations without dispute. It is also not hidden that human sciences are simply too vast and abundant for a student to hear them all from a teacher, or read them to one, and so these sciences become imprinted within books and volumes. In this way, masses of people benefit from them directly in the manner of discovery (wijādah),[2] consulting them directly to draw information, reference and cite what they contain.

But this process of discovery has two basic shortcomings: first, that it makes one independent of teachers and guides, and second, it lacks the depth, accuracy and precision of real learning. Consider how widespread the problem of alteration of books is, in terms of additions, omissions, distortions and mistakes. Beyond that, consider how many books are even put together by other than their original authors.

For these reasons, ḥadīth scholars were overly cautious in this matter and warned against it greatly. They did not allow people to quote or transmit books without having heard them from or read them to teachers, unless they were authorized to do so by teachers (through ijāzah) who were known to possess proper chains of transmission for those particular books.

The Ijāzah was, therefore, a methodology that followed audition and recital in lower rank. Moreover, it was qualified by the precondition of comprehension of content and uprightness of persons involved. In other words, it was not allowed for the receiver of ijāzah to grant it to another person unless he knew the subject matter and was morally upright with respect to transmitting it to others.

But laxity and negligence have crept into the Ijāzah system, which you are well aware of. You are absolutely correct but should know that these two deficiencies are not confined to ijāzah alone but have also affected audition and reading as well. How many teachers listen to their students without paying attention, or perhaps even without comprehending, what is being recited. Similarly, how many students are unaware of or do not understand what they are reciting? Laxity and negligence are abundant in all sciences, religious and non-religious. They are elements that weaken reports according to the masters of this craft.

We have understood the value of Ijāzah, but why is there so much emphasis on them, and what is the utility of having so many of them? Haven't you seen writers refer to one or two sources, or to many sources in a comprehensive way? When multiple sources are used, they simply support or strengthen one another.

[2] Wijādah in the terminology of ḥadīth referred to relating reports from books or manuscripts that were 'discovered' or found. Since the element of Ijāzah or permission was bypassed, this method of relating reports was considered surreptitious and frowned upon by ḥadīth experts.

Similarly, multiple ijāzahs support and mutually strengthen one another. When these paths of transmission become numerous and multiple dimensions begin to emerge, it becomes easier to compare them all and find balance, and to prefer one report over another, or some chains over others.

What is the benefit of these extended and low ijāzah chains? For we have seen a person narrate the Ṣaḥīḥ through the people of India to Abū al-ʿAbbās Aḥmad b. Abū Ṭālib al-Ḥajjār, or through the chains of the people of Ḥijāz and Syria to al-Ḥajjār, or through the chains of Egyptians and North Africans from al-Ḥajjār, comparing them and joining some of them to another, from al-Ḥajjār to Bukhārī. Shouldn't they confine themselves to one chain going to al-Ḥajjār? Don't you see writers refer to original sources and supplement those with important secondary sources, including those that are popular as well as those that are lesser known?

The same goes for ijāzah and isnād chains, for the scholars of this discipline were concerned to present all chains of later scholars, including those that were well-known and those that were not. They sought to document the transmission from Ibn Ḥajar to al-Ḥajjār, the transmission of Ibn Nāṣir al-Dīn to him, and others. They sought the support of chains of famous latter-day scholars of Egypt, Arabia, Syria, North Africa, and India. The basic principle here was simply reinforcement and support.

We see people boasting about the number of their ijāzahs and isnād chains. Why should they be singled out for blame? Are they not like writers who in their books cite multiple works and are proud of the quality of their sources and references?

How does a ḥadīth scholar grant Ijāzah to one who is not a scholar, or even to children? This question occurs due to not distinguishing between the meaning of ijāzah and shahādah. A shahādah is the issuing of a certificate to a student documenting what they attained in terms of books, fields of study, or other type of learning, such as an ʿĀlimiyyah or Faḍīlah degree,[3] or any other university degree. The ijāzah, however, is not simply a shahādah, but a permission to the student to transmit on condition of competency. There is a qualitative difference between the state of acquiring knowledge and transmitting it through audition

[3] This refers to the formal Islamic scholarship degree granted by religious seminaries inspired by the Dār al-ʿUlūm model of Muslim India, which are loosely based upon the Niẓāmī curriculum.

or recital. A child can thus attain an ijāzah—without being able to transfer it to others at the time—just as the one who acquires any knowledge through hearing, reading, ijāzah, or any other means need not be a scholar nor even an advanced student at the time.

Critical Annotation of Ibn Ḥajar's Nuzhat al-Naẓar

Lexicon (*iṣṭilāḥ*) refers to the agreement of individuals upon a new meaning for words and expressions that manages to retain some connection to older meanings. Every discipline has its own particular lexicon, or unique set of terminologies that are widely used within their field. For instance, Arabic grammarians have their own particular terms such as *iʿrāb* (word declension), *rafʿ*, *naṣb*, and *jarr* (three case endings of words that indicate their grammatical position); the field of jurisprudence has *farḍ*, *sunnah*, *ḥarām*, *makrūh*, and *mubāḥ* (which refer to the spectrum of jurisprudential values attached to every human action ranging from prohibited to obligatory); and the science of tafsīr has *muḥkam* (clear and unequivocal Qurʾānic verses), *mutashābih* (more ambiguous Qurʾānic verses), and *sabab nuzūl* (the historical occasions or immediate reasons for the revelation of specific verses).

In this manner, ḥadīth experts developed their own technical terms, such as ṣaḥīḥ, ḥasan, ḍaʿīf, marfūʿ, mawqūf, and their likes. Many books were authored to explain the prevailing terminology among ḥadīth scholars, and one of the most renowned of these was *Nuzhat al-Naẓar fī Tawḍīḥ Nukhbat al-Fikr fī Muṣṭalaḥ Ahl al-Athar*[1] of the ḥadīth expert Aḥmad b. ʿAlī b. Muḥammad b. Ḥajar, better known as Ibn Ḥajar al-ʿAsqalānī (773/1372—852/1449). He was the author of numerous beneficial works, the greatest of which was *Fatḥ al-Bārī*, a commentary on Ṣaḥīḥ Bukhārī.

With God's grace, I have had the honor of teaching *Nuzhat al-Naẓar*, with detailed commentary, numerous times in Oxford, London, and other places. I have done so with important critical observations and corrections to Ibn Ḥajar's

---

[1] '*Nuzhat al-naẓar* is a detailed commentary of a much shorter treatise written by Ibn Ḥajar, entitled *Nukhbat al-fikr fī muṣṭalaḥ ahl al-athar*. The original work consists of only a few pages. In his introduction to *Nuzhat al-naẓar*, Ibn Ḥajar explains that his contemporaries asked him to offer a brief overview of ʿilm al-ḥadīth. Ibn Ḥajar duly obliged in the form of *Nukhbat al-fikr*, but he was then later asked to expand on this work. The result was *Nuzhat al-naẓar*. Though in reality the *Nuzhah* is two separate works (*Nuzhat al-naẓar* and *Nukhbat al-fikr*), Ibn Ḥajar wrote his final piece in an amalgamated style. The result is that it can be read as if it is one piece of work.' —Dr. Ather Shahbaz Hussain, *The Nuzhah of Ibn Ḥajar al-ʿAsqalānī: A Translation and Critical Commentary*.

thought, disagreeing with him on some key points. Some of my companions asked me to compile my critical observations in order to help students of ḥadīth develop their understanding of this discipline. I am hopeful that this academic critique leads some people to review the prevailing understandings of ḥadīth lexicon.

Figure 1 Translator's ijāzah from author in the Nuzhah

My critique is based upon four observations. First, Ibn Ḥajar followed the approach of post-classical scholars under the heavy influence of Greek logic in defining and classifying ḥadīth-related terms. Second, this necessarily led to his inclusion of some matters that had no relation to the ḥadīth lexicon of early ḥadīth experts. Third, he defined some terms in a way that significantly differed from the prevailing definitions of earlier ḥadīth experts. Finally, he mentioned some rulings which were not researched properly while providing no evidence or examples for them.

Definitive versus Controvertible Knowledge

Ibn Ḥajar states the following on the matter of definitive (ḍarūrī) versus controvertible (naẓarī) knowledge: **'This is the trusted opinion: that khabar mutawātir (mass-transmitted report) gives the benefit of definitive**

knowledge. This [knowledge] forces a person to accept it in such a way it is not possible to refute.'[2] On the mashhūr report, he states: '**Amongst those who have asserted that it gives the benefit of controvertible knowledge are Abū Manṣūr al-Baghdādī, Abū Bakr b. Fūrak, and others.**'[3] On defining naẓar (contemplation): '**Contemplation (naẓar) requires the ordering of known or presumed facts, leading to [further] facts or presumptions.**'[4] On the difference between definitive and controvertible knowledge, he states: '**With this discussion, the difference between definitive knowledge and controvertible knowledge is clear: definitive knowledge gives benefit without evidence-building and controvertible knowledge gives benefit but with evidence-building. And controvertible knowledge can only be attained by the one who has the ability to contemplate.**'[5] After insisting that the reports of Bukhārī and Muslim lead to controvertible knowledge, he states: '**Amongst the scholars who clarify that whatever the two shaykhs have recorded gives the benefit of controvertible knowledge are the al-Shaykh Abū Isḥāq al-Isfarā'īnī, and from the experts of ḥadīth Abū 'Abdullah al-Ḥumaydī, Abū al-Faḍl b. Ṭāhir and others.**'[6]

Ibn Taymiyyah stated: 'They divided knowledge into definitive and controvertible. Controvertible knowledge relies on definitive knowledge, and definitive knowledge is that which is compelling and necessarily binding upon created beings with no recourse away from that. This is the definition of the judge Abū Bakr b. al-Ṭayyib and others. It means that definitive knowledge forces a person to accept something in a way that it is impossible to deny.'[7]

However, the fact is that the division of knowledge into definitive and controvertible is one of the worst and most corrupt statements of logicians and philosophers, and all those theologians and scholars of uṣūl that followed their path. It arose from their erroneous understanding of the sources of knowledge. What is that 'definitive knowledge is that which is necessarily binding upon

---

[2] *Nuzhah*, pg 42. Translation from Hussain, pg 57. All subsequent translations of the Nuzhah are bolded and taken from Dr. Hussain's work.

[3] Ibid, pg 83.

[4] Hussain, pg 58.

[5] Ibid, pg 58.

[6] Ibid, pg 82.

[7] *Majmū'*, vol 13, pg 70. Ibn Taymiyyah here was pointing this out, not necessarily endorsing it.

created beings with no recourse away from that'? God says: ﴾*God has brought you forth from your mothers' wombs not knowing anything, and then gave you hearing, sight and thinking hearts so that you may give thanks.*﴿ [8] Humans were originally created not knowing anything and then endowed with certain means to attain knowledge based upon their fiṭrah (innate nature). These means include the five senses, the faculty of reasoning, and revelation. There is no knowledge in human beings at the time of their creation except for the inclinations of their fiṭrah. Over time, they acquire knowledge through the five senses, their intellect, and through revelation.

The proper way to classify knowledge, then, is between innate (fiṭrī) and acquired (kasbī). Acquired knowledge could be divided into knowledge based upon senses (empirical), that which is based upon rational faculties, and the heavenly revealed knowledge that comes through prophets. This division was known to the early predecessors, and its details are in another chapter.

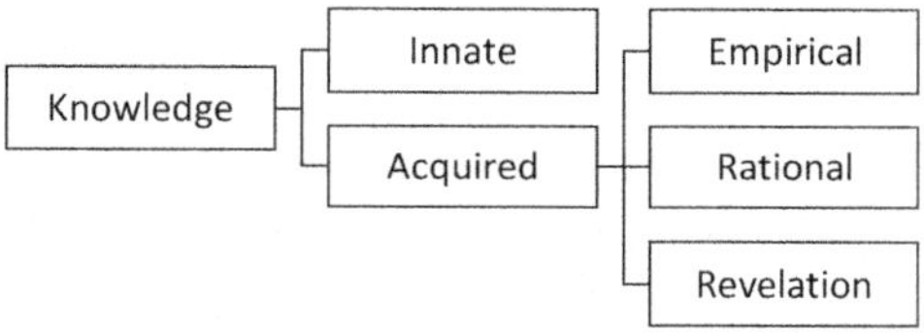

Figure 2 Divisions of Knowledge

Certain Knowledge

On the issue of certain (yaqīnī) knowledge, Ibn Ḥajar states: **'So the first is mutawātir with its conditions. This gives the benefit of certain knowledge ('ilm al-yaqīn). [By mentioning this], this excludes controvertible knowledge ('ilm al-naẓar), which will soon be explained. And *yaqīn* is strong belief corresponding [to the truth].'**[9]

In fact, however, certainty (yaqīn) does not come from anything external. The mere sight of an object, for example, does not establish the existence of the object. There must be additional requirements, such as certain specific matters on the part of the onlooker like sound and accurate vision, absence of any

[8] Qur'ān 16:78.

[9] Hussain, pg 57.

obstruction or impediment in front of the object, the intention of looking, and significant viewing experience.

The same applies to every branch of knowledge. Knowledge does not represent mere words and expressions whose definitions are to be memorized, but it represents accurately correlating these words and expressions with their realities. The procedure of connecting terms with their realities is quite difficult and is named, from one angle, the process of trial and error.

And in fact, all of knowledge can be termed probabilistic (ẓannī), because realities, whether they are physical or immaterial, are far greater than any single experience or explanation of them. This goes to the extent of something as simple as a human finger, whose full reality is far greater than what any expert could know about it. People can comprehend the reality of something from one particular aspect but realities always have other dimensions that are beyond—partially or completely—comprehension or awareness.

Certainty never comes to a person in the beginning of their quest for knowledge, for certainty is never linked to subject-matters themselves but to the persons studying these subjects. An object of study, however real it may be, does not cause the student to be certain about it until that person goes through many stages in the path of learning.

The proper path to knowledge follows the following trajectory: first, if the object of learning is sound, it then finds reception in the innate nature (fiṭrah) of a person, after which its comprehension is further augmented through the five senses and rational faculties. This allows one to arrive at some level of knowledge, which gradually increases farther and farther based upon practice and more experience.

As an example, consider the verse that is read by people: ﴾*I hear and answer the prayer of the supplicant, when he calls upon Me.*﴿ [10] This reality is well-known, certain and truthful. After reading this, a person turns his attention to their Lord and makes duʿāʾ (supplication). After gaining more and more experience making duʿāʾ, their knowledge of this verse steadily increases, until it reaches certainty or close to that.

---

[10] Qurʾān 2:186.

Therefore, ḥadīth experts were committed to the soundness of ḥadīth reports, not to the number of their isnāds, mutawātir or otherwise. If any ḥadīth was deemed to be sound, it led to knowledge, which further increased in individuals based upon comprehension, understanding and practice.

Knowledge, therefore, always begins as probabilistic (ẓannī). If one were to hope never to act upon anything unless they had certain knowledge about it, they would be hoping for the impossible.

Ḥadīth Terminology Works

On the history of works on ḥadīth lexicon, Ibn Ḥajar states: '**Amongst the first to write in this area was al-Qāḍī Abū Muḥammad al-Rāmahurmuzī (d. 360/971),[11] his book called *al-Muḥaddith al-fāṣil*. However, he did not complete this work.**'[12]

Here, Ibn Ḥajar should have mentioned those who actually founded much of this lexicon, such as Imām Shāfiʿī in his *al-Risālah*, Imām Muslim in his Muqaddimah to his Ṣaḥīḥ, and Imām Tirmidhī in his *al-ʿIlal*. Ibn Ḥajar himself alluded to this in the biographical entry of his teacher Ibrāhīm al-Tannūkhī: 'I read to him *al-Muḥaddith al-fāṣil* . . . which is the first book authored on the science of ḥadīth as is mostly presumed, even though there were individual works prior to his on some aspects of this science, but this was the most comprehensive one in his time.'[13]

However, this is not entirely correct as Rāmahurmuzī did not author his work on ḥadīth lexicon per se but on highlighting differences between the transmitter and the scholar. He states in his introduction, after relating a ḥadīth report with his isnād:

> Here, the Prophet ﷺ himself distinguished between the transmitter of the sunnah and the one who really understood it, and alluded to the superiority of the scholar through his statement: *Many a bearer of knowledge conveys it to one who is more versed than he is; and many*

[11] Abū Muḥammad al-Ḥasan b. ʿAbd al-Raḥmān b. Khallād was a Persian-origin judge and renowned ḥadīth expert who was author of this celebrated book in ḥadīth sciences.

[12] Hussain, pg 32.

[13] Ibn Ḥajar, *al-Majmaʿ al-muʾassis*, vol 1, pg 186.

> *a bearer of knowledge is not versed in it.* Virtue for any of these two necessitates virtue for the other. As an example, when you compare Mālik b. Anas with ʿUbaydullah al-ʿUmarī, or Shāfiʿī with ʿAbd al-Raḥmān b. Mahdī, or Abū Thawr with Ibn Abī Shaybah, the truth forces you to grant each person the virtue they deserve, which is the fair and just approach for those who seek it and for the teachers of truth to those who follow it without transgression. [14]

The book is actually quite comprehensive in its scope, with respect to its subject-matter, as any glance at its most important topics would prove. Dhahabī described it as follows: 'What an excellent book is *al-Muḥaddith al-fāṣil.* It is even said that Silafī[15] could almost never let the book out of his hands for a portion of his life.'[16]

Ibn Ḥajar also comments on Ḥākim's *Maʿrifat ʿulum al-ḥadīth*: **'Then came al-Ḥākim Abū ʿAbdullah al-Nīsābūrī but the book was not ordered systematically or refined.'**[17]

This could not be farther from the truth. Ḥākim's book is in our hands and it represents his best and most-developed work. It is in fact the first complete book in this discipline. It is highly refined and exceptionally structured. The problem is that latter-day scholarship has become so tainted by artificial constructs that it cannot see the beauty in what does not follow its own patterns. The same applies to grammar, jurisprudence, uṣūl al-fiqh, and other disciplines. Ibn Khaldūn said it best: 'Many scholars authored works in the science of ḥadīth,

---

[14] *Al-Muḥaddith al-fāṣil*, pg 168.

[15] Abū Ṭāhir Aḥmad b. Muḥammad al-Silafī (d. 576/1180), born in Isfahan in 475/1183, was a great ḥadīth expert and author of numerous works, including a biography of 600 of his teachers entitled *Muʿjam Isfahan*. He earned the unique title al-Silafī from his grandfather who was called Silaf from a Persian word (*sih labi*) which means three lips (he had suffered an accident). He traveled widely in pursuit of knowledge despite having limited means, staying in guest houses and even walking barefoot at times. He eventually settled in Alexandria, where he married a wealthy and pious lady Sitt al-Ahl. In 544 AH, he presided over the first school for teaching Shāfiʿī fiqh in Egypt, known as al-Silafiyyah. His sole child was his daughter Khadījah, who became a scholar in her own right and was the teacher of the ḥadīth expert al-Mundhirī. Due to his prolific scholarship, wide travels, and long life, al-Silafī possessed the highest chains in the world for Qurʾān, ḥadīth and other disciplines, and became a recurring node in worldwide isnāds. He died close to a hundred years of age in 576/1180.

[16] *Siyar*, vol 16, pg 73.

[17] Hussain, pg 34.

and from its most luminary scholars and experts was Abū ʿAbdullah al-Ḥākim. His works in this discipline are well-known, and he is the one who refined and properly systematized the whole field.'[18] Although Ibn Khaldūn was no expert in this field, his expertise and familiarity with the history and development of the sciences, compels me to highlight this aspect of Ḥākim's scholarship from his words.

The Issue of Tawātur

Ibn Ḥajar extensively discusses the issue of tawātur, defining it and setting its conditions throughout his work.

But the fact is that this notion of tawātur was unfamiliar to early ḥadīth experts, and even to experts of jurisprudence from that era. It is a notion foreign to the discipline and has absolutely no utility at all. Actually, mutawātir ḥadīth according to this conception does not even exist at all. No one included the term within ḥadīth sciences prior to Khaṭīb (392/1002—463/1071),[19] who stated:

> Reports can encompass within them truth and falsehood. They are divided into mutawātir and āḥād. A mutawātir report is one that is reported by such a large group of individuals that it becomes necessarily known through this witnessing that they could not have all lied together, that their simultaneous collusion during the period that the reports disseminated from them would be unfeasible,[20] that the contents of their reports from the source does not accept any distortion or doubt, and that motives for lying such

[18] Ibn Khaldūn, *Tārīkh,* vol 1, pg 559.

[19] The son of a preacher (khaṭīb), Abū Bakr Aḥmad b. ʿAlī b. Thābit, better known as al-Khaṭīb al-Baghdādī ('the preacher of Baghdad'), was a renowned ḥadīth expert and Ḥanbalī-turned-Shāfiʿī jurist who wrote some of the most influential works in the discipline of ḥadīth.

[20] This notion was first stipulated in a prototype form by the founder of the Muʿtazilite group Wāṣil b. ʿAṭāʾ (d. 121), who posited as one of four sources of knowledge that constitute proof as being concurred-upon reports (khabar mujtamaʿ ʿalayhi), which is every report 'in which collusion (tawāṭuʾ), mutual exchange (tarāsul) and coincidental agreement (ittifāq) are not possible.' From this group, the notion spread to the discipline of kalām, uṣūl al-fiqh, and ultimately, even to ḥadīth. See Dr. Suheil Laher, *Twisted Threads: Genesis, Development and Application of the Term and Concept of Tawātur in Islamic Thought,* pg. 25. This work, which served as Dr. Laher's PhD dissertation at Harvard University, is a brilliant academic treatment of the history of tawātur in Islamic scholarship.

> as compulsion is not possible from them. When reports become widely transmitted in such a way from anyone, this decisively establishes their truthfulness and necessitates definitive and incontrovertible knowledge.[21]

Ibn al-Ṣalāḥ (d. 643/1245)[22] states in his Muqaddimah:

> From the types of mashhūr (widespread) reports is the mutawātir, which was mentioned by scholars of fiqh and uṣūl al-fiqh. Ḥadīth scholars, however, did not mention this term in this specific meaning and sense. Though Khaṭīb used the term, his words convey a sense that he was following scholars from disciplines outside of ḥadīth. This was likely due to the fact that the notion of tawātur is not encompassed within the discipline of ḥadīth and is hardly found among their reports. The term is used for reports transmitted by reporters knowledge of whose veracity reaches the level of definitive knowledge, and this condition must be repeated at each level of the isnād beginning to end.
>
> And whoever would ask to illustrate examples of this among ḥadīth reports would be frustrated in his quest. The ḥadīth: '*Actions are by intentions*' is not an example of that in any way, though it was transmitted by a large number which did reach or exceed the requirement of tawātur, but this occurred in the middle of the chain and not the beginning. Yes, the ḥadīth: '*Whoever lies upon me intentionally is guaranteed a seat in the Fire*' is an illustration of that, because a large group of Companions reported it from the Prophet, as it appears in Bukhārī and Muslim.[23]

---

[21] *Al-Kifāyah*, pg 16.

[22] Abū ʿAmr ʿUthmān b. ʿAbd al-Raḥmān al-Shahrazūrī, better known as Ibn al-Ṣalāḥ, was a Kurdish Iraqi ḥadīth expert and author of the most influential work on the study of ḥadīth , Kitāb maʿrifat anwāʿ ʿilm al-ḥadīth (Muqaddimah). Dr. Eerik Dickinson rightfully states, 'Indeed, it would be no exaggeration to say that to his day most ḥadīth scholarship is directly or indirectly based on this one work.'

[23] Ibn al-Ṣalāḥ, *al-Muqaddimah*, pg 453-5.

As for his illustration of the ḥadīth: '*Whoever lies upon me . . .*', I see little utility in that. Its status of mutawātir does not affect its ruling in any way. What concerns us is soundness and correctness. This ḥadīth is simply elaboration of God's words: {*Who is more unjust than the one who invents lies against God.*} [24] There are numerous other examples of Qur'ānic verses which disparage lying against God and condemn falsehood.

Anwar Shāh Kashmīrī divides tawātur into four types: tawātur of isnād (which is the domain of the ḥadīth scholars), tawātur of generations (which applies to the Qur'ān), tawātur of actions and inherited traditions (like the use of siwāk and the five prayers), and an implicit tawātur of shared destinies (like the Prophetic miracles).[25] This division also has little utility and serves to prove nothing. In fact, it even stems from not fully comprehending the meaning of history and reports. Historical truth is never established by continuous traditions transmitted from generation to generation. How many beliefs and traditions are widespread among disbelievers and polytheists which represent nothing but falsehood and lies against God and His prophets?

The truth on this matter lies in the way of early ḥadīth scholars, who exhaustively research the soundness of ḥadīth reports which, upon verification, necessitate acting upon them through the details and conditions established by experts of ḥadīth and fiqh.

Mashhūr Reports

Ibn Ḥajar defines mashhūr reports as those having more than two paths of transmission: **'The second—and this is the first division of al-āḥād—is that which has limited chains but more than two. This is mashhūr, according to the ḥadīth scholars.'**[26]

In fact, this form of definition was also never part of the lexicon of early ḥadīth experts. Ibn Ḥajar delineated the condition of more than two paths in order to distinguish these reports from 'azīz, which is a report with exactly two paths of transmission. Ḥadīth experts never used the term in this way, and it was

[24] Qur'ān 6:21.

[25] Kashmīrī, *Ikfār al-mulḥidīn fī ḍarūriyyāt al-dīn*, pg 5-6.

[26] Hussain, pg 68.

never a part of their own lexicon. For this reason, Ibn al-Ṣalāḥ does not even put forth a definition for mashhūr in his Muqaddimah, but suffices with the following:

> 'The meaning of being widespread (shuhrah) is well understood. It is divided into ṣaḥīḥ, such as the report: *Actions are judged by intentions,* and non-ṣaḥīḥ, such as the report: '*Seeking knowledge is obligatory on every Muslim. . .*' From another angle, this is divided into that which was known to scholars of ḥadīth as well as other disciplines, like the report: '*A Muslim is one from whose hands and tongue other Muslims are safe,*' and those reports which were known only to scholars of ḥadīth.[27]

ʿAzīz Reports

Ibn Ḥajar states: **'The third is ʿazīz. This is where a minimum of two reporters narrate from two others.'**[28]

No early ḥadīth scholar defined it such. Ibn al-Ṣalāḥ quotes the expert Ibn Mandah: 'Gharīb reports are like the reports of solitary students of experts like Zuhrī and Qatādah. When single students report from them, their reports are termed gharīb; when two, three or more students relate from them they are termed ʿazīz. When multiple individuals report from them, the reports are termed mashhūr.'[29]

The status of gharīb, ʿazīz, and mashhūr is not judged by looking at something that occurs from the beginning to the end of the chain, but at any specific point. For instance, if one student is alone in reporting from Zuhrī, who is known for many students reporting from him, this report would be considered gharīb. If that lone student were to find support in another student or two also reporting from Zuhrī, the report would be ʿazīz. If there were even more students from Zuhrī, the report would be mashhūr.

---

[27] Ibn al-Ṣalāḥ, *Muqaddimah,* pg 265-6.

[28] Hussain, pg 73.

[29] *Muqaddimah,* pg 270.

Ibn Ḥajar continues: ʿ**Azīz is not a condition for the ṣaḥīḥ, as opposed to whoever assumes so. This is Abū ʿAlī al-Jubbāʾī of the Muʿtazila. The writings of al-Ḥākim Abū Abdullah also indicate this opinion.**'[30]

Actually, Ḥākim's words do not indicate that at all, for he states: 'The characteristic of a ṣaḥīḥ ḥadīth is that it is reported from the Prophet by a known Companion, and from him by two upright Followers, and from them the report is received and accepted by the people of ḥadīth to our times, with witness after witness.'[31]

Ḥākim's qualification of two upright Followers is simply an interpretation of the principle of removing ambiguity from the Companion and not part of the definition of ṣaḥīḥ ḥadīth. Secondly, this condition only applies to the lesser known Companions. Those Companions whose identity and Companionship is established through other evidences, their reports appear in Ṣaḥīḥ Bukhārī even if they had a solitary reporter from them. Bukhārī and Muslim both report many ḥadīth from Companions with only single narrators. Those who have not looked deeply into the issue consider it a binding condition for Bukhārī and Muslim to report from additional Companions with single reporters.

Moreover, the removal of ambiguity does not rest upon specific numbers. Ibn Rajab says:

> Yaʿqūb b. Shaybah reports that he asked Ibn Maʿīn as to how many reporting students are required for a reporter to be considered known. He replied: 'When scholars such as Ibn Sīrīn and Shaʿbī report from a person, he is no longer considered unknown.' Yaʿqūb asked: 'What if the likes of Simāk b. Ḥarb or Abū Isḥāq reported from someone?' He replied: 'These people reported from unknown persons.'
>
> This is a good explanation which opposes the view of Muḥammad b. Yaḥyā al-Dhuhalī and latter-day scholars who followed him in requiring two or more reporters in order to remove the ambiguity from a person.[32]

---

[30] Hussain, pg 73.

[31] Ḥākim, *Maʿrifah ʿulūm al-ḥadīth*, pg 61.

[32] Ibn Rajab, *Sharḥ ʿilal al-Tirmidhī*, pg 377-8.

I have discussed this issue at length in the introduction to my commentary on Ṣaḥīḥ Muslim.

Gharīb Reports

Ibn Ḥajar defines gharīb as follows: **'This is where one person is alone his narration, regardless of where the singularity occurs in the isnād.'**[33]

Gharīb is not used in this sense but only with respect to a specific individual at a particular point in the chain: a sole reporter from otherwise prolific teachers with many students, as indicated by Ibn Mandah.

Ṣaḥīḥ Reports

Ibn Ḥajar states: **'The khabar al-āḥād with the transmission of upright and completely accurate [narrators], coupled with the continuation of the isnād, without it [being] shādh or mu'allal, is [called] ṣaḥīḥ li dhātihī.'**[34]

Ibn al-Ṣalāḥ defines ṣaḥīḥ as: 'a supported ḥadīth with a contiguously connected chain of upright and accurate reporters from beginning to end that is neither anomalous (shādh) nor defective (mu'allal).' Nawawī defined ṣaḥīḥ ḥadīth as one 'that has a chain that is fully connected with upright and accurate transmitters and is neither anomalous nor defective.'

This definition only applies to the primary corpus reports of the Ṣaḥīḥayn, and not to their supporting material. In addition, there are ḥadīth reports that were deemed ṣaḥīḥ by Bukhārī and Muslim that are outside their Ṣaḥīḥayn, and ḥadīth deemed ṣaḥīḥ by Tirmidhī that are also not in the Ṣaḥīḥayn. These definitions do not apply to them.

As I clarified in the previous chapter on the meaning of ṣaḥīḥ ḥadīth, the term ṣaḥīḥ has three usages: reports of the Ṣaḥīḥayn, other non-Ṣaḥīḥayn reports deemed ṣaḥīḥ by Bukhārī, Muslim, Tirmidhī and others from their generation, and reports deemed ṣaḥīḥ by later scholars such as Ibn Khuzaymah, Ibn Ḥibbān, Ḥākim and others. The usage of ṣaḥīḥ from the late second and third centuries predominantly were for the second usage, while the first usage could be termed

---

[33] Hussain, pg 79.

[34] Hussain, pg 98.

'primary-tier ṣaḥīḥ' (*aṣaḥḥ al-ṣaḥīḥ*). The third types of reports include many ḥasan and ḍaʿīf—even munkar—reports.

Preferring Some Ṣaḥīḥ Reports Over Others

Ibn Ḥajar states: **'Related to this superiority is that which the two shaykhs have agreed upon in [recording it in their] compilations, in relation to what [only] one of them has recorded. [This is followed by] what al-Bukhārī has recorded alone in relation to what Muslim has recorded alone.'**[35]

This is not true in an absolute sense. There could be a report that was related by one of them alone that could be preferred over another that both of them reported. As an example, the ḥadīth of Jibrīl as reported by Abū Hurayrah was related by both Bukhārī and Muslim while the same ḥadīth reported through ʿUmar b. al-Khaṭṭāb was related by Muslim alone. Ḥadīth experts basically agree that the report of ʿUmar is the more sound one. For this reason, Muslim related this report first in the chapter, following it with that of Abū Hurayrah. In fact, the ḥadīth of ʿUmar is the very first one in the entirety of Ṣaḥīḥ Muslim. Most ḥadīth experts followed Muslim in preferring this ḥadīth. Bukhārī had opted out of relating this ḥadīth due to a reason that did not compromise its authenticity in a major way, which I have explained in my commentary on Ṣaḥīḥ Muslim.

He also stated: **'Then, preferred in terms of soundness is that which complies with both of its conditions. . . . If [the narration] complies with both of their conditions together, it will be less than what Muslim narrates or his likes. If [the narration] complies with one of their conditions, then the report that complies with al-Bukhārī alone is preferred over the one that complies with Muslim alone, following the principle for each. Thus, derived from this [account] are six types that differ in rank of soundness. Then there is a seventh type; and that is what complies with neither of their conditions, collectively and individually.'**[36]

This is a mere assumption on Ibn Ḥajar's part. There is simply no ḥadīth that fulfills their conditions that they did not relate, and this applies to Bukhārī and Muslim. Abū ʿAbdullah al-Ḥākim followed this assumption in his *al-Mustadrak*

[35] Hussain, pg 113.

[36] Hussain, pg 119.

'alā al-Ṣaḥīḥayn, which he filled with defective, shādh and munkar reports. This he did despite having said elsewhere: 'A ṣaḥīḥ report is not known by its narration alone but by comprehension, preservation and frequent audition. This type of knowledge is most strengthened by reviewing matters with those who have deep comprehension and awareness, in order to make apparent subtle defects in reports. If such ḥadīth are found that have sound chains but are not reported in the two books of the experts Bukhārī and Muslim, a person must investigate its defect and review the matter with proper scholars so that the defect may become apparent.'[37] I have discussed this in great detail in my commentary on Ṣaḥīḥ Muslim.

He also said: **'If, for instance, one type is preferred over another through a means which necessitates preference, then it is preceded, as sometimes a factor features which makes it higher in ranking. Like [for example] a ḥadīth with Muslim that is mashhūr though short from the stage of mutawātir, that possesses a factor which makes it give the benefit of knowledge; undoubtedly this is preferred to a ḥadīth that al-Bukhārī records alone. Similarly, a ḥadīth that neither have recorded but has been deemed as the 'most sound of chains' like Mālik, from Nāfi', from Ibn 'Umar; for indeed this is preferred over that which only one of them records, especially when their isnād contains a reporter in which there is doubt.'**[38]

This whole passage is another assumption with no evidence or examples.

On Preferring Bukhārī over Muslim

Ibn Ḥajar categorically prefers Ṣaḥīḥ Bukhārī over Muslim:

> **The attributes upon which the soundness rotates is more complete and rigid in the book of al-Bukhārī than in the book of Muslim. His conditions in it are stronger and firmer.**
>
> **As for preferring al-Bukhārī in terms of the continuity [of the isnād], his condition is that the meeting of the reporter from**

[37] *Ma'rifat 'ulūm al-ḥadīth*, pg 238-9.

[38] Hussain, pg 119-20.

> **whom he heard from must be proven, even if it is [only] once. Muslim merely depended on them being contemporaries.**
>
> **As for his preference in terms of the credibility and accuracy [of the reporters], the men who have been criticised from the men of Muslim are more in number than the men of al-Bukhārī along with the fact that al-Bukhārī did not utilise them often. In fact, most of them are his own shaykhs who he [directly] took from and was familiar with their reports. [This is] as opposed to Muslim in both matters. As for [al-Bukhārī's] preference in terms of not being shādh or muʿallal, the reports of al-Bukhārī that have been criticised are less than the reports of Muslim that have been criticised. This along with the consensus of the scholars upon the fact that al-Bukhārī was more competent than Muslim in the disciplines, more learned in ḥadīth and that Muslim was his student and graduate who continued to take benefit from him and follow his footsteps. To the extent that al-Dāruquṭnī said: 'If al-Bukhārī had not [existed], there would never have been Muslim.[39]**

I have discussed this issue in further detail in the forthcoming chapter 'The Soundest Book of All,' but I wish to emphasize here that Bukhārī and Muslim did not differ in their conditions for soundness at all, but only differed on occasion in its practical implementation on specific reports.

There is no difference between them, for instance, in the condition of isnād continuity. In fact, Muslim designated an important chapter in his Muqaddimah to the Ṣaḥīḥ to refute a novel and invented view on the issue of muʿanʿan[40] reports. The consensus of ḥadīth experts up until the time of Muslim was that these reports are considered connected if three conditions existed: that the contiguous reporters be contemporaries, that there be no explicit evidence against their reporting, and that the reporter using *ʿan* not be known for tadlīs.

---

[39] Hussain, pg 115-6.

[40] Reports in which reporters related from their teachers with the ambiguous connector *ʿan*, meaning 'from' or 'on the authority of' rather than a term that explicitly conveys the manner of reporting like 'I heard from . . .' or 'he reported to me.'

After that time, there arose some individuals who began to claim that these reports could not be accepted unless there exist explicit evidence indicating meeting and audition on the part of these reporters. Muslim stood up to reject this as a novel and innovated position, and his refutation was thorough and decisive. After him, Qāḍī ʿIyāḍ and many others until our times, began to believe that the position which Muslim was refuting was in fact that of Bukhārī and his teacher ʿAlī b. al-Madīnī. This assumption is entirely false, as I have elaborated on in my commentary on Muslim.

Similarly, there is no difference between them on the conditions of ʿadālah and ḍabṭ, and it is not true that the number of criticized reporters is greater in Ṣaḥīḥ Muslim than in Ṣaḥīḥ Bukhārī. It is also not true that there are less criticized reports in Ṣaḥīḥ Bukhārī than in Ṣaḥīḥ Muslim. Most of the criticized reporters and disputed reports in Ṣaḥīḥ Muslim are part of his secondary corpus (supporting ḥadīth material). It is well-known that his supporting ḥadīth do not meet his own primary-tier conditions. As for primary corpus reports, disputed reports are far less in number in Ṣaḥīḥ Muslim than in Ṣaḥīḥ Bukhārī.

Tirmidhī's Compound Expression Ḥasan-Ṣaḥīḥ

Ibn Ḥajar states: **'Thus if they both gather, namely ṣaḥīḥ and ḥasan in one description; like the saying of al-Tirmidhī and others: '[this is a] ḥasan ṣaḥīḥ ḥadīth,' then this results in confusion for the mujtahid in its transmission. Does it entail the conditions of ṣaḥīḥ or not? This is the case when the report in question is solitary.... When it is not, namely when the narration is not solitary, then the calling of two attributes simultaneously on one report is done according to it possessing two chains; one of them is ṣaḥīḥ and the other is ḥasan.'**[41]

Anyone who studies the book of Tirmidhī will realize that there is no confusion on his part, for he uses this compound expression for many reports that are undoubtedly primary-tier ṣaḥīḥ and part of the Ṣaḥīḥayn. Also, the expression is clearly not used for two separate isnāds.

As for the purpose of the compound expression, this indeed is somewhat problematic. He may be using ḥasan in a more general meaning, as defined by

---

[41] Hussain, pg 124-5.

Khaṭṭābī: 'Ḥasan is that whose sources are known and its reporters famous.' So the combination of these attributes would be actual (affirming both words), as has been explained previously.[42]

Shādh-Maḥfūẓ and Munkar-Maʿrūf Reports

Ibn Ḥajar defines shādh as: '**Thus if it is opposed (i.e. the narrator of a ḥasan or ṣaḥīḥ), because [in contrast] a narration is to be found which has more accuracy in the narrator, or more in number or other reasons of preference are found, then the preferred is called maḥfūẓ and the rejected is called shādh . . . . shādh is where an accepted narrator is opposed by someone more authoritative. This is the established definition of shādh according to [ḥadīth] terminology.**'[43]

He also defined munkar as follows: '**If the opposition occurs with the weak [reporter], then the preferred is called maʿrūf and the opposing one is called munkar. . . . It is known from this that between shādh and munkar is [a relation of]** *ʿumūm wa khuṣūṣ min wajh* **(general versus specific from one respect), because between them there is similarity in terms of opposition and there is difference in that shādh is the narration of an authoritative or truthful and munkar is the narration of a weak. Ignorant are those who made them synonymous.**'[44]

The usage of shādh and munkar by ḥadīth experts was broader than that envisioned by Ibn Ḥajar, and sometimes the terms were even used synonymously. The best explanation is that of Ibn al-Ṣalāḥ in his discussion of section thirteen and fourteen in the Muqaddimah, parts of which are reproduced as follows:

> Shāfiʿī stated that a shādh ḥadīth is not one that a reliable reporter is alone in narrating, but one where a ḥadīth of a reliable reporter opposes [that of] a large group of [reliable] reporters. . . .
>
> The doctrines of the ḥadīth authorities which we mentioned and those which we did not should make it plain to you that the

[42] See chapter: 'The Meaning of Ḥasan Ḥadīth.'

[43] Hussain, pg 134.

[44] Hussain, pg 137.

question of the anomalous report is not as clear cut as Abū Yaʿlā and Ḥākim represent it. Rather the question requires making the distinction which we will explain. . . .

Beyond that, the anomalous ḥadīth oscillate between various levels according to the state they are in. If the transmitter who was alone in relating the anomalous ḥadīth is not far from the level of the retentive and precise transmitter whose unparalleled transmissions are accepted, we regard that ḥadīth of his as ḥasan and we do not put it in the category of weak ḥadīth. If he falls far short of that level, we reject the ḥadīth he alone transmits, and it is considered an unfamiliar anomalous ḥadīth (*al-shādh al-munkar*). From that, it may be deduced that there are two subcategories of the rejected anomalous ḥadīth. One is the contradictory isolated ḥadīth (*al-fard al-mukhālif*). The second is the isolated ḥadīth the transmitter of which does not possess sufficient reliability and precision to counteract the unfamiliarity and weakness that isolation and anomaly engender.[45]

Munkar basically means the same thing as shādh.[46]

As for maʿrūf and maḥfūẓ, they are rarely used as opposites of shādh and munkar.[47]

Mursal Reports

Ibn Ḥajar defines mursal reports as **'where there is a drop after the successor (tābiʿī).'**[48] On the difference between munqaṭiʿ and mursal, he says: **'Similar to**

---

[45] Ibn al-Ṣalāḥ, *An Introduction to the Science of Ḥadīth*, pg 57-8.

[46] Ibid, pg 59.

[47] The essence of the critique of Ibn Ḥajar is that his definitions here are highly technical and precise, which does not reflect the broader usage of early ḥadīth experts such as Shāfiʿī and even leads to alteration of key details. On this, Dr. Akram is pointing out that Ibn al-Ṣalāḥ is more nuanced and accurate. For him, shādh and munkar are not as distinct as Ibn Ḥajar would make them out to be. Also, for Ibn Ḥajar, the key notion in shādh is the conflict with stronger evidence whereas for Ibn al-Ṣalāḥ it is the lone report. That is, a shādh report does not always have to openly conflict with stronger reports but it could be a non-conflicting report from a lone reporter whose accuracy is not strong enough to warrant his lone reports being accepted.

[48] Hussain, pg 168.

this difference is munqaṭiʿ and mursal. Are they different or not? Most scholars [agree] upon its difference, but [only] in terms of its usage as a noun. As for usage as the derived verb, they use irsāl only.'[49]

Khaṭīb states: 'As for mursal, it is a report whose chain is disconnected in a way that some of its reporters did not hear from those above them, whereas the predominant usage is for the report of a Follower who quotes the Prophet directly. . . . Munqaṭiʿ is like the mursal, though it is used predominantly for those who are not Followers who report from Companions, like Mālik b. Anas relating from Ibn ʿUmar, or Sufyān al-Thawrī relating from Jābir b. ʿAbdullah, or Shuʿbah b. al-Ḥajjāj relating from Anas b. Mālik.'[50]

The issue of how early scholars saw the difference between mursal and munqaṭiʿ is an extremely difficult one, as is the case of the difference between the noun and derived verb. Muslim, for instance, in his Muqaddimah uses the terms mursal/irsāl in the meaning of munqaṭiʿ/inqiṭāʿ:

> If this person were to claim that there is evidence for his view, we would ask him to produce it. If he were to respond: 'I claimed so because I found reporters from past to present relating from one another without having seen or heard those reports. When I saw them permitting the relating of ḥadīth from one another in this way, through irsāl and not hearing directly—and the basic principle for us and other scholars is that mursal reports are not evidence—I decided to verify the hearing of each reporter. If I find evidence of hearing even the smallest amount in any reporter, I then accept all his reports as having been heard. If it becomes difficult to ascertain this, I suspend judgment about the report, which does not represent evidence due to the possibility of irsāl in it.' Then we would say to him . . .

The correct position in my eyes is that mursal is the same as munqaṭiʿ and that its first usage arose in the time of the junior Followers. They would say, for example, 'Saʿīd b. al-Musayyab reported it directly (*arsala*) from the Prophet.'

[49] Hussain, pg 90.
[50] *Al-Kifāyah*, pg 21.

Some people began to assume that irsāl only applied to the case that a Follower reported from the Prophet directly, but that is not the case. The early experts also used the term in describing the reporting of Ibrāhīm al-Nakhaʿī from Ibn Masʿūd, for instance, and other junior Followers who narrated from Companions they had not met.

Muḍṭarib

Ibn Ḥajar said: **'Or if the opposition is with the changing of a narrator and there is no means of preferring one report over the other, then this is muḍṭarib.'**[51]

For early experts, muḍṭarib was used for a ḥadīth whose isnād or matn was differed over without any clear evidence for preferring one over another.

Accusations of Innovation

On the issue of rejecting a report due to innovations of reporters, Ibn Ḥajar said: **'Hence the trusted opinion is that the narration of someone who denies the multiply-attested (mutawātir) matters of sharīʿah, known in religion through conviction will be rejected. And similar is the case for one who does the opposite (in that he believes in something which is definitively known to be forbidden in sharīʿah). As for someone who is not of this attribute, coupled with the fact that he is careful in what he reports with awareness and piety, then there is no hindrance to accepting his report.'**[52] Ibn Taymiyyah responds to this:

> Hardly any report can be verified from Shīʿah reporters due to the preponderance of lying among them. For this reason, compilers of Ṣaḥīḥ collections do not utilize their reports. Bukhārī only relates the ḥadīth of ʿAlī from his family, including his children such as Ḥasan, Ḥusayn, and Muḥammad b. al-Ḥanafiyyah; his scribe ʿAbdullah b. Abī Rāfiʿ; or from the companions of Ibn Masʿūd like ʿUbaydah al-Salmānī, al-Ḥārith al-Taymī, Qays b. ʿAbbād and their

[51] Hussain, pg 230.

[52] Ibid, pg 258-9.

> likes, since these were truthful in reporting from ʿAlī. For this reason, the authors of Ṣaḥīḥ collections related these reports.[53]

The issue of innovation is a complex one. Ḥadīth experts did relate in their Ṣaḥīḥ collections from many reporters who were known for innovation, and concerning whom evidence exists to warrant rejecting their reports. Khaṭīb relates from ʿAlī b. al-Madīnī: I said to Yaḥyā b. Saʿīd al-Qaṭṭān: ʿAbd al-Raḥmān b. Mahdī said: I abandon among the ḥadīth reporters all those who were known for championing innovation. Yaḥyā b. Saʿīd laughed and asked: What would he do with Qatādah? What would he do with ʿUmar b. Dharr al-Hamadānī, or Ibn Abī Rawwād? Yaḥyā began to list people, including some that I would not mention. Yaḥyā then said: If ʿAbd al-Raḥmān would leave people in this way, he would leave out so many.[54]

Khaṭīb also relates from ʿAlī b. al-Madīnī: 'If I were to leave the reports of Baṣrah in order to prevent the heresy of Qadr, and the reports of Kūfah for their Shīʿism, the books would become completely ruined.' Khaṭīb explains: 'Ruin of those books refers to loss of ḥadīth reports.'[55]

Bukhārī, Muslim, and other compilers of primary ḥadīth texts reported from ʿUbaydullah b. Mūsā and others who were accused of major innovations. In his Ṣaḥīḥ, Bukhārī even relied for support on ʿAbbād b. Yaʿqūb al-Rawājinī, about whom Ibn Khuzaymah said while relating from him: 'ʿAbbād b. Yaʿqūb, who was accused of heresy but was reliable in his ḥadīth, reported to us . . .'[56]

Here, Ibn Khuzaymah testified to the veracity of ʿAbbād b. Yaʿqūb (d. 250 AH), who was accused with the worst of Rawāfiḍ heresy. The ḥadīth expert Muḥammad b. al-Muẓaffar said: al-Qāsim al-Muṭarriz reported to us: I entered upon ʿAbbād in Kūfah. He used to test his students [before accepting them]. He asked me: 'Who excavated the seas?' I replied: 'God.' He replied: 'Yes he did, but who excavated them?' I said: 'Let the teacher tell us.' He said: 'ʿAlī excavated them. Now who makes them flow?' I replied: 'God.' He said: 'Yes, but who makes them flow?' I replied: 'Let the teacher benefit us.' He replied: 'Ḥusayn

---

[53] *Majmūʿ*, vol 13, pg 32.

[54] *Al-Kifāyah*, pg 128.

[55] Ibid, pg 129.

[56] Ṣaḥīḥ Ibn Khuzaymah: Kitāb al-imāmah fī al-ṣalāh—Bāb dhikr kitābat ajr al-muṣallī bi al-mashī ilā al-ṣalāh.

makes them flow.' The teacher was blind, and I saw a sword and shield in his house. I asked him: 'Whose are these?' He replied: 'I prepared them so I can fight alongside the Mahdī.' After I finished, I came back another day, and, not recognizing me, he asked me once again: 'Who dug the seas?' I replied: 'Muʿāwiyah excavated them, and ʿAmr b. al-ʿĀṣ makes them flow.' I then jumped away. He cried out loud: 'Catch that transgressor and enemy of God, and kill him!' Dhahabī comments after relating this story: Its isnād is ṣaḥīḥ. I do not know how they allowed accepting reports from someone whose state is like this! But they deemed him truthful.[57]

[57] *Siyar,* vol 11, pg 538.

Abrogation

Ibn Ḥajar mentions after discussing how abrogation is recognized: **'Amongst [the means of identification] is that which the Companion states is the latter. [This is] like the saying of Jābir, 'The last of the two orders from the Messenger of Allah was the abandoning of ablution for what is touched by fire.'**[58]

This was reported by many scholars, including Abū Dāwūd:

BOOK OF PURITY—CHAPTER: NOT PERFORMING ABLUTION FOR [FOOD] COOKED BY FIRE Ibrāhīm b. al-Ḥasan al-Khathʿamī reported to us: Ḥajjāj reported to us: Ibn Jurayj said: Muḥammad b. al-Munkadir reported to me: I heard Jābir b. ʿAbdullah say: I presented bread and meat to the Prophet ﷺ. He ate them and called for ablution water. He performed ablution and offered the noon (Dhuhr) prayer. He then called for the remaining food and ate it. He then got up and prayed and did not perform ablution.

Mūsā b. Sahl Abū ʿImrān al-Ramlī reported to us: ʿAlī b. ʿAyyāsh reported to us: Shuʿayb b. Abī Ḥamzah reported to us: from Muḥammad b. al-Munkadir: from Jābir: The last of the two orders from God's Messenger was not to perform wuḍūʾ for that which was cooked by fire.

سنن أبي داود - كتاب الطهارة - باب في ترك الوضوء مما مست النار

حَدَّثَنَا إِبْرَاهِيمُ بْنُ الْحَسَنِ الْخَثْعَمِيُّ، قَالَ: ثَنَا حَجَّاجٌ، قَالَ ابْنُ جُرَيْجٍ، أَخْبَرَنِي مُحَمَّدُ بْنُ الْمُنْكَدِرِ، قَالَ: سَمِعْتُ جَابِرَ بْنَ عَبْدِ اللهِ يَقُولُ: قَرَّبْتُ لِلنَّبِيِّ صَلَّى اللهُ عَلَيْهِ وَسَلَّمَ خُبْزًا وَلَحْمًا فَأَكَلَ، ثُمَّ دَعَا بِوَضُوءٍ فَتَوَضَّأَ بِهِ، ثُمَّ صَلَّى الظُّهْرَ، ثُمَّ دَعَا بِفَضْلِ طَعَامِهِ فَأَكَلَ، ثُمَّ قَامَ إِلَى الصَّلَاةِ وَلَمْ يَتَوَضَّأْ.

حَدَّثَنَا مُوسَى بْنُ سَهْلٍ أَبُو عِمْرَانَ الرَّمْلِيُّ، قَالَ: ثَنَا عَلِيُّ بْنُ عَيَّاشٍ، قَالَ: ثَنَا شُعَيْبُ بْنُ أَبِي حَمْزَةَ، عَنْ مُحَمَّدِ بْنِ الْمُنْكَدِرِ، عَنْ جَابِرٍ قَالَ: كَانَ آخِرُ الْأَمْرَيْنِ مِنْ رَسُولِ اللهِ

[58] Hussain, pg 154.

صَلَّى اللهُ عَلَيْهِ وَسَلَّمَ تَرْكَ الْوُضُوءِ مِمَّا غَيَّرَتِ النَّارُ، قَالَ أَبُو دَاوُدَ: وَهَذَا اخْتِصَارٌ مِنَ الْحَدِيثِ الأَوَّلِ .

This is a summary of the first ḥadīth.[59]

Ibn Ḥajar used the condensed form of the ḥadīth which was mentioned by Abū Dāwūd. The ḥadīth occurs in the context of the woman who cooked sheep for the Prophet, who ate from it, performed ablution, and prayed the Ẓuhr prayer. He then ate from it and prayed ʿAṣr. It could be that the wuḍūʾ for Ẓuhr was for a reason other than eating from the sheep. For this reason, Abū Dāwūd and others say: The intended meaning of *amr* here could be the matter or story at hand, and not necessarily order (i.e. 'the last of the two matters from the Messenger . . .').

I will end my discussion with this, though there are other similar matters for which I have critiqued Ibn Ḥajar in my lessons. This is not a disparagement of him, for he is in my eyes the best of the later scholars in knowledge, insight, virtue, and understanding of the sciences of ḥadīth. Some of these mis-notions and mistakes overtook him due to his following the views of others or from the preoccupation of latter scholarship with artificial, invented sciences, as previously alluded to.

[59] Abū Dāwūd: Kitāb al-ṭahārah—Bāb fī tark al-wuḍūʾ fī mā massat al-nār.

Principles of Ḥadīth in the Ḥanafī School

We have learned ḥadīth from you and its principles in exhaustive detail. You have laid out for us its rules and principles in an easy manner and detailed for us the differences of trustworthy scholars and proficient experts in authentication and weakening of ḥadīth reports. You have drawn comparisons for us between the positions of the earliest scholars—along with their methodological commitment to diligence, precision, accuracy and consistency—and the carelessness of later scholars, so full of confusion, bias, inconsistencies and discrepancies. We are grateful to you for your counsel and your efforts for the sake of our wellbeing.

Please bring to our ears something new in the discipline of ḥadīth which is in concordance with the Ḥanafī school of law. What a terrible request this is! You have accompanied me for so long and have still not understood my position with respect to this confusion, which is tainted by partisanship and prejudice? Don't you perceive the element of injustice in it and its departure from the well-known path of knowledge and awareness, and its transgression to the paths of truth?

But Ḥanafī scholars have preceded us in addressing this topic. These innovated statements and strange views have grabbed the attention and temptation of the masses. And then the disease has even exceeded that by affecting the learned ones without their being aware of the underlying distortion of concepts, sound thinking, balance, and standards.

We have gained from you the correct thinking and positions in the sciences, arts and etiquette, but still find ourselves facing deviant and alien thoughts and need to be wary and protected from them. The call to the formulation of the principles and study of ḥadīth according to the Ḥanafī school betrays an ignorance of the meaning of the terms *ḥadīth*, *fiqh*, and the term *principles*. You need to fully understand the following two issues:

1. Know that ḥadīth and fiqh are two separate topics. Ḥadīth is reporting and history, whereas fiqh is philosophy and reasoning. Ḥadīth has its own particular standards to verify its reports, while fiqh has its own criteria to arrive at a correct or sound position free of errors and mistakes. Muddling these two concepts causes confusion and deviation.

In chapter four, I have discussed the difference between ḥadīth and philosophy, which you may refer to.

2. Know that every science has principles and parameters specific to that discipline and craft which are supposed to be independent from bias and alternate perspectives, and free of affiliation to schools or specific sensitivities. It would be foolish and even shameful for intelligent people to study grammar based upon the methodology of medicine, medicine based upon principles of grammarians, mathematics by way of jurists, fiqh by way of mathematics, and so on.

Know that soundness of ḥadīth is dependent upon two matters: first, that it is transmitted by trustworthy individuals from generation to generation; and second, in case reliable reporters differ over any ḥadīth in its isnād or matn, either by deficiency or excess (in details or wordings), we prefer the reports of some of them over others according to their degree of precision or their numbers. We refer to the rejected one as anomalous (shādh),[1] or sometimes detested (munkar).[2] When Mālik and Ibn ʿUyaynah differ in their narrations from Zuhrī, for instance, we prefer the narrations of Mālik due to his greater strength as a narrator from Zuhrī. But when Ibn ʿUyaynah agrees with other more reliable students of Zuhrī, like ʿUqayl, Yūnus, Maʿmar and Shuʿayb, in that case we would accept the greater number over the lesser.

This is the standard that is observed in verifying reports for ḥadīth scholars and historians, which is even used by other faith traditions. There really is no substantial difference on this. What has been narrated from scholars of the Ḥanafī school is that they followed this same standard. Sufyān al-Thawrī narrates that Abū Ḥanīfah used to accept sound reports of trustworthy narrators.[3] Qāḍī Abū Yūsuf said, 'Take ḥadīth which are known by the majority, and be wary of anomalous reports.'[4]

---

[1] A shādh, or anomalous, narration is one that is otherwise sound but conflicts with stronger narrations. See chapter 10.

[2] A munkar narration, like the anomalous one, conflicts with stronger evidence, but contains deeper, less benign, contradictions with often negative connotations or meanings. See chapter 10.

[3] Ibn ʿAbd al-Barr, *al-Intiqāʾ*, pg 142.

[4] Abū Yūsuf, *al-Radd ʿalā siyar al-Awzāʿī*, pg 24.

CHAPTER 16: ḤANAFĪ PRINCIPLES OF ḤADĪTH

Please clarify some of the errors of writers on the subject of ḥadīth principles of the Ḥanafī school. They have erred in two matters: taṣḥīḥ (authentication of ḥadīth reports) and tarjīḥ (the process of preferring differing reports).

On the first issue, they believed that principles of sound ḥadīth differed in the Ḥanafī school from those of other ḥadīth scholars. For example, they claimed that ḥadīth scholars saw mursal ḥadīth as constituting a defect that compromised its soundness, whereas Ḥanafī scholars did not see it as such.

This view is not rooted in any difference among schools of jurisprudence, but it simply arose from the fact that ḥadīth scholars exerted themselves in verifying the continuity of isnāds, because if there were any missing links, it would not be known if that unknown person was trustworthy, precise, and accurate, or inclined to negligence, laxity, forgetfulness or mistakes. And since a mursal ḥadīth was basically disconnected in its chain, most ḥadīth scholars rejected such ḥadīth. Some of them, however, held the position that if a major Companion was the one quoting the Prophet without directly hearing from him, then this constituted no serious defect. From that, they extrapolated the position of accepting mursal reports of senior Successors who were known for relating mursal reports only when they were sure of the content of these reports. This view was adopted by major scholars of Madīnah and Kūfah from the virtuous, early generations.

Al-Jaṣṣāṣ (d. 370/981)[5] said: 'As for those about whom we know that they narrate mursal reports from those who are unreliable, it is not allowed to take knowledge from them, and their mursal ḥadīth are not acceptable to us. But our view (on accepting mursal reports) applies to those who are known to narrate mursal reports only from the trustworthy and reliable.'[6]

This is a mainstream view, but what would be more correct is that we be more stringent in verifying isnād continuity in Prophetic reports. Reporting from him is not like reporting from anyone else. This was the view of the two Imāms Bukhārī and Muslim, and all those that followed them in this field, may God shower them with His mercy and be pleased with them.

---

[5] Abū Bakr Aḥmad b. ʿAlī al-Rāzī al-Jaṣṣāṣ hailed from Rayy and was the senior Ḥanafī scholar of his time who authored an important jurisprudential tafsīr work entitled *Aḥkām al-Qurʾān.*

[6] Jaṣṣāṣ, *al-Fuṣūl fī al-uṣūl.* Vol 3, pg 155.

As for the second issue of tarjīḥ, they believed that differences among some trustworthy narrators did not affect their ḥadīth narrations as a whole, and so anomalous narrations were not considered a defect for them. Because of this, they sometimes accepted anomalous narrations and rejected preserved ones.

Do they have any proof for this? Yes, they would reject some sound reports if they were to contradict the Qur'ān; mass-transmitted or widespread sunnah practices; fundamental, well-known religious matters; scholarly consensus; or the dictates of reason. And they would accept some disparaged reports if they were confirmed or supported by any of the aforementioned evidence.

Are you convinced by their arguments? No. *Why not?* Because none of these are from ḥadīth principles. I have explained this further elsewhere.

PART 3: ḤADĪTH BOOKS

Ḥadīth Books

We discussed in the chapter on ḥadīth documentation the widespread authorship of works in this field. The best of them were the Muwaṭṭa', Ṣaḥīḥ Bukhārī, Ṣaḥīḥ Muslim, Sunan Abī Dāwūd, Sunan Tirmidhī, Sunan Nasā'ī, Sunan Ibn Mājah, Muṣannaf 'Abd al-Razzāq, Musnad Abī Dāwūd al-Ṭayālisī, Musnad Aḥmad b. Ḥanbal, Muṣannaf Ibn Abī Shaybah, Musnad Isḥāq b. Rāhawayh, Musnad al-Ḥumaydī, Ṣaḥīḥ Ibn Khuzaymah, Musnad al-Bazzār, Ṭaḥāwī's Sharḥ Ma'ānī al-Āthār, Ṣaḥīḥ Ibn al-Sakan, Sunan Dāruquṭnī, Muntaqā of Ibn al-Jārūd, the Mu'jam works of Ṭabarānī, Ṣaḥīḥ Ibn Ḥibbān, Ḥākim's Mustadrak, and Bayhaqī's al-Sunan al-Kubrā.

Those interested in further details on these works should consult *Bustān al-muḥaddithīn* of Shāh 'Abd al-'Azīz al-Dihlawī in Persian, which I translated into Arabic with a few essential modifications and additions, or *al-Risālah al-mustaṭrifah* of one of our senior teachers the eminent scholar and ḥadīth expert Muḥammad b. Ja'far al-Kattānī. However, I will provide here a brief description of the Muwaṭṭa' and the six primary collections.

Muwaṭṭa' of Imām Mālik

Abū 'Abdullah Mālik b. Anas was the Imām of Dār al-Hijrah (the Abode of Hijrah, i.e. Madīnah). His work encompasses fully connected Prophetic ḥadīth, disconnected mursal reports, mawqūf reports, maqṭū' reports, statements of jurists among the Followers, balāgh reports,[1] and his own jurisprudential rulings based upon prevailing practice in Madīnah, qiyas or principles of Sharī'ah.

He began authoring the Muwaṭṭa' at the prime of his life and continued working on it until his final days. Our teacher Shaykh 'Abd al-Fattāḥ Abū Ghuddah, however, wrote in the introduction to *al-Ta'līq al-Mumajjad* that Mālik authored the Muwaṭṭa' after the year 147 and completed it sometime after 158.

Abū 'Abdullah Muḥammad b. Ibrāhīm al-Kattānī al-Aṣfahānī said: I asked Abū Ḥātim al-Rāzī why the Muwaṭṭa' of Mālik was named such, and he replied:

---

[1] Imām Malik often uses reports that begin with *balaghanī* ('It has reached me . . .').

'It was something he authored and made easy (in Arabic, *waṭṭa'a*) for people, so it became known as the Muwaṭṭa' of Mālik, just like it is said the Jāmi' ('compilation') of Sufyān.'[2]

Abū al-Ḥasan b. Fihr reports from 'Alī b. Aḥmad al-Khalanjī: I heard some teachers say: Mālik said: I presented this book of mine to seventy jurists of Madīnah, and they all agreed with me (*wāṭa'a*) concerning it, so I named it the Muwaṭṭa'.[3]

Abū Bakr al-Abharī said: The total number of reports in the Muwaṭṭa' from the Prophet, Companions and Followers are 1,720. Six hundred of them are related with full isnāds, 222 are mursal reports, 613 are mawqūf reports, and 285 are reports from the Followers.[4]

There are eighty-five Companions that appear in the isnāds of the Muwaṭṭa', including twenty-three women.

Mālik reports from some individuals outside of Madīnah, including Abū al-Zubayr of Makkah (eight connected reports), Ḥumayd al-Ṭawīl of Baṣrah (seven connected reports and one mawqūf one), Ayyūb al-Sakhtiyānī of Baṣrah (four connected, one mursal report), 'Abd al-Karīm b. Mālik al-Jazarī[5] of Iṣṭakhr, Persia (one report), 'Aṭā' of Khurāsān (one report), and Ibrāhīm b. Abī 'Ablah of Syria (one report).

'Abd al-Raḥmān b. Mahdī said: 'There is no book after the Qur'ān more beneficial to people than the Muwaṭṭa'.'[6] Imām Shāfi'ī said: 'There is no book on earth after God's book that is more sound than the Muwaṭṭa' of Mālik b. Anas.'[7]

The Muwaṭṭa' became widely transmitted throughout the world, and these transmissions are mentioned in *Bustān*.

---

[2] Zarqānī, *Sharḥ Muwaṭṭa'*, vol 1, pg 62.

[3] Ibid, pg 62.

[4] Ibid, pg 61.

[5] The appellation al-Jazarī refers to Jazīrah Ibn 'Umar, Romanized as Cizre, a city in southeastern Anatolia located on the Tigris River on the border of Syria-Turkey-Iraq.

[6] Ibn 'Abd al-Barr, *al-Tamhīd*, vol 1, pg 87.

[7] Ibn 'Abd al-Barr, *al-Istidhkār*, vol 1, pg 12.

The Six Primary Collections of Ḥadīth

It is reported in Ibn ʿAsākir's *History of Damascus* and al-Mizzī's *Tahdhīb al-Kamāl* that people asked the ḥadīth expert of Baghdad Abū ʿAlī Saʿīd b. ʿUthmān b. al-Sakan, better known as Ibn al-Sakan to summarize for them the books of ḥadīth which had become too numerous. After hesitating at first, he responded by mentioning four in order, saying the following: The fundamentals of Islam are contained in four: the book of Bukhārī, the book of Muslim, the book of Abū Dāwūd, and the book of Nasāʾī.'[8]

Later a fifth name became added and accepted widely: the Jāmiʿ of Tirmidhī. From these five books, the ḥadīth expert Abū al-ʿAbbās Aḥmad b. Thābit b. Muḥammad al-Ṭarqī al-Azdī (d. 521/1127) compiled a comprehensive index work (aṭrāf). Then Zayn al-Dīn Abū Bakr Muḥammad b. Mūsā al-Ḥāzimī (d. 584/1188) authored a book entitled *Conditions of the Five Books.*

Abū Ṭāhir al-Silafī (d. 576/1180)[9] states in his introduction to Sunan Abī Dāwūd in Khaṭṭābī's commentary: 'The book of Abū Dāwūd is one of the five books which were unanimously accepted and declared sound by the leading jurists and noble ḥadīth experts.'[10]

Ultimately, the notion of 'Six Books' arose. At first, the sixth book was disputed. The people of North Africa considered the sixth to be the Muwaṭṭaʾ, whereas others added Sunan al-Dārimī, until finally the Sunan of Ibn Mājah was uniformly accepted. The ḥadīth expert Abū al-Faḍl Muḥammad b. Ṭāhir al-Maqdisī authored a book, *Conditions of the Six Books.* ʿAbd al-Ghanī al-Maqdisī followed him in that in his own book *al-Kāmil fī asmāʾ al-rijāl.* This has been the popular convention until our times. Zarkashī states: 'The six books are: the Ṣaḥīḥayn, the Jāmiʿ al-Tirmidhī, and the Sunan of Abū Dāwūd, Nasāʾī, and Ibn Mājah.'

---

[8] Mizzī, *Tahdhīb al-kamāl,* vol 1, pg 167.

[9] See footnote 15 on page 119.

[10] Khaṭṭābī, *Maʿālim al-sunan,* vol 4, pg 357.

Two Types of Ḥadīth Books

The compilations and works of ḥadīth from the first century to our day have become numerous, including the Ṣaḥīfah collections of Companions and Followers[1]*; the Jāmi'*[2] *collections of Ma'mar, Sufyān al-Thawrī, Awzā'ī, Ibn 'Uyaynah and Wakī'; the Muwaṭṭa'*[3] *collections; the Musnad*[4] *compilations of Abū Dāwūd al-Ṭayālisī, Musaddad b. Musarhad*[5]*, Aḥmad b. Ḥanbal, Baqīyy b. Makhlad*[6]*, and Abū Ya'lā*[7]*; the two Muṣannaf*[8] *compilations of 'Abd al-Razzāq and Ibn Abī Shaybah; the Ṣaḥīḥayn of Bukhārī and Muslim; and the Books of the Sunan.*[9] *Are all of these books related to one another in anyway? Are they similar in their methodologies and aims, or do they differ significantly?*

They actually represent many different kinds of works, which I will divide into two broad classifications. Recognizing this distinction is indispensable. Historically, not doing so has led to great error and confusion, even on the part of otherwise great individuals, not to mention those lesser than them.

---

[1] Many Companions and Successors were known to have kept written compilations known as Ṣaḥīfah collections. See section 'Preserving Ḥadīth Through Writing' in chapter 6.

[2] The Jāmi' is a comprehensive ḥadīth compilation inclusive of not only legal rulings, but also additional topics such as tafsīr, aqīdah and heart softeners.

[3] The Muwaṭṭa' was famously compiled by Imām Mālik of Madīnah (d. 179/795)—with others following him—and represented a subclass of the Muṣannaf genre of ḥadīth works, which were topically arranged fiqh-oriented ḥadīth works that represented the first organized works of Islamic scholarship. See previous chapter.

[4] These ḥadīth works were organized by the isnād, usually grouped by Companions, and occurred in the backdrop of greater attention on the isnād in the 3rd century. These musnad works were storehouses and comprehensive collections of narrations, sometimes with little regard for authenticity. —Dr. Jonathan AC Brown, Hadith: Muhammad's Legacy in the Medieval and Modern World. Oneworld Publications. 2009.

[5] See footnote 13 in chapter 12.

[6] Abū 'Abd al-Raḥmān Baqīyy b. Makhlad (d. 276/889) was a ḥadīth scholar of Cordoba, Spain, who famously traveled the width of the Muslim world to learn ḥadīth from Imām Aḥmad. He compiled a multi-volume Musnad work—now lost—which was thought to possibly be the largest book of ḥadīth ever compiled.

[7] Abū Ya'lā al-Mauṣilī (d. 307/919) was a ḥadīth expert of Mauṣil, Iraq.

[8] See footnote 3 above.

[9] Representing the pinnacle of ḥadīth scholarship, these later works (Ṣaḥīḥ and Sunan) combined the two earlier genres (Muṣannaf and Musnad) to produce topically arranged works with full isnāds and greater regard for authenticity. Sunan compilations are topically arranged, legal ḥadīth works. Unlike the Muṣannaf genre, they only contain Prophetic ḥadīth, reflecting their aim to collate ḥadīth rather than fiqh.

What are these two types?

1. Ḥadīth Registers (Mudawwanāt)[10]

The first are the ḥadīth registers (in Arabic, *mudawwanāt* or *dawāwīn*). These were compilations of certain scholars who simply aimed to record their ḥadīth reports or those of their teachers. Their primary goal was to record these ḥadīth, either in their entirety or by way of more particular selections. These were compiled without any intended order or sometimes with an order or arrangement that arose spontaneously or incidentally. They were devoid of demonstrating any practical applications or advancing comprehension in any major way. There was no attention paid within them, for instance, to the subtleties of ḥadīth study or analysis, and no section introductions that included evidence or supporting material.

The authors relied upon these records solely for the purpose of audition and recital (hearing and reading reports in ḥadīth teaching sessions. They were often intermingled with commentary from their teachers as well as their own rulings, interpretations and clarification of potential defects. Teachers presented these works to those learning ḥadīth from them, either through narration or dictation. These books were recorded only for a specific time and for specified individuals. The only ones who were able to benefit from these works are those who took them from their teachers/authors, hearing from them directly or reading the texts back to them.

2. Ḥadīth Works Proper (Muṣannafāt)

Then there were works compiled by scholars as properly authored books independent from time and space. They were inclusive of practical application, designed for the aim of comprehension, and contained alerts to potential defects within reports. These scholars organized their books with chapter prefaces and headings containing proofs and supporting evidence. They aimed for a clear higher order and were inclusive of full detail. They paid particular attention to

[10] In Arabic, *mudawwanāt* or *dawāwīn*.

deriving rulings, extracting other benefits, and linking subsidiary matters with their foundational principles. These were not mere registers of ḥadīth but designed, rather, to fulfill specific goals and objectives as intended by their authors.

Please elaborate for us what these two types are, with examples. The first type (registers) includes the books of Sufyān al-Thawrī, Awzāʿī, Sufyān b. ʿUyaynah and Wakīʿ, in which they recorded their ḥadīth narrations for their students to hear from them or read back to them. Their companions in turn recorded personal copies for themselves or made selections therefrom. Over time, many of these books eventually became parts of subsequent works in later generations.

The best examples of ḥadīth works proper are the Ṣaḥīḥ of Bukhārī and Muslim. Ṣaḥīḥ Bukhārī is a work separated from time and space, whose author gathered within it ḥadīth reports that fulfilled very specific conditions which are apparent throughout the book. He organized the book using chapter headings that included many benefits and rulings, extracted in such intricate ways that it astonished scholars and thinkers alike. Its astounding arrangement reinforces the notion that sound ḥadīth are sufficient for our religion. Bukhārī's book encompasses two basic aims:

1. Comprehensive compilation of sound ḥadīth with necessary clarification of potential defects and other issues relating to their chain or text, as well as reinforcing his own views and choices with supporting narrations.[11]
2. Demonstrating applications of ḥadīth and elaborating on their meanings through his arrangement and chapter headings containing proofs and evidence, affirming fundamental and peripheral principles of religion, and frequently repeating ḥadīth in order to distinguish various textual wordings and bring new benefits.[12]

---

[11] Mutābaʿāt are those secondary narrations that represent a lower degree of authenticity and are used only as supporting evidence for the primary, more authentic ḥadīth material. Similarly, muʿallaqāt are those narrations, also of lesser authenticity, which Bukhārī quotes—often without isnād—in his chapter headings to achieve the same purpose. Lack of awareness of this secondary, lesser-tier material in Bukhārī has led to much confusion among critics.

[12] The well-known saying about Bukhārī is quite apt here:

The author of Ṣaḥīḥ Muslim compiled it to comprehensively gather sound ḥadīth which, according to him, are those that were narrated by transmitters of the first rank who possessed moral uprightness, steadfastness, strong memory, and expertise, of the likes of Imām Mālik, Shuʿbah, Sufyān al-Thawrī, Ḥammād b. Zayd and others. The ḥadīth reports of this generation are exhausted comprehensively.[13] The author then follows up these ḥadīth with those of the second rank, who are lesser than the first in memory and expertise while being similar in moral uprightness. This material was not exhausted entirely, but the author chose from them what he needed for supporting evidence. And if there were potential defects in the first-tier ḥadīth,[14] he would clarify that at the ends of the chapters. Muslim excelled in this arrangement of ḥadīth and originated methodologies not used previously, making it *the single best work of ḥadīth craftsmanship*. He demonstrated the marvels of this discipline in the best way possible, surpassing all his predecessors and peers, and making it difficult for those who came after him. He left behind a singular, unique book in its field.

Those who examine these two works should really understand their aims, features and distinctions, and not treat them like the ḥadīth registers.

Which of the two types does the Muwaṭṭaʾ fall into? Into the first type.

Is this not an insult to the Muwaṭṭaʾ that it be placed among the ḥadīth registers? Of course not. What kind of insult would this be? Rather, it is from the merits of Mālik—and those who were like him—that he did not restrict people nor compel them to his book. This was the way of the scholars of Islām as well as

---

فقه البخاري في تراجمه

'The real genius of Bukhārī is found in his arrangement and chapter headings.'

The contributions of Bukhārī are therefore manifold: providing evidence that represents the highest-tier of authenticity possible, providing ample secondary evidences to bolster the primary proofs, demonstrating applications of ḥadīth through their arrangements in various chapters, spelling out his views in the chapter headings, quoting other non-ḥadīth material therein, repeating the same ḥadīth throughout the work in various chapters to support multiple applications of the same texts, and bringing out multiple textual variations of ḥadīth to support more nuanced applications.

[13] i.e. All of this primary-tier ḥadīth material is produced in the Ṣaḥīḥ in a comprehensive and all-inclusive manner.

[14] A deeper study of ḥadīth shows that is quite possible, and even common, for the bulk of a ḥadīth narration to be authentic, while the narration still suffers from some hidden defect in a smaller portion that does not affect the overall authenticity. Scholars like Bukhārī and Muslim fulfilled their responsibility diligently to point these out in their works. Muslim does this at the ends of the chapters whereas Bukhārī often utilizes the chapter headings for this purpose.

those of other traditions. Even the books of Aristotle and other philosophers represent nothing other than lessons and lectures delivered to their pupils, who in turn confined these lessons to specific works.[15]

So what then is the benefit of the ḥadīth registers? They are compilations of precise reports of specific teachers, which students heard and read to them. They did so without necessarily confining themselves to their teachers' understandings and manners of extrapolation or derivation.[16] Later, students compiled for those after them the lessons of their teachers in the application and extrapolation of ḥadīth texts.[17] And it was from this same starting point that even Aristotle began his own philosophical school, and some of the most intelligent people followed him.[18]

What is the confusion and error that results from not being aware of the difference between these two types? Many people treated ḥadīth works like ḥadīth registers, studying them and commenting upon them as mere collections of ḥadīth, without recognizing their inherent features and distinctions placed therein by their authors. For example, most commentaries of the Ṣaḥīḥayn and other books are merely explanations of their individual ḥadīth reports, like Baghawī's[19] *Sharḥ al-Sunnah* and Khaṭṭābī's *Maʿālim al-Sunan*. There would be no real difference if

---

[15] Although the Muwaṭṭaʾ is technically part of what is known as the 'muṣannaf genre' of ḥadīth works (topically-arranged fiqh-oriented ḥadīth compilations), Dr. Akram's use of muṣannaf in his mudawwanāt-muṣannafāt scheme is different: the former referring to registers of individual reports without a higher organization and the latter for ḥadīth works that reflected a higher organization and purpose with its contents. He maintains that the Muwaṭṭaʾ belongs to the former category in this scheme, as its order and organization is mostly from Mālik's various students who rendered the Muwaṭṭaʾ in their own ways, such as Muḥammad b. al-Ḥasan al-Shaybānī.

[16] To reiterate, these 'register-works' were basic skeletal compilations of ḥadīth texts, used by students to learn from their teachers in face-to-face, live instruction. They were never intended to provide the principles or methodologies of these teachers. Those principles and methodologies (i.e. comprehension) were taught in the live instruction sessions, utilizing the raw material, if you will, of these skeletal texts.

[17] It was only later on that students added to these works, or compiled separate ones, in which they added the principles, approaches and methodologies of these great teachers.

[18] Dr. Akram is pointing out that even the Hellenistic tradition had a similar origin, in that the Aristotelian school was born from initial correspondences and instructions between Aristotle and his students, and later evolving into a more coherent and systematic school.

[19] Abū Muḥammad al-Ḥusayn b. Masʿūd al-Baghawī (d. 510/1117) was a prolific scholar from the village of Bagh near Herāt who authored a number of famous works, including a tafsīr work and the above work, which is a commentary of the most widely accepted ḥadīth narrations from the various works of ḥadīth.

one were to replace the commentary in these works with commentaries from other works concerning the same ḥadīth.

Is there any commentary that is an exception to this? I refuse to accept any exception to this other than *Fatḥ al-bārī*,[20] for it is a commentary of the entirety of Ṣaḥīḥ Bukhārī, inclusive of its special features and distinctions.

Do you find in it any faults at all? Which single book is free of errors or mistakes? If the Ṣaḥīḥ of Bukhārī is the soundest book after the Book of Allah, then *Fatḥ al-bārī* is the best commentary, of the highest and noblest rank. The one who said about it, 'There is no migration after the *Fatḥ*,' was truthful.[21]

---

[20] The monumental commentary to the Ṣaḥīḥ of Bukhārī authored by the renowned ḥadīth expert Ibn Ḥajar of Aschelon (d. 852/1449).

[21] This is a well-known ḥadīth of the Prophet referring to the 'Opening' (*Fatḥ*) of Makkah, whose words were borrowed to describe this commentary, also aptly named the 'Opening':

لَا هِجرَةَ بَعدَ الفَتح

There is no migration after the Opening.

The Soundest Book of All

What is the greatest book of all? After the Book of God, the greatest book is undoubtedly the Ṣaḥīḥ of Imām Bukhārī, entitled *al-Jāmiʿ al-musnad al-ṣaḥīḥ al-mukhtaṣar min umūr rasūlillāh wa sunanihī wa ayyāmihī.* Nothing like it has ever been authored in Islam or any other tradition. It is a sound book of the highest quality, accuracy and precision. Among all works, it offers the greatest insights into understanding the Qurʾān, chains of transmission, ḥadīth sciences, fiqh, history and language. I have explained some of its unique characteristics in various articles which form a book entitled *Madkhal ilā Ṣaḥīḥ al-Bukhārī* ('Introduction to Ṣaḥīḥ al-Bukhārī').

And what is the soundest book of all? Soundness is of various degrees, which I will summarize for the sake of ease into three levels: 1. the Ṣaḥīḥ compilations of Bukhārī and Muslim; 2. those ṣaḥīḥ (sound) reports that are not within these two collections but have been deemed such by Aḥmad b. Ḥanbal, Abū Dāwūd, Tirmidhī, and even by Bukhārī and Muslim in their other works; and 3. the ṣaḥīḥ reports deemed by individuals of the likes of Ibn Khuzaymah, Ibn Ḥibbān, al-Ḥākim and others.

What is the soundest of all these works? It is enough for you that I mentioned that the soundest works after the Qurʾān are the Ṣaḥīḥ works of Bukhārī and Muslim.

Please inform us of the soundest one of these two. I am afraid that your minds would not be pleased with my view on that and not be able to reflect deeply or delve into it further. And I am afraid you will accuse me of what I am innocent of. But if you do insist, then know that the soundest of the two is the book of Imām Muslim entitled *al-Musnad al-ṣaḥīḥ al-mukhtaṣar min al-sunan bi naql al-ʿadl ʿan al-ʿadl ilā rasūlillāh.*

Why are you fond of bringing fringe, anomalous views (shādh) to the people of knowledge? You have opposed the majority of this nation, past to present. What is so anomalous about my view? Did I not explain in my previous article that an anomalous opinion is different from an anomalous report? An anomalous report is one that is related by a reliable person which opposes a larger group of reliable people, while an anomalous opinion is one that opposes another that has stronger proofs without consideration for numbers. So please do not oppose me by referencing the views of the majority, but rather, oppose me by presenting stronger proofs.

The majority of the scholars of this nation did not adopt the view of preferring Ṣaḥīḥ Bukhārī over Ṣaḥīḥ Muslim except due to evidences for that, which Ibn Ḥajar summarized in his work, Nuzhat al-naẓar:

> *In the book of Bukhārī, those features which determine soundness are present in a more complete and stringent fashion than in Ṣaḥīḥ Muslim, and Bukhārī's conditions are stronger and more correct than those in Ṣaḥīḥ Muslim.*
>
> *As for his superiority from the perspective of connectedness of chain, Bukhārī stipulated the condition of reporters having met, even if it was documented only once, while Muslim sufficed with their being contemporaries.*
>
> *His superiority in reporter integrity and accuracy is demonstrated by the fact that reporters who have been disputed are in greater number in Ṣaḥīḥ Muslim than in Ṣaḥīḥ Bukhārī. Bukhārī does not relate their reports frequently, and when he does, they are usually from his own teachers from whom he has taken ḥadīth reports and has scrutinized their ḥadīth reports. Muslim does not do the same.*
>
> *His superiority in anomalous and defective reports is demonstrated by the fact that Ṣaḥīḥ Bukhārī has fewer criticized reports than Ṣaḥīḥ Muslim.*[1]

Ibn Ḥajar's point about the superiority of Bukhārī in connectedness of chains is not acceptable. The truth is that both Ṣaḥīḥ collections have the very same conditions of connectedness, as Imām Muslim has explicitly clarified in his introduction to his Ṣaḥīḥ. This was a matter that was agreed upon by proficient ḥadīth experts, who have never disputed this. Muslims states in his introduction:

> Some claimants to knowledge of ḥadīth from our contemporaries have spoken regarding the authentication and weakening of chains,

[1] *Nuzhat,* vol 1, pg 74-5.

which, if we were to avoid mentioning it and pointing out its falsity, it might have become a strong opinion and sound approach. Surely ignoring a corrupt view is the best way to put it to rest and make its proponent less known. It is best not to draw attention to such a view for those who were unaware of it. However, because we fear the consequences and because the ignorant may be deceived by their innovations and rush to believe their mistakes and flawed arguments, we decided to expose their flawed views and refute their opinions as much as is appropriate. That is better for the people and will bring better results, God-willing.

The claimant whose flawed arguments we mentioned at the beginning of our discussion, claims that any ḥadīth in which the chain says, 'so and so narrated from so and so,' and it is well established that they were contemporaries who could have met one another, and that the narrator could have heard it directly from the one from whom he narrated it, or he could have spoken with him directly, but we have no proof that he heard any report from him, and we have not found anything in any report to show that they met at all or spoke to one another—then it cannot be authentic, unless he has some proof that they met during their lifetimes once or more, or spoke to one another, or there is some report which shows that they met once in their lifetimes or more. If he has no proof to that effect, and there is no sound report which says that this narrator met the other or heard something from him—if this is the case, then this report cannot be authentic. In his view, the report is mawqūf, unless it is proven to him in a report that he heard some reports, a few or many, from him.[2]

Muslim's description of 'claimants to knowledge of ḥadīth' refers to some pretenders who entered the field of ḥadīth and falsely claimed to be part of it.

[2] Ṣaḥīḥ Muslim, Muqaddimah, vol 1, pg 79-80. Darrusalam translation. It should be noted that the Muslim's Muqaddimah is complex and has lent itself to much misunderstanding. Hence, it is in need of a critical arrangement to increase clarity of Muslim's purpose and thought, a project which Shaykh Akram is working on.

We do not know the names of whom he was referring to, nor is there any pressing need to determine that, because their view is an invented one that opposed the consensus of ḥadīth experts. This was the case until Qāḍī ʿIyāḍ claimed otherwise in his commentary on Ṣaḥīḥ Muslim: 'The view which Muslim refuted is that of experts of this discipline such as ʿAlī b. al-Madīnī, Bukhārī and others.'[3] After him, nearly all commentators and authors in ḥadīth, including Nawawī and Ibn Ḥajar, began to repeat this assertion to our times.

This is an important chapter in Muslim's introduction, compiled to refute this false argument surrounding the muʿanʿan report. The unanimous view of experts up until Muslim's time was that the muʿanʿan report is considered connected if it fulfills three conditions: 1. that the one reporting in such a manner (with ʿan) is contemporary to the one he is reporting from, 2. that there exist no clear proof contrary to that person's hearing of the report, and 3. that the one reporting in a such a manner is not known for tadlīs. Then there arose some individuals who began to claim that there had to exist positive proof of meeting and audition for a muʿanʿan report to be accepted. Muslim took the initiative to stand up and refute this newly invented position, and he did that in the most firm and decisive way.

There is no doubt that Muslim's position was the correct one and the same one espoused by Bukhārī, ʿAlī al-Madīnī and others. I have expounded on this at length in my commentary on Ṣaḥīḥ Muslim.

As for the other two points, Ibn Ḥajar was certainly correct, for the number of disputed reporters are indeed greater in Ṣaḥīḥ Muslim than in Ṣaḥīḥ Bukhārī, while disputed reports are fewer in Ṣaḥīḥ Bukhārī than in Ṣaḥīḥ Muslim. But this does not prove the superiority of Ṣaḥīḥ Bukhārī over Ṣaḥīḥ Muslim.

Why do you deny obvious facts based upon your own views? Is not reveling in your views a blameworthy and illogical matter? You should know that Ṣaḥīḥ Muslim, as the author has indicated in his own introduction and is obvious to anyone who has looked into the book, includes three types of ḥadīth reports: 1. primary corpus ḥadīth (uṣūl), which are reports of primary-tier narrators in integrity and precision; 2. supporting ḥadīth (mutābaʿāt), which are reports of narrators of a similar level of integrity but lesser precision; and 3. defective ḥadīth reports

[3] Qāḍī ʿIyāḍ, *Ikmāl al-muʿallim bi fawāʾid Muslim*, pg 307-12.

(muʿallal), which are sometimes related by Muslim only to highlight their defects.

The ṣaḥīḥ reports are undoubtedly the primary corpus ones, which Muslim has exhaustively included in his work and bolstered with supporting narrations. As for the disputed reporters in Ṣaḥīḥ Muslim, they are primarily from second-tier supporting reports, while the disputed reports of Ṣaḥīḥ Muslim are mostly from supporting and defective ḥadīth reports.

The disputed reporters among Muslim's primary corpus reports are exceedingly rare. Moreover, these disputes concerning their status do not affect the soundness of their reports at all, and this is not the place to expound on this.

The summary of the matter is that Ṣaḥīḥ Muslim—i.e. its primary corpus material—is purer and sounder than Ṣaḥīḥ Bukhārī. I have only preferred Ṣaḥīḥ Muslim over Ṣaḥīḥ Bukhārī in the matter of soundness, while in all other matters, Bukhārī's work is undoubtedly greater and far more outstanding.

Whoever follows Muslim's methodology closely in his Ṣaḥīḥ will find that his ordering and arrangement of isnāds in the chapter is absolutely amazing, showing the depth of his mastery and proficiency in the knowledge of isnād and its defects. He always begins with the soundest isnāds, following them up with those that come after them in soundness. He also brings isnāds with support before those without any support or lesser support, and higher isnāds (those with fewer intermediaries) before lower ones. He will bring those isnāds united by reporters of a common region or tribe before those that do not follow such a pattern.

You should know that Bukhārī and Muslim related the most sound ḥadīth reports in their books which fulfilled certain conditions, and excluded other sound ḥadīth which did not fulfill these conditions. They were also united in the conditions whose fulfillment deems a report ṣaḥīḥ, though they may have differed in their practical application in specific cases. Every single report that they included in these two works, and excluded from them, was based upon evidence.

The ḥadīth expert Abū al-Faraj Ibn al-Jawzī states, after refuting those who considered Imām Aḥmad's statement that 'there are 700,000 ṣaḥīḥ reports from the Prophet' to refer to matn of ḥadīth reports rather than isnāds:

Similar to this is the heedlessness of those who claim that Bukhārī did not relate every ṣaḥīḥ report but only a selection or sampling in order to not make his work lengthy. The likes of Abū Bakr al-Ismāʿīlī held this view and attributed to Bukhārī the following statement: 'I have left out many reports from my Ṣaḥīḥ.' In fact, what Bukhārī meant by this was specific isnāds. This is proven by the fact that Dāruquṭnī, the master of all ḥadīth experts, attempted to compile all reports which Bukhārī and Muslim failed to include, and came up with very few reports. Had the matter been as claimed, he could have produced volumes. Also, his title *Ilzāmāt* (meaning, 'that which was necessary' [for Bukhārī and Muslim to report]) is explicit proof for this, for the one who produces a mere selection is not bound by anything.[4]

[4] Ibn al-Jawzī, *Ṣayd al-khāṭir*, pg 164.

Kitāb al-Āthār

What is the soundest of all books? I don't find it useful to entertain such queries, but if you insist, you should know that the soundest books are the Ṣaḥīḥayn of Bukhārī and Muslim along with the Muwaṭṭa' of Imām Mālik (the Prophetic reports therein).

Are you not a follower of the Ḥanafi school? Of course, but does the soundness of books vary from school to school? Or has there come to you a strange anomalous view which you wish to broadcast through your discussions?

Didn't one of your own teachers, the ḥadīth scholar Shaykh 'Abd al-Rashīd Nu'mānī, advocate the view that the soundest book of all was Kitāb al-Āthār of Imām Abū Ḥanīfah? Yes, Shaykh 'Abd al-Rashīd Nu'mānī, may God have mercy on him and forgive him, passionately advocated this view. I have spoken with him on a number of occasions and debated him in a forceful and contentious way. *Did he moderate his stance in any way?* No, he lived and died upon this stance without budging from it in any way. *Was there any solid or indisputable evidence which motivated his stance?* No, the only evidence he had was that Abū Ḥanīfah was a Follower and hence chronologically before Imām Mālik, which made Abū Ḥanīfah's work more worthy of being considered the soundest work after the Qur'ān.

Where you persuaded and why not? No, can any one be persuaded by that? Firstly, there is no proof that Kitāb al-Āthār was authored by Abū Ḥanīfah. Had it really been his own work, people would have flocked to him to hear the book and read it to him, as in the case of Mālik's Muwaṭṭa'. In fact, no report has reached us that anyone ever heard the book from him or read it to Abū Ḥanīfah.

Secondly, it is filled with āthār (non-Prophetic reports), maqṭū' (reports of Followers) and mursal reports. The Prophetic reports in it are very few. In fact, many of the Prophetic reports related in the Ṣaḥīḥayn are found in this work in defective forms (as mawqūf, mursal and disconnected reports). Of course, the Muwaṭṭa' also contains such reports, but they are there to provide context and balance between ḥadīth and fiqh.

Thirdly, many of its reports are from reporters with compromised accuracy and precision (ḍabṭ). These reports contradict those of the known and reliable experts of narration, and they contain an abundance of mistakes.

Can you provide some examples of these mistakes?

Muḥammad b. al-Ḥasan reported: Abū Ḥanīfah reported to us: Manṣūr b. Zādān reported to us: from Ḥasan al-Baṣrī: from the Prophet ﷺ: *Whoever laughs should repeat his wuḍū ʾ and prayer.* Abū Yūsuf reported in his own rendition of Kitāb al-Āthār: from Abū Ḥanīfah: from Manṣūr b. Zādān from Ḥasan from Maʿbad.

This is clearly a mistake. This report is proven only from Abū al-ʿĀliyah as a mursal report. The inclusion of Ḥasan al-Baṣrī in the isnād of Manṣūr is a mistake. Dāruquṭnī states in al-Sunan:

> Abū Ḥanīfah reported this ḥadīth from Manṣūr b. Zādān from Ḥasan from Maʿbad al-Juhanī as a mursal report from the Prophet ﷺ. Abū Ḥanīfah reported it from Manṣūr in a mistaken way. In fact, Manṣūr reports it from Muḥammad b. Sīrīn from Maʿbad, who was not a Companion. It is said that he was the first Follower to advocate the view of al-Qadr. Those who reported it from Manṣūr with his isnād to Ibn Sīrīn included Ghaylān b. Jāmiʿ and Hushaym b. Bashīr, both of whom were more accurate in knowledge of isnād than Abū Ḥanīfah.[1]

Dāruquṭnī stated after relating the isnāds of Abū al-ʿĀliyah, Ḥasan, Ibn Sīrīn, Ibrāhīm al-Nakhaʿī, Zuhrī and others, and showing evidence that all paths go through Abū al-ʿĀliyah: All these ḥadīth reports that have been mentioned on this topic go back to Abū al-ʿĀliyah al-Riyāḥī, who reported this directly from the Prophet without naming the intermediary.[2]

Can you provide another example? From Muḥammad b. al-Ḥasan's Kitāb al-Āthār, he states: Abū Ḥanīfah reported to us: Abū al-Ḥasan Mūsā b. Abī ʿĀʾishah reported to us: from ʿAbdullah b. Shaddād b. al-Hād: from Jābir b. ʿAbdullah

---

[1] Sunan al-Dāruquṭnī, vol 1, pg 306.

[2] Sunan al-Dāruquṭnī, vol 1, pg 314.

who reported that the Prophet said: *Whoever prays behind an imām, the recitation of the imām serves as his own recitation.*

In fact, the mention of Jābir here is a mistake. Ibn Abī Ḥātim stated: My father said: There is no dispute among scholars that those who report the isnād of Mūsā b. Abī ʿĀʾishah from Jābir are mistaken. Ibn Abī Ḥātim said: I asked my father if the one who made this mistake is Nuʿmān b. Thābit (Abū Ḥanīfah), and he replied: Yes.[3]

Abū Zurʿah in *al-Ḍuʿafāʾ* stated: This ḥadīth is from the reports of Abū Ḥanīfah, who added 'from Jābir.' Dāruquṭnī in al-Sunan said: No one provided a complete isnād to the Prophet from Mūsā b. Abī ʿĀʾishah other than Abū Ḥanīfah and al-Ḥasan b. ʿAmmārah, and both of them are weak.

Ibn ʿAbd al-Barr said: 'This ḥadīth was reported by Abū Ḥanīfah from Mūsā b. Abī ʿĀʾishah from ʿAbdullah b. Shaddād b. al-Hādī from Jābir from the Prophet ﷺ, and no one else reported it with a complete isnād to the Prophet. But Abū Ḥanīfah according to ḥadīth experts was not accurate in preservation. The experts who opposed him included Sufyān al-Thawrī, Shuʿbah, Sufyān b. ʿUyaynah, and Jarīr, all of whom reported it thus: from Mūsā b. Abī ʿĀʾishah from ʿAbdullah b. Shaddād from the Prophet. The correct version is as a mursal report.'[4]

Do ḥadīth experts agree on the weak status of Abū Ḥanīfah? No. *They why did they deem him weak?* They deemed him weak due to the abundance of mistakes in his reports.

You agree with the abundance of mistakes in Abū Ḥanīfah's reports but you disagree with his status as a weak reporter. What is the secret behind that? You should know that Abū Ḥanīfah did not author any of the works that are attributed to him. Rather, he referred to ḥadīth reports during the course of his discussions on jurisprudence with his companions and students. It was they who captured these reports and placed them into written works, which subsequently began to be transmitted from these students. This caused many people to mistakenly believe that these were Abū Ḥanīfah's own works. Had Abū Ḥanīfah intended to author them he would have followed the principles of writing and likely

---

[3] Dāruquṭnī, *al-ʿIlal*, pg 370.

[4] *Al-Tamhīd*, vol 11, pg 48.

recorded them with accuracy and precision as Mālik and others had done in their books. In this, there was no fault on the part of Abū Ḥanīfah or his students, but the blame is on later Ḥanafīs who began to ascribe the books to Abū Ḥanīfah. They believed they were doing good, but the truth is that they wound up harming this great, peerless Imām, may God have abundant mercy upon him.

Abū Ḥanīfah was not alone in these mistakes, for there exist many supporting reports from other isnāds that share in these. Do not be impressed by these supporting reports, for they either come from very weak reporters whose reports have no proof-value at all, or from a single source such that they are not supporting reports at all but the same report (mistakenly presented as multiple isnāds).

An example is in the above ḥadīth concerning laughter. Abū Ḥanīfah reported it from Ḥasan as a supporting isnād for the isnād of Abū al-ʿĀliyah. Others provided supporting isnāds from Zuhrī, Ibrāhīm al-Nakhaʿī, and others. But these are not supporting isnads. Dāruquṭnī relates in his Sunan from ʿAlī b. al-Madīnī:

> ʿAlī b. al-Madīnī reported: ʿAbd al-Raḥmān b. Mahdī said to me: this ḥadīth rests upon Abū al-ʿĀliyah.
>
> I said to him: Ḥasan also reported it in mursal form from the Prophet ﷺ. ʿAbd al-Raḥmān replied: Ḥammād b. Zayd reported to me: from Ḥafṣ b. Sulaymān al-Minqarī, who said: I am the one who reported it to Ḥasan from Ḥafṣah from Abū al-ʿĀliyah.
>
> I then said: Ibrāhīm also reported it as a mursal report. He replied: Sharīk reported to me: from Abū Hāshim: I am the one who reported it to Ibrāhīm from Abū al-ʿĀliyah.
>
> I then said: Zuhrī also reported it as a mursal report. He replied: I read in the book of Zuhrī's nephew: from Zuhrī from Sulaymān b. Arqam from Ḥasan.[5]

We are convinced by your views and recognize the mastery of ḥadīth experts. We realize that the attribution of Kitāb al-Āthār and other works to Abū Ḥanīfah diminishes his stature. We are fearful of committing this offense on such a great Imām of the Muslims.

---

[5] Sunan al-Dāruquṭnī, vol 1, pg 302.

If only people sufficed themselves with knowing the lofty rank and stature Abū Ḥanīfah attained in the discipline of fiqh, they would be pleased and not commit such disgraceful excesses. We love Abū Ḥanīfah for the sake of God due to his deep understanding, character, piety, and devotion, God's vast mercy be upon him.

Transmission of Books from their Authors

What are the number of narrations of Mālik's Muwaṭṭa'? Countless individuals from a span of generations across diverse lands heard the Muwaṭṭa' from Mālik, but the ones who really circulated the book and surpassed all others include about twenty individuals. The most eminent of them, and best known for accuracy and proficiency, were 'Abd al-Raḥmān b. Mahdī, 'Abdullah b. Wahb, Ma'n b. 'Īsā al-Qazzāz, 'Abdullah b. Yūsuf al-Tinnīsī, 'Abdullah b. Maslamah al-Qa'nabī, Yaḥyā b. Yaḥyā al-Tamīmī al-Naysāpūrī, Yaḥyā b. Yaḥyā al-Laythī, Muḥammad b. al-Ḥasan al-Shaybānī, and Muḥammad b. Idris al-Shāfi'ī, may God have mercy on them all.

Do these abundant and interwoven transmissions increase certainty in the attribution of the Muwaṭṭa' to Mālik? Yes, the proliferation of reports certainly increases certainty as they mutually strengthen and support one another, as in the case of supporting isnāds for ḥadīth.

Abū Ḥanīfah's Kitāb al-Āthār has also been abundantly transmitted from him, including by his son Ḥammād, Abū Yūsuf, Muḥammad b. al-Ḥasan al-Shaybānī, Zufar b. al-Hudhayl, al-Ḥasan b. Ziyād al-Lu'lu'ī, Ḥafṣ b. Ghiyāth, and Muḥammad b. Khālid al-Wahbī. Doesn't this increase certainty in the ascription of the work to Abū Ḥanīfah? No. *Why the distinction between the two books? Why have you considered the multiple transmitters of the Muwaṭṭa' to increase this certainty but not for Abū Ḥanīfah's book?* You have not understood the matter of book transmission, which is the source of your confusion.

Know that the transmission of books occurs in two ways.

First, some books are transmitted directly from their own authors, like the Muwaṭṭa' of Malik and the six primary ḥadīth works of Bukhārī, Muslim, Tirmidhī, Abū Dāwūd, Nasā'ī, and Ibn Mājah. This also includes Sibawayh's al-Kitāb, Shāfi'ī's Risālah, and Muḥammad b. al-Ḥasan al-Shaybānī's Kutub Ẓāhir al-Riwāyah.

Second, many works represent the transmission in book form of ideas and teachings from certain individuals, who are the proponents of those teachings but not the authors of those books. Examples are the Mashyakhah[1] of Ibn al-

[1] Mashyakhah, plural of *shaykh,* is a term for a work cataloguing one's teachers and their reports.

Bukhārī[2] compiled by Ibn al-Ẓāhirī[3] (which represents content of Ibn al-Bukhārī and not Ibn al-Ẓāhirī), and the Arbaʿīn (forty ḥadīth) collection of Ibn Taymiyyah compiled by Dhahabī (which represents Dhahabī's compilation of forty reports from Ibn Taymiyyah). These types of works are extremely common. Students would often compile reports of their teachers, which others would then take and read to these teachers directly, so that all could share in these transmissions.

For example, Shaykh Ziyād al-Tuklah compiled *Nayl al-amānī bi fahrasat musnid al-ʿaṣr ʿAbd al-Raḥmān al-Kattānī*,[4] which is now used by students of ʿAbd al-Raḥmān al-Kattānī to relate from him, though he is neither the author nor did they hear the book from him. Also, Shaykh Muḥammad ʿAbdullah al-Rashīd's *Imdād al-Fattāḥ bi asānīd wa marwiyāt al-shaykh ʿAbd al-Fattāḥ* is used to relate from Shaykh ʿAbd al-Fattāḥ Abū Ghuddah directly.

The books attributed to Abū Ḥanīfah were authored by his students and then copied by others and used to relate from Abū Ḥanīfah in order to share in this loose sense of transmission from him (with the contents and topics attributed to Abū Ḥanīfah). Some of these works were even compiled by individuals several generations removed from Abū Ḥanīfah.

In my view, Kitāb al-Āthār was really authored by Muḥammad b. al-Ḥasan al-Shaybānī and used by students of Abū Yūsuf, al-Ḥasan b. Ziyād, and Zufar to relate from them to Abū Ḥanīfah directly, or by some through their teachers through Muḥammad b. al-Ḥasan al-Shaybānī to Abū Ḥanīfah. The latter is documented in Ibn Ḥajar's *Lisān al-Mīzān*: 'Muḥammad b. Najīḥ al-Balkhī reported Kitāb al-Āthār from al-Ḥasan b. Ziyād al-Luʾluʾī from Muḥammad b. al-Ḥasan from Abū Ḥanīfah.'[5]

There were other works that were related from him but authored by others. For example, Abū Bakr al-Sarakhsī states about *Kitāb al-ʿAyn wa al-Dayn*: 'Know that this book's topics and their arrangement were the work of Muḥammad b. al-Ḥasan al-Shaybānī, while tracing the isnād to Abū Ḥanīfah and their details

---

[2] Abū al-Ḥasan Fakhr al-Dīn ʿAlī b. Aḥmad b. ʿAbd al-Wāḥid al-Anṣārī al-Maqdisī, better known as Ibn al-Bukhārī, was a prolific ḥadīth scholar who died in 690/1291.

[3] Abū al-ʿAbbās Jamāl al-Dīn Aḥmad b. Muḥammad b. ʿAbdullah, better known as Ibn al-Ẓāhirī, was a Ḥanafī scholar from Aleppo, student of Ibn al-Bukhārī, who lived from 626/1229—696/1297.

[4] Published by Dār al-Ḥadīth al-Kattānīyyah in Morocco.

[5] *Lisān al-Mīzān*, vol 5, pg 31.

were the work of al-Ḥasan b. Ziyād, who had a unique mastery over mathematics among Abū Ḥanīfah's students. However, due to his quarrelsome personality and his young age, he did not spend much time with Muḥammad b. al-Ḥasan but wrote alone. Later Muḥammad b. al-Ḥasan secretly discovered his books and copied many details into his own work. Many books of mathematics were like this, especially this one, which contains many insights into fiqh and mathematics that others don't have.'[6]

But the narrators of Kitāb al-Āthār include Abū Yūsuf and al-Ḥasan b. Ziyād, who were older than Muḥammad b. al-Ḥasan al-Shaybānī. How could they relate a book authored by someone younger than them? There is nothing strange in that, for in our times, individuals such as Muḥammad ʿAwwāmah, Muḥammad Niẓām Yaʿqūbī, and Muḥammad b. Nāṣir al-ʿAjamī all relate the book *Nayl al-Amānī* from ʿAbd al-Raḥmān al-Kattānī, though they are all older than Muḥammad Ziyād.

So how do we verify the attribution of early books to their authors? There are three basic conditions through which we verify the attribution of books to their authors. First, there must be clear and explicit mention of the authorship and composition by the individual from his own words or from his peers. Second, there must be evidence of students hearing the book from the author himself or reading it to him. Third, there must exist numerous students that reported the book from the author.

If any of these conditions is compromised, then the attribution of the work to the author is either invalidated or placed in doubt. This applies to the Musnad of Abū Ḥanīfah and Shāfiʿī, for we are certain that these were not authored by them but compiled by later students who selected reports of these Imāms and attributed these to back to them. There is no confusion about this for anyone who is blessed with any share of knowledge.

[6] *Al-Mabsūṭ*, vol 28, pg 110.

PART 4: PEOPLE OF ḤADĪTH

From Whom Ḥadīth is Taken: Three Tiers of Reporters

An important question to reflect over is the following: From whom would we learn medicine, astronomy, engineering, or any other field? The simple and obvious answer is that every discipline is learned from its own particular teachers who specialize in that field. Medicine is learned from physicians, astronomy from astronomers, engineering from engineers, and so on. None of these are learned from speakers, preachers, story tellers or laypersons.

Perhaps a more familiar example would be as follows: If you desire mastering the art of poetry, you would not frequent a doctor, engineer, local mosque imām, or any person known only for his piety. You will try your best to find a poet who has published his work, demonstrated familiarity with the craft, and has expertise in its meters and patterns. Here, you will not achieve success through your wishes alone, but you will have to rely on those have memorized verses, acquired a taste for poetry, are able to transmit great lines with precision and accuracy, and are able to distinguish well-crafted from defective poetry. These individuals would then be able to teach you what beautiful language is, help you appreciate its taste, and give you the capacity to distinguish between fine and coarse verse.

If you bypass this established practice, however, and acquire poetry from other than these, you will expose yourself and the entire field to distortion—and the world is filled with those who sow corruption. When a poet recited some weak verses to Bashshār b. Burd and asked him what he thought, he replied: 'It is good that you brought them out of your chest, for had you left them, you would have suffered a stroke!'[1]

If you understand this, then you should know that ḥadīth represents information that comes from the Prophet ﷺ and the sciences relating to him ﷺ. The sciences that are transmitted from the Prophet include: the Qur'ān, Sunnah, fiqh, his life and character (sīrah), his battles, his leadership, and his politics. Some of his Companions were intimately familiar with all of these, while others

---

[1] *Ḥadā'iq al-azhār*, pg 94.

focused on only some of them. And then there were some Companions who did not focus on any of these formal sciences but were included along with the others for their companionship, faith and struggle. Because of this, the Companions were the best of creation after the prophets and messengers, peace be upon them all.

An obvious and self-evident principle is that ḥadīth is never taken from the following:

1. known liars whose reports are known to be fabricated (mawḍūʿ)
2. those who are disparaged and whose reports are abandoned (matrūk)
3. those who are weak and made mistakes, whose reports conflicted with reliable ones (wāhī, munkar).

Three Essential Tiers

Ḥadīth is only taken from upright individuals (ʿudūl), who exist in three levels. Bukhārī relates the following in his Ṣaḥīḥ:

BOOK OF KNOWLEDGE—CHAPTER: VIRTUE OF THE ONE WHO LEARNS AND TEACHES Muḥammad b. al-ʿUlāʾ reported to us: Ḥammād b. Usāmah reported to us: from Burayd b. ʿAbdullah: from Abū Mūsā:

The Prophet ﷺ said: The example of the guidance and knowledge Allah sent me with is like abundant rain falling on the earth, some of which is fertile soil that absorbs the rain-water and brings forth vegetation and green grass in abundance. Some of it is hard ground which only holds the water which Allah uses to benefit people: for drinking, feeding their animals and irrigation. And some of it is high and barren, neither

صحيح البخاري - كتاب العلم -
باب فضل من علم وعلم
حَدَّثَنَا مُحَمَّدُ بْنُ الْعَلاَءِ، قَالَ حَدَّثَنَا حَمَّادُ بْنُ أُسَامَةَ، عَنْ بُرَيْدِ بْنِ عَبْدِ اللَّهِ، عَنْ أَبِي بُرْدَةَ، عَنْ أَبِي مُوسَى، عَنِ النَّبِيِّ صلى الله عليه وسلم قَالَ مَثَلُ مَا بَعَثَنِي اللَّهُ بِهِ مِنَ الْهُدَى وَالْعِلْمِ كَمَثَلِ الْغَيْثِ الْكَثِيرِ أَصَابَ أَرْضًا، فَكَانَ مِنْهَا نَقِيَّةٌ قَبِلَتِ الْمَاءَ، فَأَنْبَتَتِ الْكَلأَ وَالْعُشْبَ الْكَثِيرَ، وَكَانَتْ مِنْهَا أَجَادِبُ

holding water nor bringing forth vegetation. The first is the example of the person who comprehends Allah's religion and benefits from what Allah has revealed through me, for he learns and teaches others. The last example is a person who does not care for it and does not take accept Allah's guidance revealed through me.[2]	أَمْسَكَتِ الْمَاءَ، فَنَفَعَ اللَّهُ بِهَا النَّاسَ، فَشَرِبُوا وَسَقَوْا وَزَرَعُوا، وَأَصَابَتْ مِنْهَا طَائِفَةً أُخْرَى، إِنَّمَا هِيَ قِيعَانٌ لاَ تُمْسِكُ مَاءً، وَلاَ تُنْبِتُ كَلأً، فَذَلِكَ مَثَلُ مَنْ فَقِهَ فِي دِينِ اللَّهِ وَنَفَعَهُ مَا بَعَثَنِي اللَّهُ بِهِ، فَعَلِمَ وَعَلَّمَ، وَمَثَلُ مَنْ لَمْ يَرْفَعْ بِذَلِكَ رَأْسًا، وَلَمْ يَقْبَلْ هُدَى اللَّهِ الَّذِي أُرْسِلْتُ بِهِ.

Ibn Ḥazm comments on this ḥadīth:

> In this report, the Prophet ﷺ combined all the levels of scholarship without leaving anything out. The pure and fertile ground represents the jurist who is an expert in relating the meanings and understandings of the words of the texts and is able to refer people's disputes back to these clear texts of the Qurʾān and Sunnah.
>
> As for the hard land that holds water which people are then able to use, it refers to those who are able to preserve through memory or writing all that they learn and are able to relate that learning accurately to others without change. They do not, however, have an understanding of the meanings of the words in these reports and teachings, nor can they refer people's disputes back to these texts of the Qurʾān and Sunnah that they relate. Yet God still benefits many people through their conveying of these teachings, and they are able to convey these to those who are able to comprehend them, which the Prophet ﷺ himself alluded to: '*God brighten a man who hears something from us and conveys it to others as*

[2] Ṣaḥīḥ Bukhārī: Kitāb al-ʿilm—Bāb fadl man ʿailma wa ʿallama; Ṣaḥīḥ Muslim: Kitāb al-faḍāʾil—Bāb bayān mithl mā baʿatha Allāh bihi al-nabī.

he heard it, for many a one to whom it is brought retains it better than the one who heard it.'; 'Many a bearer of knowledge is not versed in it'

As for the one who does not accurately preserve what he learns, he is neither like the fertile soil nor the hard ground that holds water, but he is one who is totally deprived, excused, or even blamed, like the elevated and barren ground which can neither sprout vegetation nor hold water. This is a sufficient explanation, and God is the source of success.

Whoever is able must strive to be like the pure and fertile ground, and whoever cannot, should be like the second type of ground. Beyond that, there is no virtue or eminence.[3]

First-Tier Reporters

The first tier, then, represents those who are experts in what they transmit. They are known to ḥadīth scholars as people of top precision and accuracy. In this, the reports concerning sīrah and battles are taken from its experts, while reports concerning sunnah and fiqh are taken from its own experts. I will elaborate on this last type because the majority of ḥadīth reports that explain and apply the Qur'ān are those of sunnah and fiqh.

First-Tier Companions of Fiqh

The foremost Companions in the understanding of sunnah and fiqh were the four Rightly Guided Caliphs, Ibn Mas'ūd, Ubayy b. Ka'b, Mu'ādh b. Jabal, Zayd b. Thābit, 'Ā'ishah, Umm Salamah, and Asmā' bint Abī Bakr.

After them come Ibn 'Umar, Ibn 'Abbās, Abū al-Dardā', 'Ubādah b. al-Ṣāmit, Abū Mūsā al-Ash'arī, Maymūnah, Ḥafṣah, and Sawdah.

After them come Abū Hurayrah, Mu'āwiyah, 'Abdullah b. 'Amr b. al-'Āṣ, Jābir b. 'Abdullah, Abū Sa'īd al-Khudrī, Anas b. Mālik, Umm Ḥabībah, Fāṭimah bint Qays, Umm Sulaym, and Umm 'Aṭiyyah. God be pleased with them all.

---

[3] *Al-Iḥkām,* vol 1, pg 139-40.

First-Tier Followers of Fiqh

The senior Followers in this field were Saʿīd b. al-Musayyab, ʿAlqamah, Aswad, ʿUrwah b. al-Zubayr, ʿUbaydullah b. ʿAbdullah b. ʿUtbah b. Masʿūd, ʿAmrah bint ʿAbd al-Raḥmān, Muʿādhah al-ʿAdawiyah, and ʿĀʾishah bint Ṭalḥah.

The middle tier includes ʿUmar b. ʿAbd al-ʿAzīz, al-Qāsim b. Muḥammad b. Abūbakr, Sālim b. ʿAbdullah b. ʿUmar, Nāfiʿ, Ibrāhīm al-Nakhaʿī, ʿĀmir al-Shaʿbī, ʿAṭāʾ b. Abī Rabāḥ, Ḥasan al-Baṣrī, Muḥammad b. Sīrīn, and Ḥafṣah bint Sīrīn.

The lower tier of Followers includes Ibn Shihāb al-Zuhrī, ʿAmr b. Dīnār, Abū al-Zinād, Muḥammad b. al-Munkadir, Ayyūb al-Sakhtiyānī, ʿAwn b. ʿAbdullah, Manṣūr b. al-Muʿtamir, Aʿmash, Qatādah, Hishām b. ʿUrwah, and Fāṭimah bint al-Mundhir. May God have mercy on them all.

First-Tier People of Understanding from Subsequent Generations

From the next generation the foremost were ʿUbaydullah al-ʿUmarī, Misʿar b. Kidām, Sufyān al-Thawrī, Shuʿbah, Mālik b. Anas, Awzāʿī, Ḥammād b. Zayd, Layth b. Saʾd, Sufyān b. ʿUyaynah, and Isrāʾīl.

These were followed by ʿAbdullah b. al-Mubārak, Wakīʿ b. al-Jarrāḥ, Yaḥyā b. Saʿīd al-Qaṭṭān, ʿAbd al-Raḥmān b. Mahdī, Abū Nuʿaym al-Faḍl b. Dukayn, and Ismāʿīl b. ʿUlayyah.

These were followed by their students Aḥmad b. Ḥanbal, ʿAlī b. al-Madīnī, Abū Bakr b. Abī Shaybah, Yaḥyā b. Maʿīn, Ḥumaydī, and then Bukhārī, Abū Ḥātim al-Rāzī, Abū Zurʿah al-Rāzī, Muslim b. Ḥajjāj, Abū Dāwūd, Tirmidhī, and then al-Nasāʾī, Ibn Khuzaymah, and Ṭabarī.

If a ḥadīth report concerning sunnah and fiqh is related through these above individuals in each generation, then it is fully sound to the highest degree. Yaḥyā b. Bakr once said to Abū Zurʿah al-Rāzī: 'O Abū Zurʿah! This isn't about Zaʿzaʿah relating from Zawbaʿah,[4] but you are lifting the curtain to look at the Prophet ﷺ and the Companions, when you report from Mālik from Nāfiʿ from

[4] i.e. random, unknown individuals.

Ibn ʿUmar.'[5] This is the type of report that the ummah has uniformly accepted. Abū Isḥāq al-Shīrāzī said when discussing solitary (āḥād) reports: 'As for the solitary reports which were uniformly accepted by the ummah, their truthfulness is certain, whether they were acted upon by all scholars or alternately explained by others. It is binding to act upon these reports, and they comprise knowledge and evidence.[6]

Sarakhsī said: 'Know that reporters are two types: well-known and relatively unknown. Well-known reporters are also of two types: those known for deep insight and acumen in deriving rulings (fiqh and ijtihad), and those known for accuracy and preservation while not possessing this degree of knowledge. The former includes the likes of the four Rightly-Guided Caliphs, the four ʿAbdullahs (Ibn ʿUmar, Ibn ʿAbbās, Ibn al-Zubayr, and Ibn ʿAmr b. al-ʿĀṣ), Zayd b. Thābit, Muʿādh b. Jabal, Abū Mūsā al-Ashʿarī, ʿĀʾishah and others well-known for jurisprudence from the Companions. Their reports are a binding proof that establish certain knowledge and necessitate action, irrespective of whether it agrees with qiyas or not.[7]

These reports represent binding proof for the one who hears them. These are the reports relied upon by Bukhārī and Muslim in their primary corpus, and they comprehensively compiled these reports, not leaving any out.

Those who reject these reports fall into mistakes, heresy, and innovation, and close the doors to good. Imām Shāfiʿī said: 'If anything is established from Allah's Messenger ﷺ, then it is obligatory on all who are aware of that to accept it and nothing else shall be accepted in place of that, for God has given no one else authority to give an order contrary to the Prophet's order.'[8]

The Second Tier of Reporters

The second tier of upright individuals are those known for accuracy and precision but are not specialists in fiqh or sunnah. They are like teachers of poetry whom while not being poets themselves can appreciate fine verse and are

---

[5] *Al-Kifāyah,* pg 399 (Maktabah ʿIlmīyyah).

[6] *Al-Lumaʿ,* pg 72.

[7] Uṣūl al-Sarakhsī, vol 1, pg 338-9.

[8] *Al-Risālah,* pg 330.

familiar with the art of poetry. Similarly, this tier of individuals, while not being specialists in fiqh or sunnah, are known for their basic understanding of it and transmitting it faithfully and accurately. Though some jurisprudential rulings may be known from them, they were really distinguished by their trustworthiness and accuracy in transmission.

From the Companions, these individuals were Sa'd b. Abī Waqāṣ, Zubayr b. al-'Awwam, Ṭalḥah b. 'Ubaydullah, 'Amr b. al-'Āṣ, Abū Ayyūb al-Anṣārī, Ḥudhayfah b. al-Yamān, Salmān al-Fārsī, 'Ammār b. Yāsir, Abū Bakr al-Thaqafī, al-Mughīrah b. Shu'bah, al-Miswar b. Makhramah, al-Miqdād b. al-Aswad, Sahl b. Sa'd al-Sā'idī, Jubayr b. Muṭ'im, Nu'mān b. Bashīr, Rāfi' b. Khudayj, 'Imrān b. Ḥusayn, Abū Ḥumayd al-Anṣārī, Umm Ḥarām bint Milḥān, Asmā' bint 'Umays, and Umm Ḥabībah bint Jahsh. God be pleased with them all.

From the Followers, they were 'Abdullah b. Dīnār, Abū Ṣāliḥ, Muḥammad b. Ziyād, Abū Burdah, Ḥumrān the freed slave of 'Uthmān, 'Abd al-Raḥmān b. Hurmuz al-A'raj, 'Īsā b. Ṭalḥah, Hammām b. Munabbih, 'Abdullah b. al-Ṣāmit, Yaḥyā b. Abī Kathīr, Abū Isḥāq al-Sabī'ī, 'Ikrimah, Mujāhid, Abū al-Zubayr, Yazīd b. al-Aṣamm, 'Awf b. Abī Jamīlah, Ṣafiyyah bint Shaybah, 'Ā'ishah bint Sa'd b. Abī Waqāṣ, Nadbah the freed slave of Maymūnah, and Mussah al-Azdiyyah.

In the next generation, there were the following: Fulayḥ, Suhayl b. Abī Ṣāliḥ, Dāwūd b. Abī Hind, Simāk b. Ḥarb, Ḥammād b. Salamah, al-'Alā' b. 'Abd al-Raḥmān, and Hishām al-Dastuwā'ī.

The reports of this second tier of individuals are not like those of the first. These reports are relied upon only in the absence of the first-tier reports. These reports are used only infrequently in the primary corpus of ḥadīth books and more frequently as secondary supporting evidence. Ibn al-Qayyim says:

> In this way, those that came after consisted of two types. The first were the experts known for precision and accuracy in relating what they learned, but they did not derive rulings nor extract gems from what they had preserved. The second were those who deeply understood the texts and were devoted to deriving and extracting rulings from them. The former included Abū Zur'ah, Abū Ḥātim, and Ibn Wārah. The latter included Mālik, Shāfi'ī, Awzā'ī, Bukhārī,

Aḥmad b. Ḥanbal and others who combined deep comprehension and the ability to extract rulings with the ability to transmit accurately. These two groups are the most fortunate people who accepted the revelation that God sent through the Prophet ﷺ and devoted themselves to it.[9]

The Third Tier of Reporters

The third tier of reliable reporters are those not known for their knowledge and teaching. Some of them were known for their participation in battles, preaching, story-telling, or for their great piety and worship. Most of them rarely reported ḥadīth.

From the Companions, there were some such individuals known for their participation in battles and many that were not known at all. There were some that saw the Prophet ﷺ but did not accompany him in any substantial way. This group of Companions was not known to transmit any knowledge, and no leading experts or scholars from the Successors reported anything from them. May God be pleased with them all.

From the Followers, they were individuals such as Muṣʿab b. Saʾd, ʿAnbasah b. Abī Sufyān, ʿAṭāʾ b. al-Sāʾib, Wāʾil b. ʿAlqamah, Yazīd b. Abī Ziyād, Layth b. Abī Sulaym, ʿAbd al-Jabbār b. Wāʾil, ʿĀṣim b. Kulayb, Kathīr b. Sulaym, Ashʿath b. ʿAbd al-Malik al-Ḥamrānī, Abū Sufyān, Zādān, Umm Dharrah, Jasrah bint Dajājah, Umm Ghurāb, Qamīr the wife of Masrūq, and Umm Farwah.

After their generation, there were ʿAbdullah al-ʿUmarī, Jubārah b. al-Mughallis, ʿAbdullah b. Muḥammad b. ʿUqayl, Maṭar al-Warrāq, ʿAmr b. Shuʿayb, Bahz b. Ḥākim, and Shurayk.

These reporters are qualitatively less than the second-tier individuals. Their reports are not utilized in the primary corpus of chapters concerning fiqh and sunnah, but they may be used only as supporting evidence, in which case they can potentially be collectively raised to *ṣaḥīḥ ligahyrihī* or *ḥasan lighayrihī*. There were those scholars who accepted all reports of this tier in the subject of virtues, but the right approach is that of ḥadīth experts—that solitary reports from this

[9] *Al-Wābil al-Ṣayyib*, pg 59.

category are not accepted in any subject, from rulings to virtues. Muslim in his Muqaddimah was referring to this group when he said:

> When we examine the reports of this group of narrators (*Muslim here would be referring to the first tier and most of the second tier according to my division in this chapter*), we bring after them in rank those reports in whose chains exist some individuals not known for accuracy or precision like those of the previously described group. Although they fell below what we described (of the first group), the overall designation of being protected, trustworthy, and involvement in knowledge still applies to them. They included the likes of ʿAṭāʾ b. al-Sāʾib Yazīd b. Abī Ziyād, Layth b. Abī Sulaym among the reporters of ḥadīth.
>
> So even though they possessed what we described as protection, trustworthiness, and being well-known among people of knowledge, their peers whom we mentioned for their precision and accuracy in reporting were above them in status and rank because this first category is a high rank and noble trait according to the people of knowledge.
>
> Can you not see that when you compare the likes of these three people we just mentioned—ʿAṭāʾ, Yazīd, and Layth—with Manṣūr b. al-Muʿtamir, Sulaymān al-Aʿmash, and Ismāʿīl b Abī Khālid in ḥadīth accuracy and soundness, you will find them dissimilar and not close. There is no dispute on that among the experts of ḥadīth since the accuracy of preservation and precision of Manṣūr, Aʿmash and Ismāʿīl was well known to experts, while such was not known from ʿAṭāʾ, Yazīd, and Layth.
>
> In the same manner, when you compare the levels of Ibn ʿAwn and Ayyūb al-Sakhtiyānī with ʿAwf b. Abī Jamīlah and Ashʿath al-Ḥamrānī—and all of them were the students of Ḥasan and Ibn Sīrīn—then there is great disparity and distance between these two levels in terms of virtue and soundness of transmission, even though ʿAwf and Ashʿath are still known for truthfulness and honesty by

> people of knowledge. But the matter is as we described regarding their levels.[10]

In conclusion, when a ḥadīth is presented to you, first look to its contents and then to its transmitters to see if they were known for their competence and mastery of that topic. If they are known to be so, then accept that ḥadīth and hold on to it firmly. If not, then leave it and do not utilize it, for the consensus of experts of guidance is that knowledge is a central matter of religion that requires great caution in terms of the sources from where it is taken from. Imām Mālik said:

> Truly this knowledge is religion, so be careful from whom you take your religion. I have met seventy people quoting the Prophet ﷺ at this pillar—and he pointed to the mosque of the Prophet—and yet, I did not take anything from them. Were they to be entrusted over financial affairs they would prove trustworthy, but they simply did not possess expertise in this discipline.[11]

[10] Muslim, *Muqaddimah.*

[11] Ibn ʿAbd al-Barr, *al-Intiqāʾ*, vol 1, pg 16.

Ranking the Companions and Later Generations

Who are the closest human beings to God? The prophets and messengers of God. *Who is next?* The Companions of the Prophet Muḥammad ﷺ, who possessed the purest hearts, the deepest knowledge, the least pretensions, the firmest guidance, and the best states. God Himself revealed concerning them: ﴾*And thus have We willed you to be a community of the middle way, so that [with your lives] you might bear witness to the truth before all mankind.*﴿ (2:143); ﴾*You are indeed the best community that has ever been brought forth for [the good of] mankind.*﴿ (3:110)

Don't these verses include all Muslims until the Day of Judgement? Of course, but the two verses apply most to the Companions of the Prophet, who are most deserving of this honor, followed by those after them that share in those attributes of the middle path and the presence of good. This is what the Prophet ﷺ meant when he said: 'The best of generations is my generation, and then those that followed them, and then those that followed them.'

What were their levels? The Companions were in three ranks:

1. Muhājirīn (Emigrants)
2. Anṣār (Helpers)
3. Companions who embraced Islam after the conquest of Makkah until the passing of the Prophet ﷺ

God says in the Qur'ān:

> ﴾*It also belongs to the poor Emigrants who have been driven out of their homes and their possessions, those who seek Allah's favor and good pleasure, and help Allah and His Messenger. Such are the truthful ones. It also belongs to those who were already settled in this abode (of Hijrah) having come to faith before the (arrival of the) Emigrants. They love those who have migrated to them and do not covet what has been given them; they even prefer them over themselves though poverty be their own lot. And whosoever are preserved from their own greed, such are the ones that will prosper. And*

it also belongs to those who came after them, and who pray: 'Lord, forgive us and our brethren who have preceded us in faith, and do not put in our hearts any rancor towards those who believe. Lord, You are the Most Tender, the Most Compassionate.'} (59:8-10)

Who are the best of them? The four Rightly-Guided Imāms: Abū Bakr, ʿUmar, ʿUthmān, ʿAlī, as well as the rest of the ten who were promised Paradise.

Is there any standard which we can use to determine their virtues? That would be the extent of their closeness to God which comes from their taqwā and ṣabr. *But that is hidden matter known only to God. Is there any other way to measure their rankings more precisely?*

Ibrāhīmic Devotion versus Mosaic Strength

The best of the prophets and messengers are Ibrāhīm and Mūsā, and Ibrāhīm is the better of the two. Both of them share in some attributes and differ in others.

Ibrāhīm was distinguished by his pure devotion to God (ḥanīfiyyah), truthfulness (ṣiddīqīyyah), forebearance (ḥilm), and uprightness (rushd). Mūsā was distinguished by his ability to separate truth from falsehood, express truth openly, destroy falsehood, become angry for God's sake, and be stern on God's path, all of which was tempered by his humility and readiness to stop at God's limits. Our Prophet ﷺ combined the qualities they missed like leadership (imāmah), being chosen, and closeness to God.

Among the first two Caliphs, Abū Bakr was the closest to Ibrāhīm, while ʿUmar was closest to Mūsā. Among the latter two, ʿUthmān was closest to Ibrāhīm, and ʿAlī to Mūsā. Among the two most beloved wives to the Prophet ﷺ, the closest to Ibrāhīm was the mother of the believers Khadījah, and the closest to Mūsā was ʿĀʾishah.

Among the rest of the Companions, the closest to Ibrāhīm were Abū ʿUbaydah b. al-Jarrāḥ, ʿAbd al-Raḥmān b. ʿAwf, the mother of the believers Umm Salamah, Muʿādh b. Jabal, Ibn Masʿūd, Abū al-Dardāʾ, Salmān al-Fārisī, Abū Mūsā al-Ashʿarī, and Ḥasan son of ʿAlī.

Among the Followers, the closest to Ibrāhīm were ʿAlqamah, Aswad, Ibrāhīm al-Nakhaʿī, Ayyūb al-Sakhtiyānī, and Ibn ʿAwn.

After them the closest to Ibrāhīm were Abū Ḥanīfah, Sufyān al-Thawrī, ʿAbd al-Raḥmān b. Mahdī, Aḥmad b. Ḥanbal, Bukhārī, Abū al-Ḥajjāj al-Mizzī, and others.

Among our teachers in contemporary times, the closest was Abū al-Ḥasan ʿAlī Nadwī, God's mercy be upon all of them.

Among the rest of the Companions the ones who resembled Mūsā the most were Zubayr b. al-ʿAwwām, Ṭalḥah b. ʿUbaydullah, Ubayy b. Kaʿb, and Ḥusayn son of ʿAlī.

Among the Followers, the closest were Saʿīd b. al-Musayyab, Ḥasan al-Baṣrī, and Ibn Sīrīn.

After them, they were Ibn Abī Dhiʾb, Mālik, Shuʿbah, Shāfiʿī, Yaḥyā b. Maʿīn, Abū Ḥātim al-Rāzī, Muslim b. Ḥajjāj, Ibn Taymiyyah, Aḥmad Sirhindī, Muḥammad b. ʿAbd al-Wahhāb, Shāh Ismāʿīl Shahīd, and others. Among our teachers it was Muḥammad Yūnus Jawnpūrī, God's mercy be on them all.

What would you advise us with respect to the Companions? Learn about their lives, follow their example, pray for them, and love them, for you are with the ones you love.

What do you say about those who have problems with the Companions? They are the most unfortunate people and farthest removed from God's mercy. Whenever they insult or harm a Companion, their own good deeds are transferred to them. Insults to the Companions only serve to raise their rank and dignity even further, while the insulters only increase in misery, defamation and blame.

Abū Hurayrah and Some Ḥanafī Jurists

There has been disparagement by some Ḥanafī jurists of the great Companion, jurist, Imām and expert Abū Hurayrah, may God be pleased with him, when they did not consider him to be from the Companions who possessed deep understanding (fiqh) and the ability to issue rulings (fatwā). They advocated abandoning his reports in favor of qiyās whenever there were conflicts.

I have previously written about this issue in my critique of *Uṣūl al-Shāshī.* The author was not correct, nor were other Ḥanafī jurists, in not placing Abū Hurayrah among the ranks of those Companions who possessed the ability to reason (ijtihād) and issue rulings (fatwā). Dhahabī refutes this by saying:

> There is no basis for this, for Muslims of the past and present were united in accepting his reports due to his accuracy, eminence and insight. Moreover, the likes of Ibn ʿAbbās learned from him and used to say: 'Issue fatwā, O Abū Hurayrah.'[1]
>
> Other Companions and individuals from subsequent generations readily accepted his reports in opposition to prevailing qiyās on many matters, for instance, his report from the Prophet ﷺ: 'A woman cannot be taken as a co-wife alongside her paternal or maternal aunt.' Also, the practice of Abū Ḥanīfah, Shāfiʿī and others was to follow his ḥadīth that the one who ate forgetfully while fasting should continue to complete his fast (without expiation). Abū Ḥanīfah's qiyās was that eating forgetfully broke a person's fast, but he later abandoned that in favor of Abū Hurayrah's report. In fact, he gave up his qiyās for lesser reports than those of Abū Hurayrah, such as the matter of laughing in prayer (which was deemed to break one's ablution) due to a mursal report.
>
> Abū Hurayrah was in fact extremely accurate in his reports, and we do not know of him ever making a mistake in a single ḥadīth.[2]

---

[1] Ṣaḥīḥ Bukhārī: Kitāb al-nikāḥ—Bāb lā tunkaḥu al-marʾatu ʿalā ʿammatihā; Muslim: Kitāb al-nikāḥ—Bāb taḥrīm al-jamʿ bayna al-marʾati wa ʿammatihā aw khālatihā fī al-nikāḥ.

[2] *Siyar,* vol 2, pg 578-632.

The great ḥadīth scholar and jurist Muḥammad ʿAbd al-Ḥayy of Lucknow listed Abū Hurayrah among the Companions who were frequent in issuing rulings: 'This negates the position of some Ḥanafī scholars of uṣūl al-fiqh that Abū Hurayrah was not a jurist, because Abū Hurayrah issued fatāwā in the lifetime of the Prophet ﷺ and beyond, and no one did so in that time except for those who were jurists. From our companions who also refuted this notion was Ibn al-Humām Muḥammad b. ʿAbd al-Wāḥid, the author of *Fatḥ al-qadīr*, who discussed this in his book *Taḥrīr al-uṣūl*.'[3]

The scholar and jurist ʿAbd al-ʿAzīz al-Bukhārī said: 'We do not acknowledge the assertion that Abū Hurayrah was not a jurist, for he did not lack any of the qualifications for ijtihād. He used to issue rulings in the time of the Companions, and no one did so in those times except for a jurist who possessed the ability for ijtihād. He was from the best of the Companions of the Prophet ﷺ.'[4]

Ibn al-Humām said: 'Abū Hurayrah was a jurist.'[5] Ibn Amīr Ḥāj said: 'He did not lack any of the qualifications for ijtihād. He used to issue rulings in the time of the Companions, and no one did so in those times except for a mujtahid.'[6] Abū Hurayrah's qualifications were highlighted by a number of other Ḥanafī jurists.

Ibn Taymiyyah was asked about a discussion between two individuals concerning muṣarrāt (un-milked animals) transactions[7] and the permissibility of returning the item after it is sold. The one who considered this permissible relied on the ḥadīth of Abū Hurayrah reported in the Ṣaḥīḥayn,[8] to which his opponent replied that 'Abū Hurayrah was not a jurist and that even ʿUmar had disliked his prolific narration of ḥadīth and forbade him from doing so. Also, Ibn ʿAbbās

[3] See *Ẓafr al-amānī bi sharḥ mukhtaṣar al-Sayyid al-Sharīf al-Jurjānī*, edited by our Shaykh ʿAbd al-Fattāḥ Abū Ghuddah, pg 543.

[4] *Kashf al-asrār*, vol 2, pg 708.

[5] *Al-Taḥrīr*, pg 319.

[6] *Al-Taqrīr*, vol 2, pg 251.

[7] This was the practice of retaining milk in live-stock animals for sale through means such as tying their udders or not milking them for days in order to give the impression to potential buyers that they provided lots of milk.

[8] According to the ḥadīth, the Prophet gave two options to the purchaser of such an animal: retain the animal, or return it with a handful of dates.

and ʿĀʾishah had rejected some matters from him. Ibn Taymiyyah responded to these statements concerning Abū Hurayrah:

> This person is mistaken from a number of angles. The first is his statement that Abū Hurayrah was not a jurist. In fact, ʿUmar had placed him in charge of Baḥrayn, a land that consisted of the best of Muslims, who had sent a delegation to the Prophet ﷺ led by ʿAbd al-Qays.
>
> Abū Hurayrah was the governor over these people and provided rulings for them with his keen insights. One of them was on the issue of a divorced women of less than three divorces with whom her husband has sexual relations. Does the divorce return to one out of three, as is the position of Ibn ʿAbbās, Ibn ʿUmar, the school of Abū Ḥanīfah, and ʿUmar in a report from him? This is built upon the principle that sexual relations with a revocably divorced spouse (of less than three divorces) reverses the divorce. The other position is that of ʿUmar, some senior Companions, Mālik, Shāfiʿī, and Aḥmad (in what is widely known from him) . . . Abū Hurayrah ruled by this latter position and then brought this to ʿUmar's attention, who affirmed his ruling and said: 'Had you ruled any other way, I would have disciplined you.'
>
> Abū Hurayrah issued rulings on a number of delicate matters of fiqh along with other jurist Companions like Ibn ʿAbbās. The reported wordings of his rulings bear witness to that. Though ʿUmar and ʿAlī were more knowledgeable than ʿImrān b. Ḥuṣayn and Abū Mūsā al-Ashʿarī, that does not expel the latter from being jurists. Similarly, though Muʿādh, Ibn Masʿūd and their likes were more knowledgeable than Abū Hurayrah, Ibn ʿUmar, and others, it does not exclude the latter from being jurists.
>
> Secondly, it is known that all scholars of the ummah acted upon the reports of Abū Hurayrah even when they conflicted with explicit qiyās. All scholars acted upon Abū Hurayrah's ḥadīth from the Prophet ﷺ: 'A woman cannot be taken as a cowife to her paternal or maternal aunt.' Abū Ḥanīfah, Shāfiʿī, Aḥmad, and others acted upon his ḥadīth from the Prophet ﷺ that 'Whoever eats or drinks forgetfully should complete his fast, for it is God that provided food and drink.' It was known that Abū

Ḥanīfah's qiyās was that eating forgetfully does break the fast, but he left that in favor of this report. There are numerous such examples. Mālik, Shāfiʿī, and Aḥmad acted upon the ḥadīth of Abū Hurayrah that indicated that one must wash the container licked by a dog seven times, though Mālik's qiyās was that it need not be washed because the dog was not impure. In fact, scholars left their opinions for reports lesser than those of Abū Hurayrah, as Abū Ḥanīfah had left his qiyās that laughing does not affect ablution in favor of a mursal report whose Companion is not known. The reports of Abū Hurayrah are far stronger than such reports by the agreement of all scholars.

Third, it can be stated that the one who reports a ḥadīth accurately through his memory, it does not harm him if he does not understand it fully. This includes those who teach the words of the Qurʾān, adhān, tashahhud and similar matters. The Prophet ﷺ stated: '*God brighten a man who hears a report and conveys it to those who did not hear it, for many are those who transmit knowledge (fiqh) but do not understand it, and many are able to carry knowledge to those who can understand it better.*' This proves clearly that one can take a matter of knowledge and understanding from those who do not understand it fully. However, transmitters who relate by way of meaning and not exact wording must be able to understand their reports fully, lest they wind up inadvertently changing the report.

Abū Hurayrah had one of the most accurate memories among the Companions, for the Prophet ﷺ had prayed for his memory. He himself admitted that he never forgot a thing after that prayer of the Prophet ﷺ. As such, he was able to relate his reports, such as the report of muṣarrāt, exactly as the Prophet had said them.

Fourth, all Companions accepted the reports of Abū Hurayrah, including ʿUmar, Ibn ʿUmar, Ibn ʿAbbās, ʿĀʾishah and others. Whoever studies ḥadīth books knows that well.

Fifth, no single Companion rejected anything that Abū Hurayrah reported by claiming that he made a mistake, not ʿUmar nor anyone else. In fact, Abū Hurayrah used to sit and teach by ʿĀʾishah's house, and once said to her, 'O owner of the chamber, do you object to anything that I say?' After ʿĀʾishah finished her prayers, she only said the following: 'Allah's Messenger ﷺ did not relate ḥadīth in this rapid manner of yours. Rather, he used to talk so clearly that if somebody wanted to count the number of his words, he could do so.' She had objected to his manner of teaching, not the content.

Similarly, when Ibn ʿUmar was asked if he objected to the reports of Abū Hurayrah in any way, he replied, 'No, for he relates and we (sometimes) respond.' In fact, Abū Hurayrah once asked: 'What is my crime, that I memorize and cannot forget?' He related so prolifically that others considered it unusual. Abū Hurayrah himself said:

> People say that Abū Hurayrah narrates too many reports. In fact, Allah knows whether I say the truth or not. They also ask, 'Why don't the Emigrants or Helpers narrate as he does?' In fact, my brothers who were emigrants were busy trading in the markets, and my brothers from the Anṣār were busy with their properties. I, however, was a poor man keeping the company of Allah's Messenger ﷺ and was satisfied with what filled my stomach. So, I used to be present while they were absent, and I used to remember while they forgot. One day, the Prophet ﷺ said, 'Whoever spreads his sheet until I finish this statement of mine and then draws it upon his chest will never forget anything of my statement.' So, I spread my covering sheet which was the only garment I had, till the Prophet ﷺ finished his statement and then I gathered it over my chest. By Him Who has sent him with the truth, since then, I have never forgotten a single word of that statement of his until today. By Allah, had it not been for two verses in Allah's Book, I would never have related any narration: ﴾*Indeed, those who conceal what We sent down of clear proofs and guidance after We made it clear for the people in the Scripture - those are cursed by Allah and cursed by those who curse, except for those who repent and correct themselves and make evident [what they concealed]. For those I will accept their*

repentance, and I am the Accepting of repentance, the Merciful.} (2.159-160)[9]

It is reported from Abū Hurayrah that he divided his nights into three portions: one-third for prayer, one-third for reviewing ḥadīth, and one-third for sleep. It is apparent that the reasons for his strong preservation of ḥadīth were his devotion to the Prophet ﷺ exclusively, cutting off all other relationships, and the prayer of the Prophet ﷺ for him. ʿUmar used to request ḥadīth from him, asking him about them. He never forbade him from relating any knowledge that was needed from the Prophet ﷺ nor did he reprimand him for that. He was simply following the approach of caution and verifying ḥadīth, not wanting people to become bold enough to increase ḥadīth [such that they would fall into mistakes]. For this reason, he had once asked Abū Mūsā al-Ashʿarī if anyone else had corroborated a report of his, though Abū Mūsā was among the senior and most learned Companions.

Six, Companions even consulted in matters of fiqh those who were lesser than Abū Hurayrah, as ʿUmar had consulted Ḥamal b. Mālik and others on the blood-money of the fetus, and ʿUthmān b. Affan had consulted Farīʿah bint Mālik on the matter of the widow staying in the home of her deceased husband. Similarly, ʿUmar had questioned Ḍaḥḥāk b. Sufyān al-Kilābī about the woman inheriting the blood-money of her husband, and Zayd b. Thābit had consulted a woman of the Anṣār about missing the farewell ṭawāf due to menstruation. Once, Ibn Masʿūd had ruled a certain way specifying customary dowry for a woman who was married without a dowry whose husband later died. When some people from the Ashjaʿ clan testified that they had witnessed the Prophet ﷺ give the exact same ruling concerning Birwaʿ bint Wāshiq, Ibn Masʿūd was extremely elated to hear that (his ijtihad had coincided with the Prophet's practice). Abū Bakr made the grandmother inherit based upon the ḥadīth of al-Mughīrah b. Shuʿbah and Muḥammad b. Salamah. There are many such examples.

Seven, the opponent of Abū Hurayrah's report on the muṣarrāt transaction holds that the report opposes established principles and analogy.

---

[9] Ṣaḥīḥ Bukhārī: Kitāb al-muzāraʿah—Bāb mā jāʾa fī al-ghars. Though Ibn Taymiyyah does not relate the full ḥadīth in his passage, I have done so for the sake of clarity.

However, the matter here is like all others in which the texts are followed. This ḥadīth concerns a case that opposes norms rather than following them, and qiyās represents the equivalency of matters that are identical and the differentiation of those things that are different.

The opponent deems the existence of a defect to warrant the return of the defective item, either by its replacement if it is such an object or by returning its value. In this report, accountability is placed, without replacement or return of value, on the buyer, and profit should follow liability.

The response is that the return is assured due to the deceptive nature of the practice and differing of the product from its description, and this is agreed upon by experts. Deceit on the part of the buyer can occur by his false description of an object, in which case the option of return is different from that of a defective object.

It should also be made clear that the buyer is not responsible for any new milk that is produced during his ownership but is responsible for the mild that was already in the udders. When he buys the animal with full udders, and the milk is then extracted during his possession, then he is responsible for that older milk. The Legislator approximated a substitute because the old milk is difficult to distinguish from the new such that its exact equivalent be determined. Therefore, the Legislator determined an approximate substitute to eliminate dispute (as per the ḥadīth, a ṣāʿ of dates to replace the extracted older milk). There are other examples in the Sharīʿah, such as the blood-money of persons and bodily injuries. In general, the exact amount is due whenever it can be determined with certainty, and otherwise, the Sharīʿah designates an approximate substitute to eliminate dispute. Sometimes, it calls for an approximation based upon estimation rather than certainty, when exact measurement or weighing is difficult. At other times, it even calls for drawing lots in cases of complete ambiguity. [10]

---

[10] *Majmūʿ*, vol 4, pg 532-9.

The Meaning of the Revival Ḥadīth

What is the meaning of the ḥadīth that speaks about revival (tajdīd) of religion? This ḥadīth is a popular one among laymen and scholars alike, many of whom have endeavored to provide their own commentary and explanation. The ḥadīth was reported by Abū Dāwūd:

BOOK OF BATTLES—CHAPTER: WHAT HAPPENS IN EACH CENTURY Sulaymān b. Dāwūd al-Mahrī reported to us: Ibn Wahb reported to us: Sa'īd b. Abī Ayyūb reported to me: from Sharāḥīl b. Yazīd al-Ma'āfirī: from Abū 'Alqamah: from Abū Hurayrah: from the Prophet ﷺ (as far as I know):

Allah will raise for this ummah at the head of every hundred years one who will renew its religion for it.

Abū Dāwūd added: 'Abd al-Raḥmān b. Shurayḥ al-Iskandarānī has also transmitted this tradition, but he did not exceed Sharāḥīl (in the isnād).[1]

سنن أبي داود - كتاب الملاحم -

باب ما يذكر في قرن المائة

حَدَّثَنَا سُلَيْمَانُ بْنُ دَاوُدَ الْمَهْرِيُّ، أَخْبَرَنَا ابْنُ وَهْبٍ، أَخْبَرَنِي سَعِيدُ بْنُ أَبِي أَيُّوبَ، عَنْ شَرَاحِيلَ بْنِ يَزِيدَ الْمَعَافِرِيِّ، عَنْ أَبِي عَلْقَمَةَ، عَنْ أَبِي هُرَيْرَةَ، فِيمَا أَعْلَمُ عَنْ رَسُولِ اللَّهِ صلى الله عليه وسلم قَالَ إِنَّ اللَّهَ يَبْعَثُ لِهَذِهِ الأُمَّةِ عَلَى رَأْسِ كُلِّ مِائَةِ سَنَةٍ مَنْ يُجَدِّدُ لَهَا دِينَهَا. قَالَ أَبُو دَاوُدَ رَوَاهُ عَبْدُ الرَّحْمَنِ بْنُ شُرَيْحٍ الإِسْكَنْدَرَانِيُّ لَمْ يَجُزْ بِهِ شَرَاحِيلَ .

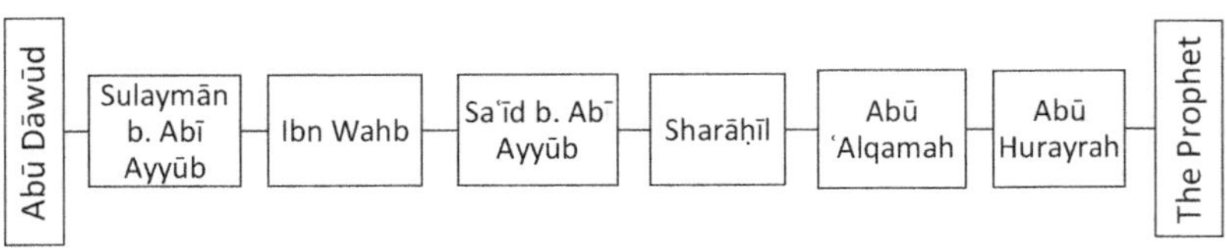

[1] Abū Dāwūd: Kitāb al-malāḥim—Bāb mā yudhkaru fī qarn al-mi'ah.

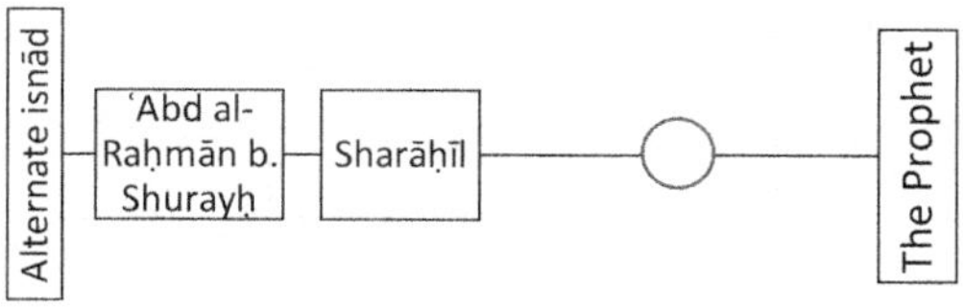

The words *'from the Prophet ﷺ (as far as I know)'* are probably those of Abū ʿAlqamah or another reporter below him. What this means is that 'I believe that Abū Hurayrah reported this from the Prophet ﷺ and not from himself.'

Abū Dāwūd adds the comment that ʿAbd al-Raḥmān b. Shurayḥ al-Iskandarānī has also transmitted this tradition, meaning from Sharāḥīl, but he did not exceed him in the isnād. The ḥadīth is thus considered muʿḍal (problematic), since ʿAbd al-Raḥmān b. Shurayḥ dropped Abū ʿAlqamah and Abū Hurayrah from the isnād. ʿAbd al-Raḥmān was deemed reliable whose reports were accepted by both Bukhārī and Muslim. Similarly, Saʿīd b. Abī Ayyūb, who related the connected isnād to the Prophet, was also deemed reliable. In the end, we have a difference of two trustworthy reporters with respect to the connection of the chain, and the broken isnād is likely the correct one since the connected isnād is not related from the Prophet ﷺ with decisive wording.

Sharāḥīl b. Yazīd al-Maʿāfirī was not utilized by any of the authors of the six primary ḥadīth books except for Abū Dāwūd, who related from him only this single ḥadīth. No one else related from him or deemed him reliable except for Ibn Ḥibbān who listed him among the reliable reporters. Bukhārī stated: 'Sharāḥīl b. Yazīd al-Maʿāfirī heard from Muslim b. Yasār from Abū ʿAlqamah. ʿAbd al-Raḥmān b. Shurayḥ and Saʿīd b. Abī Ayyūb related from him.'[2] Bukhārī did not affirm his hearing from Abū ʿAlqamah but placed Muslim b. Yasār as an intermediary between them.

Abū al-Qāsim Ṭabarānī reported in al-Muʿjam al-Awsat reported the ḥadīth through ʿAbdullah b. Wahb and commented: 'This ḥadīth is not reported from the Prophet ﷺ except through this isnād, and Ibn Wahb is alone in that.'

What is your opinion about those who authenticated this ḥadīth? Most of them have deemed it ṣaḥīḥ did so on the basis of their belief that the reporters in the

[2] *Al-Tārīkh al-kabīr*, vol 4, pg 255.

isnād are all reporters of Muslim, but they are mistaken in that, for Muslim only utilizes Sharāḥīl for one single ḥadīth in the Muqaddimah and nowhere else in his book. It is known that Muslim's conditions in the Muqaddimah are less strict than those of the rest of the book, which great scholars and experts have clarified.

Clearly, the ḥadīth is related in a solitary manner and is a weak one whose attribution to the Prophet ﷺ is questionable. What is strange and odd (and strange and odd things never cease to occur) is that people have bound the notion of tajdīd to one hundred years, even to the point that someone like Jalāl al-Dīn al-Suyūṭī (d. 911/1505)[3] went as far as naming the revivalists in every century in a poem entitled *Tuḥfat al-muhtadīn bi akhbār al-mujaddidīn*. However, he confined the matter after the time of Imām Shāfiʿī to Shāfiʿī scholars alone, mentioning, for example, Ibn Surayj (d. 306/918)[4] and Ashʿarī in the third century while forgetting the role of Imām Aḥmad b. Ḥanbal, who was without doubt the best one who stood for reform and revival in that time.

Suyūṭī then went on to nominate himself for the position in his own era, with the following verses:

وهَذِهِ تَاسِعَةُ المِئِينَ قَدْ / أَتَتْ وَلَا يُخْلَفُ مَا الهَادِي وعَدْ

وَقَدْ رَجَوْتُ أَنَّنِي المُجَدِّدُ / فِيهَا فَفَضْلُ اللهِ لَيْسَ يُجْحَدُ

And now the ninth century has come
Without designating or listing a guide

I hope that I am the revivalist of this time
and the grace of God cannot be opposed[5]

After that, Suyūṭī closed the door of revival by saying:

وآخِرُ المِئِينَ فِيما يَأْتِي / عِيسى نَبِيُّ اللهِ ذُو الآياتِ

[3] Jalāl al-Dīn ʿAbd al-Raḥmān b. Abī Bakr b. Muḥammad al-Khuḍayrī, better known as Imām al-Suyūṭī, was one of the most prolific Muslim scholars and authors who has left no field untouched. He lived from 849 to 911.

[4] Shāfiʿī scholar of Baghdad.

[5] *ʿAwn al-Maʿbūd*, vol 11, pg 265.

CHAPTER 25: ḤADĪTH OF REVIVAL

The last century is the one in which will come
ʿĪsā the prophet of God, bearer of signs[6]

A question that must be raised here is the following: don't people in every time need and deserve someone who would rectify the matter of their religion? Why should they await the end of the century for a reformer to come? Moreover, the Hijrī calendar did not exist at the time the Prophet ﷺ uttered these words.

What is the proper position on this matter? The basic principle is established by a ṣaḥīḥ ḥadīth related in the Ṣaḥīḥayn from Muʿāwiyah:

From ʿAbd al-Raḥmān b. Yazīd b. Jābir: ʿUmayr b. Hāniʾ reported to me: that he heard Muʿāwiyah say: I heard the Prophet ﷺ say:

There will never cease to be a group among my ummah that establishes Allah's orders. They will not be harmed by those who reject them or oppose them until Allah's command comes (the Last Day) while they are still on the right path.[7]

عَن عَبدِ الرَّحمَنِ بنِ يَزِيدَ بْنُ جَابِرٍ، قَالَ حَدَّثَنِي عُمَيْرُ بْنُ هَانِئٍ، أَنَّهُ سَمِعَ مُعَاوِيَةَ، يَقُولُ سَمِعْتُ النَّبِيَّ صلى الله عليه وسلم يَقُولُ لاَ يَزَالُ مِنْ أُمَّتِي أُمَّةٌ قَائِمَةٌ بِأَمْرِ اللَّهِ، لاَ يَضُرُّهُمْ مَنْ خَذَلَهُمْ وَلاَ مَنْ خَالَفَهُمْ حَتَّى يَأْتِيَهُمْ أَمْرُ اللَّهِ وَهُمْ عَلَى ذَلِكَ ". قَالَ عُمَيْرٌ فَقَالَ مَالِكُ بْنُ يُخَامِرَ قَالَ مُعَاذٌ وَهُمْ بِالشَّأْمِ. فَقَالَ مُعَاوِيَةُ هَذَا مَالِكٌ يَزْعُمُ أَنَّهُ سَمِعَ مُعَاذًا يَقُولُ وَهُمْ بِالشَّامِ.

This ḥadīth report is explained in more detail by the following:

---

[6] Ibid.

[7] Ṣaḥīḥ Bukhārī: Kitāb al-ʿilm—Bāb man yuridillāhu bihi khayran yfaqqihhu fī al-din; Kitāb al-manāqib—Bāb ḥaddathanī Muḥammad b. al-Muthannā; Kitāb al-tawḥīd—Bāb qawl Allāh innamā qawlunā li shayʾin idhā aradnāhu; Ṣaḥīḥ Muslim: Kitāb al-imārah—Bāb qawluhu lā tazālu ṭāʾifah min ummatī ẓāhirīna ʿalā al-ḥaqq.

From Ibrāhīm b. ʿAbd al-Raḥmān al-ʿUdhrī: the Prophet ﷺ said: 'From every generation, the upright will carry this knowledge, purifying it from the interpretations of the ignorant, the claims of the falsifiers, and the distortion of the extremists.'[8]

وَعَنْ إِبْرَاهِيمَ بْنِ عَبْدِ الرَّحْمَنِ الْعُذْرِيِّ قَالَ: قَالَ رَسُولُ اللَّهِ صَلَّى اللَّهُ عَلَيْهِ وَسلم: يَحْمِلُ هَذَا الْعِلْمَ مِنْ كُلِّ خَلَفٍ عُدُولُهُ يَنْفُونَ عَنْهُ تَحْرِيفَ الْغَالِينَ وَانْتِحَالَ الْمُبْطِلِينَ وَتَأْوِيلَ الْجَاهِلِينَ.

We understand the expression 'one hundred years' to mean generation or group of people, and the ḥadīth to mean that in every generation and group of people there will be reformers. This was the very interpretation of Shāh Walīullah, who said:

> The Prophetic statements: '*My ummah will never unite on misguidance*' and '*Allah will raise for this ummah at the head of every hundred years one who will renew its religion for it*' are both explained by another ḥadīth: '*From every generation, the upright will carry this knowledge, purifying it from the interpretations of the ignorant, the claims of the falsifiers, and the distortion of the extremists.*'[9]

At the head of these revivalists are the experts of ḥadīth who preserved the Prophetic sunnah and fought innovations. More details on them are forthcoming in the subsequent chapter.

[8] Mursal ḥadīth of Ibrāhīm b. ʿAbd al-Raḥmān al-ʿUdhrī that is related by Bayhaqī in al-Sunan, Ibn ʿAsākir in Tārīkh Damishq, Khaṭīb al-Baghdādī in Sharaf Aṣḥāb al-Ḥadīth and by Tabrīzī in al-Mishkāt al-Maṣābīḥ #248 and others. Imām Aḥmad is one of the few early authorities who considered it ṣaḥīḥ while some later scholars like Ibn al-Qayyim followed him in authenticating it on the basis of supporting chains. Most scholars have deemed it weak, including Ibn Kathīr and Irāqī. The main issue is the disconnect in the chain from Ibrāhīm to Muʿān b. Rafāʿah, the narrator from Ibrāhīm, (whose name mistakenly appears as Muʿādh b. Rafāʿah in some printings) is generally considered weak. Albānī accepted the ḥadīth while Muqbil b. Hādī did not.

[9] *Ḥujjahtullāh al-bālighah*, vol 1, pf 289.

Ḥaddathanā: These Beloved Words

What are the best and most beloved words to you? That would be a person saying *ḥaddathanā* or *akhbaranā.*[1] The judge Yaḥyā b. Aktham said it best: 'I have was given the position of judge, then chief judge, then the ministry, and more, but nothing brings me joy like when I hear the reader (in a ḥadīth session) say: 'Who will you mention, may God be pleased with you?"[2] This is a reference to readers in ḥadīth sessions reciting the words of the ḥadīth scholar: *ḥaddathanā* and *akhbaranā*.

The full meanings and implications of these beloved words are difficult to confine to expression, but sufficient is the fact that they were uttered by the beloved of the Lord of the worlds, master of the messengers and seal of the prophets ﷺ.

I have spent long hours studying and reviewing books of ḥadīth with its devotees, and I have never tired or become bored. These beloved words have an astonishing impact on the heart and serve to transport its hearers to another world of majesty and splendor, especially for those who are aware of their tremendous value and importance. When Ayyūb al-ʿAṭṭār once heard Bishr al-Ḥāfī say: 'Ḥammād b. Zayd reported to me . . .', he remarked: 'I seek God's forgiveness, for surely mentioning isnād [can be] extreme vanity for the soul.'[3]

Yaḥyā b. Aktham relates the following: the Caliph Hārūn al-Rashīd once asked me, 'What is the noblest position?' I replied: 'The one you occupy, Oh Commander of the Believers!' He asked: 'Do you know who is better than me?' I replied: 'No.' Hārūn said: 'I do: It is a simple man uttering in his circle: '*ḥaddathanā so-and-so from so-and-so that Allah's Messenger ﷺ said such-and-such*."' I asked him: 'Oh Commander of the Believers! How could that person be better than you while you are a relative of the Prophet ﷺ, placed in charge of all Muslims?' He replied: 'Woe to you! That person is better than me, because his name is mentioned alongside the name of Allah's Messenger ﷺ, and his name

---

[1] Both are forms of relating ḥadīth, meaning 'he reported to us . . .'

[2] The readers in the ḥadīth assemblies would often ask their teachers in the beginning of the sessions as to whose ḥadīth they would be relating that day. *Sharaf aṣḥāb al-ḥadīth,* vol 1, pg 104.

[3] *al-Jāmiʿ li akhlāq al-rāwī wa ādāb al-sāmiʿ*, vol 1, pg 338.

will never die. We will die and perish, while scholars will remain so long as time remains.'[4]

The judge ʿUmar b. Ḥabīb al-ʿAdawī reported: The Caliph Maʾmūn said to me: 'Every desire of mine has been fulfilled except for ḥadīth. I would have loved to sit on a chair and it be said to me: 'Who reported to you?', and I reply: '*Ḥaddathanī fulān ʿan fulān* (So-and-so reported to me from so-and-so).'' I said to him: 'Do it, Oh Commander of the Believers! Why don't you relate ḥadīth?' He replied: 'Kingdom and Caliphate are not befitting to be combined with teaching ḥadīth.'[5]

The secret behind the power and sweetness in these beloved words which have become a symbol for ḥadīth practitioners throughout the ages is the extreme consistency they achieved between words and action, thereby becoming recipients of the love of Allah, His Messenger ﷺ, and the believers.

How does Allah love them? Allah loves them because they are embellished with traits such as uprightness, taqwā, worship, indifference to the debris of this world, and longing for the next life. In fact, their very practice of relating ḥadīth is one of the consequences of their uprightness.

When Abū Ḥafṣ ʿAmr b. Abī Salamah was asked if he loved to relate ḥadīth, he replied: 'Who would not love that their name be among records of righteous people?'[6] Ṣāliḥ b. Muḥammad al-Rāzī and others said: 'If the people of ḥadīth are not the saints, then I don't know what a saint is.'[7]

How does the Messenger's love manifest through them? Because they carry his message and work to fulfill his trust. They live the following ḥadīth: It was reported by Abū Bakrah al-Thaqafī that the Prophet ﷺ said: 'Let those who are present convey [the message] to those who are who are not here, and perhaps some of you will wind up conveying it to those who can understand it better.'[8] It was reported by al-Mughīrah b. Shuʿbah that the Prophet ﷺ said: 'Some of my followers will remain victorious until the Last Day comes while they are still

---

[4] *Sharaf aṣḥāb al-ḥadīth*, vol 1, pg 99.

[5] *Sharaf aṣḥāb al-ḥadīth*, vol 1, pg 101.

[6] Ibid, vol 1, pg 51.

[7] Ibid, vol 1, pg 49.

[8] Ṣaḥīḥ Bukhārī: Kitāb al-ʿilm—Bāb qawl al-nabī rubba muballigh awʿā min sāmiʿin.

victorious.'[9] Yazīd b. Hārūn commented: 'If these [reports] are not about the people of ḥadīth, then I don't know whom they are about.'[10]

The prayer of the Prophet ﷺ applies to them, as related by Ibn Masʿūd that he ﷺ said: 'God brighten a man who hears a statement of mine, understands it, memorizes it, and transmits it to others. And many are those who transmit knowledge (fiqh) to those who can understand it even better.'[11] Ḥumaydī reported that he heard Sufyān b. ʿUyaynah say: 'There is no one that studies ḥadīth except that there is a brightness on their face, because of the statement of the Prophet ﷺ: 'God brighten a man who hears a report and conveys it'.'[12]

These people will be the closest to the Prophet ﷺ on the Day of Judgement, because Ibn Masʿūd related that he ﷺ said: 'The closest people to me on the Day of Judgement will be those who most frequently sent blessings upon me.'[13] Abū Nuʿaym al-Isfahānī said: 'This noble status is exclusively for the reporters and transmitters of reports because frequently sending blessings upon the Prophet is not known from any group of scholars more than this one, and they do it in writing and by the tongue [in relating ḥadīth].'[14]

What about the believers love for them? Muslims have attained their desire to follow the sunnah through their work, and so, they love them as they love him ﷺ. Yūnus b. ʿAbd al-Aʿlā relates that he heard Shāfiʿī say: 'When I see a person of ḥadīth, it is as I am seeing the Prophet ﷺ alive.'[15] Sufyān al-Thawrī said: 'The angels are the guardians of the heavens, while the people of ḥadīth are the guardians of the earth.'[16] ʿAbdullah b. Dāwūd al-Khuraybī said: 'I have heard from our scholars and those above us that the people of ḥadīth and bearers of knowledge are the trustees of God upon His religion and protectors of His Prophet's sunnah which they understand and implement.'[17] Ṣāliḥ al-Rāzī said:

---

[9] Ṣaḥīḥ Bukhārī: Kitāb al-iʿtiṣām bi al-kitāb wa al-sunnah—Bāb qawluhu lā tazālu ṭāʾifah.

[10] *Sharaf aṣḥāb al-ḥadīth*, vol 1, pg 27.

[11] Tirmidhī: Kitāb—Bāb mā jāʾa fī al-ḥathth ʿalā tablīgh al-samāʿ; Abū Dāwūd: Kitāb—Bāb faḍl nashr al-ʿilm; Sunan Ibn Mājah: Kitāb al-muqaddimah; *Sharaf aṣḥāb al-ḥadīth*.

[12] *Sharaf aṣḥāb al-ḥadīth*, vol 1, pg 19.

[13] Tirmidhī related it in his Sunan in Kitāb al-witr—Bāb mā jāʾa fī faḍl al-ṣalāh ʿalā al-nabī and deemed it ḥasan gharīb. Ibn Ḥibbān also related it in his Ṣaḥīḥ.

[14] Ibid, vol 1, pg 34.

[15] Ibid, vol 1, pg 46.

[16] Ibid, vol 1, pg 44.

[17] Ibid, vol 1, pg 43.

'The trustworthy one ('adl) is not the one who guards chastity, life, or wealth, but the one who testifies about the Prophet ﷺ while his testimony is accepted.'[18]

Ḥadīth really represents provision for the next life. It is for those who are indifferent to this life while longing for the next seeking the Face of God. God grants these individuals the good pleasure of both realms. Sahl b. 'Abdullah said: 'Whoever desires this world and the next should write ḥadīth for it contains the benefit of both worlds.'[19] Sufyān al-Thawrī said: 'Hearing ḥadīth represents strength for the one seeking this life, and guidance for the one seeking the next.'[20]

The people of ḥadīth are the companions of the Prophet as well as the companions of his Companions. A'mash used to say: 'Between me and the Companions of Muḥammad is one curtain, which I remove to look at them.'[21]

Studying ḥadīth and its sciences is among the greatest acts of worship and devotion, and an extremely weighty matter which only the greatest individuals are blessed to partake in. Wakī' said: 'Had I not considered ḥadīth more virtuous than tasbīḥ, I would never have related ḥadīth.'[22] Qanabi said: 'If I knew that ṣalāh was more virtuous than ḥadīth, I would never have related ḥadīth.'[23]

How wonderful are a people whose sustenance consists of the words *qālallāhu* and *qāla al-rasūlu.* Their way of life is exclusive devotion to this discipline while shunning all else. Pages and books are their only passion, resolve and determination their guide, blessings upon the Prophet and seeking forgiveness from God their drink, and deliberation their knowledge. Deep wisdom is their logic, radiance their visage, and pure piety their inner state.

[18] Ibid, vol 1, pg 49.
[19] Ibid, vol 1, pg 61.
[20] Ibid, vol 1, pg 62.
[21] Ibid, vol 1, pg 69.
[22] Ibid, vol 1, pg 82.
[23] Ibid, vol 1, pg 84.

But Not Like My Love for Those Earlier Ones

I have examined many biographies and found none more preeminent in knowledge and practice, more steadfastness and pure in conscience, more consistent between word and action, and none whose efforts achieved as much success and whose scholarship as much precision and perfection, as the following individuals in these early generations and those that followed their footsteps:

- Manṣūr b. al-Muʿtamar, Ayyūb al-Sakhtiyānī, Sulaymān al-Taymī, ʿAbdullah b. ʿAwn, Yūnus b. Ubayd
- Sufyān al-Thawrī, Mālik, Shuʿbah, Misʿar b. Kidām
- Sufyān b. ʿUyaynah, ʿAbdullah b. al-Mubārak, Wakīʿ b. al-Jarrāḥ, Yaḥyā al-Qaṭṭān, ʿAbd al-Raḥmān b. Mahdī, Yaḥyā b. Maʿīn, ʿAlī b. al-Madīnī

After them, I found myself amazed with the following people in language and literature: al-Khalīl b. Aḥmad al-Farāhīdī, Sībawayh, Kisāʾī, Ibn Jinnī, al-Jurjānī, Zamakhsharī, Jāḥiẓ, ʿAbd al-Ḥamīd al-Kātib, Ibn al-Muqaffaʿ, and Ibn al-ʿAmīd. From contemporaries they were Muṣṭafā Luṭfī al-Manfalūṭī, Sibāʿī, Ṭāhā Ḥusayn, Aḥmad Amīn, and ʿAlī Ṭanṭāwī.

From poets, they were the authors of the Hanging Odes (muʿallaqāt), some pre-Islamic (mukhaḍram), Islamic-period and Umayyad-era poets, Abū Tamām (188/803—231/845), Buḥturī (206/821—248/897), Mutanabbī, and in Persian: Firdawsī, Saʿdī, Ḥāfiẓ, Rūmī, Amīr Khusraw; and in Urdu: Mīr Taqī Mīr, Asadullāh Ghālib, Mīr Dard, and Iqbāl.

Among philosophers, they were: Abū Nasr Fārābī, Ibn Sīnā, Rāzī, Ibn Rushd, and Mullā Ṣadr al-Dīn Shīrāzī. From the Sufis, they were Junayd, Shiblī, ʿAbd al-Qādir Jīlānī, Shihāb al-Dīn Suhrawardī, Najm al-Dīn al-Kubrā, Shaykh Aḥmad Sirhindī, and hundreds of others following in their path.

I readily profess the virtue of these notable individuals in each art and discipline. *I love them but not like my love for those earlier ones*, who were above and beyond all others, untouched and unreachable. I am exclusive in my sincerity, devotion, and love for them alone.

I am amazed by the devotion and worship of Sulaymān al-Taymī, who used to pray the entire night with the ablution of the ʿIshāʾ prayer. He and his son would make the rounds of the mosques at night, praying in each turn-by-turn, until the morning came. Ḥammād b. Salamah said: We never came upon Sulaymān al-Taymī at any hour of the day and night except that we found him engaged in some form of worship.

I am amazed by the humility and extreme regard for anonymity of Ayyūb al-Sakhtiyānī. Shuʿbah stated: I would sometimes attempt to follow Ayyūb when he would go out some errand, but his manner would not allow me to follow him, for he would dart right and left and exit from different places, so that no one would tempt him.[1]

Regarding fear and reverence, we have the example of Sufyān al-Thawrī. Qabīṣah said: 'I have never sat with Sufyān except that I have found him remembering death, and I have never come across one who remembered death as much as him.'[2]

Yūsuf b. Asbāṭ said: Once after ʿIshāʾ, Sufyān asked me for a container of water to make ablution. I brought it to him. He took it with his right hand and put his left hand across his cheek in deep contemplation. I went to sleep, and when I arose close to the time of Fajr prayer, I found the container still in his right hand and said to him: 'The time of Fajr has come.' He replied: 'I've been thinking about the next life from that moment until now.'[3]

ʿAbd al-Raḥmān b. Mahdī said: 'Sufyān used to shout when his illness became prolonged, 'O death! O death!' He would then follow-up by saying, 'We don't wish for it, nor do we ask for it.' When he was on his deathbed, he began to weep and become fearful.' I said to him, 'Abū ʿAbdullah, why do you weep?' He replied, 'ʿAbd al-Raḥmān, because of the intensity of my experience with death. Death is so hard!' I touched him and he was saying, 'The soul of the believer leaves like perspiration. I hope for that!' He then reminded himself, 'God is more merciful than a tender, loving mother. He is most Generous and Bountiful. How can I love to meet Him, while I hate death?' I myself began to

---

[1] Dhahabī, *Tārīkh al-Islām,* vol 3, pg 617.

[2] *Siyar,* vol 7, pg 240.

[3] *Siyar,* vol 7, pg 240-1.

weep until I began to choke, trying to hide my crying from him. He then began to cry out, 'Oh! Oh!' from the pangs of death.[4]

Regarding taqwā, there is the story of ʿAbdullah b. ʿAwn. Makkī b. Ibrāhīm relates: I was with ʿAbdullah b. ʿAwn when people began to curse Bilāl b. Abī Burdah (amīr of Baṣrah) for his injustice and oppression. ʿAbdullah, meanwhile, was completely silent. They said to him: We only mention him because of what he did to you. ʿAbdullah replied: 'I fear that there will be two statements that will come out of my register of deeds on the Day of Judgement: *lā ilāha illallāhu* ('no being worthy of worship save God') and 'God cursed so-and-so."[5] It was said to Ibn ʿAwn: 'Why don't you speak your words for reward?' He replied: 'Should not the speaker be content with self-sufficiency?'[6]

ʿAbd al-Raḥmān b. Mahdī said: 'If not for the fact that I hate for God to be disobeyed, I would have loved that there not remain a single person in the city who did not back-bite me. What could be more wonderful than good deeds one finds in his scales on the Day of Judgement that he had not performed.'[7]

Regarding indifference to the world and being independent from all people, Sufyān al-Thawrī relates that when ʿAbd al-Ṣamad the uncle of the ruler Manṣūr once visited him. Sufyān turned his face away and did not return the greetings. ʿAbd al-Ṣamad said to his companion: 'I think that Abū ʿAbdullah is sleeping,' to which his companion agreed. Sufyān exclaimed: 'Do not lie! For I am not asleep!' ʿAbd al-Ṣamad asked him: 'Is there anything we can help you with?'

Sufyān replied: 'Yes, three things: Don't you dare visit me again, nor attend my funeral, nor pray for me.'

Embarrassed, ʿAbd al-Ṣamad got up and left, saying: 'By God, I was ready not to leave the room without his head!'[8]

Firyābī relates from Sufyān: I visited the ruler al-Mahdī and said to him: 'It has reached me that ʿUmar spent a total of twelve dinārs during his Ḥajj, and look at your state!' He became angry and said: 'Do you want me to be in this state that you are in?' I replied: 'If you cannot be like that, then at least spend less

---

[4] *Siyar,* vol 7, pg 250.

[5] *Siyar,* vol 6, pg 369.

[6] *Siyar,* vol 6, pg 369.

[7] *Tārīkh al-Islām,* vol 4, pg 1152.

[8] *Siyar,* vol 7, pg 244.

than what you are doing now.' The minister of the ruler angrily retorted: 'You have sent us many requests in writing which we granted!' Sufyān replied: 'I have never written anything to you at all.'[9]

These are my roots, and I ascribe myself to them. They are my refuge and my solace. They are the friends of the Merciful One, proofs of God among His creation, and His signs in this world. They had praiseworthy traits, noble character, and refined natures. My best days and brightest nights are when I am studying their reports. My favorite names and states are those that resemble theirs. I am happy with their fortunes and delight in their blessings. Seeing their opponents only increases my passion for them. Those who are jealous of them only increase in their vane desires. I have promised them not to love anyone else. Their image does not escape my eyes nor their thoughts from my mind even for a moment, even as all images and thoughts are bound to vanish. I have taken a firm and solemn pledge to this effect, while asking God to make me honor my promise.

God's peace be upon you people of ḥadīth!

[9] *Siyar,* vol 7, pg 257.

PART 5: DEVOTION TO ḤADĪTH

My Journey in Ḥadīth

Please share your journey in ḥadīth.

I am merely a seeker of the noble discipline of ḥadīth who has joined its caravan and relishes hearing their reports, who contends for their inclusion among the sciences, who is enamored with their conduct and character, and who is endeared to them for my own teaching and education.

By the time I completed my ʿālimiyyah degree from Dār al-ʿUlūm Nadwat al-Ulamāʾ of Lucknow, India, in 1401, I considered all Islamic disciplines equivalent and was not able to distinguish between the offerings to determine what agreed with me and what did not. An unwitting circumstance[1] confined my choice to ḥadīth and fiqh, and I could no longer delay the hands of fate which led me to the direction of these two disciplines and the clearing of confusion for me.

I finally registered for the faḍīlah degree program in the department of ḥadīth—and I am eternally grateful to God for His facilitation and choosing of this for me.

In this stage, I learned Ṣaḥīḥ Bukhārī in its entirety and in exhaustive detail from Shaykh Ḍiyāʾ al-Ḥasan Nadwī. I learned the motives behind his divisions and chapter headings and delved into the scholarly differences of jurists. I developed a deep and earnest love for the Ṣaḥīḥ due to what it contained: pofound and profuse knowledge, insight into the sunnah, clarification of isnāds and subtle defects of reports, and many types of ḥadīth sciences.

My love for ḥadīth was increased in this early stage by studying Ṭaḥāwī's *Sharḥ maʿānī al-āthār* and through my discussions with Shaykh Shahbāz Iṣlāḥī, which were quite heated at times.

When I came to Oxford University as a researcher in 1411, I discovered in their library Dhahabī's *Siyar aʿlām al-nubalāʾ*, which I borrowed and proceeded to read it in its entirety in a totally engrossed and exclusive manner. The book

[1] This 'unwitting circumstance' occurred in the course of Shaykh Akram's discussions with his teacher Shahbāz Iṣlāḥī as to what to he should specialize in after the completion of his studies. Maulānā Shahbāz advised him to pursue fiqh because of the need for qualified muftīs but lamented the suboptimal quality of the fiqh program. Shaykh Akram thus entered ḥadīth as a process of elimination and matter of unwitting coincidence, which he fondly ascribes to God's choosing of the path for him.

exhaustively chronicles the ranks and generations (ṭabaqāt) of ḥadīth scholars, their travels, and their reports, including distinguishing sound from unsound ones. It highlights the deep knowledge, sound conduct, fear of God, good character, and longing for the Hereafter that is found in these great personalities.

I read this great book a number of times and was impressed by Dhahabī's manner of presenting biographies. He points the reader to known matters as well as more subtle points. He imparts the importance of consistency between knowledge and practice. He mentions the greatest teachers and students of each individual, highlights their life events, and discusses their virtues as well as criticisms in a balanced manner. He documents the most important ḥadīth reports of each individual, their understandings on specific issues, and the reasons for their merits. My attachment and love for Dhahabī's manner exhibited in my own compilation of extractions from his work, which I have drawn on in my work over the years whenever I needed to.

I also discovered in the Oxford Library *Fihras al-fahāris* of ʿAbd al-Ḥayy al-Kattānī, a book and author I had never heard of before. I read it and used it to study the isnāds of latter-day scholars, until a clear picture emerged in my mind of the fine art of ijāzah, musalsal ḥadīth sessions, indexing one's teachers through fahāris and athbāt works, and the highest chains and best ḥadīth narrators through whom the art of narration continued in our times. I developed an intense desire for seeking ijāzahs, and read the book a number of times until I had taken its content to heart.

I became acquainted with the historian and ḥadīth narrator Muḥammad ʿAbdullah Āl al-Rashīd after participating in an international conference in Samarqand in 1412. We developed a close and firm bond. He pointed out many scholars to me and sought ijāzah on behalf of me from many senior teachers. Through him, I developed a close association with my brother Aḥmad Āshūr, who helped me continue the journey in seeking ijāzah. I saw in Aḥmad many qualities that are rare in young people, such as balancing the knowledge of Qurʾān and Sunnah, the art of transmitting (riwāyah) and understanding (dirāyah) ḥadīth, attaining the highest chains with prolific narration, combining good conduct with noble character, and magnanimity with uprightness. I had found a companion on my journey to ḥadīth and in my journey to the next life.

I then found many other Companions whose favors upon me are well-known, and who have been mentioned elsewhere.

My research work on females involved in ḥadīth, my teaching of ḥadīth books, and my work on a commentary on Ṣaḥīḥ Muslim increased my connection with ḥadīth. For my work on female ḥadīth narrators, *al-Wafā' bi asmā' al-nisā'*, I had to consult countless biographical and historical works, works on ḥadīth and isnād, unpublished manuscripts, and registers of attendance and audition (samā'). I wound up spending a good portion of my life buried in these works, which increased my connection with ḥadīth.

My teaching of Tirmidhī and Bukhārī, and my work on a commentary on Ṣaḥīḥ Muslim solidified my mastery and understanding of the science of ḥadīth, including study of its reporters, subtle defects, and the scholarly methodologies in verifying and authenticating ḥadīth reports.

My advice to budding ḥadīth students is to study Dhahabī's *Siyar*, al-Mizzī's *Tahdhīb al-kamāl*, al-Khaṭīb's *al-Jāmi' li akhlāq al-rāwī wa ādāb al-sāmi'*, and 'Abd al-Ḥayy al-Kattānī's *Fihris al-fahāris.* This should be the first stage of ḥadīth study. No doubt, this is difficult, but you must force yourself to work hard and bear hardships in order to attain your goals. Work hard now so that you can enjoy the results later, for it is God who says: ﴾*We have created humankind in constant struggle.*﴿ (90:4); and ﴾*A person attains only what they have striven for*﴿ (53:39).

The Right Pathway to Studying Ḥadīth

Why is it that you vociferously denounce the manner of teaching noble Prophetic ḥadīth in most religious seminaries today? Yes, as a matter of fact, I do criticize this approach quite heavily for its mistakes in turning away from the expected aim. *And what is that expected aim?*

Historical Pathways to Ḥadīth Study

The Companions of the Prophet received the Noble Qurʾān from him as well as his Sunnah (religious practice) directly without intermediary. They supported these two sources, understood them deeply, and practiced them. When the next generation of Successors came, they took the Qurʾān just as the Companions had done so, preserving it well and establishing it in their lives. Yet, they differed in a significant way from Companions in their treatment of the Sunnah. This was for the simple reason that the Sunnah had now become reduced to transmission of reports and circulation of chronicles, prior to it becoming an implemented practice. Therefore, they strove first to verify the truthfulness, uprightness, accuracy and precision of the transmitters of ḥadīth; and only after that, to understand and practice what these ḥadīth reports contained.

Successive generations followed this same practice until the fourth century. As the Prophetic era was becoming more distant and the levels of intermediaries were increasing even further, adding to the sheer number of transmitters, the task of scrutiny and investigation became more dire. The proper objective, therefore, in teaching ḥadīth is two basic matters: determining the veracity of reports first and then understanding and practicing them.

In later generations, unfortunately, people became lax and negligent in the first task, and even for the first time began to strip the texts of ḥadīth from their isnād chains. In doing so, they removed the contents from the very sources upon which they rested and which determined their veracity. Their treatment of the Qurʾān and Sunnah became the same as that of the era of the Companions, with the difference being that the Companions had combined two similar matters, while these latter generations were deeming equivalent two opposing matters. The earlier ones were correct while the latter were mistaken.

Ḥadīth as Sacred Texts

The fifth century saw the rise of a new practice of treating ḥadīth reports as sacred texts rather than historical reports, especially when Imām Muḥy al-Sunnah Abū Muḥammad al-Ḥusayn b. Mas'ūd b. Muḥammad al-Farrā' al-Baghawī (433—516 AH)[1] authored his book al-Maṣābīḥ stripped from isnād. Initially, only those who were lazy accepted that, but then many scholars began to follow suit, until stripped books began to multiply and the damage became grave. Ḥadīth now began to be taught as texts that were similar to the Qur'ānic text. Ḥadīth students and their teachers focused only on the ḥadīth contents and their meanings, while deeming their isnāds cumbersome and forgetting their critical role. They were less concerned with verifying authenticity and did not distinguish between ḥadīth texts and the Noble Qur'ān, whose verses were clear and whose text was free of the need for verification.

Was this not actually a way of making things easier for the beginners, who would then further their studies by examining the Sunan works of Abū 'Īsā, Abū Dāwūd and others along with their chains, and then move on to the two Ṣaḥīḥ collections and the Muwaṭṭa'?

This pathway of study was not the correct one for them, because they had studied those ḥadīth without verifying their weakness or authenticity, until these reports had become established and sanctified in their minds. And when they eventually did get to a study of the foundational books of the Sunnah, the matter of verification was already lost for them, such that they treated all these reports with sanctity and reverence. Among the masses, they perpetuated reverence for all that was spread in the name of ḥadīth and hastened to accept all such reports, even those that were slightly weak, contradictory, extremely weak, and even false and fabricated. These reports began to fill their pages and books and adorn their speeches and words. Even great scholars fell into this, and very few were those who managed to be protected from this.

Their reverence for these treasure troves of narrations did not allow them to fully accept the notion of weakness or conflict in these reports. They resorted to accepting the veracity of every weak, conflicting and defective report—even

[1] Persian scholar of ḥadīth and tafsīr who was born in Baghshūr near Herat. His ḥadīth work became the basis for the extremely popular ḥadīth book Mishkāt al-Maṣābīḥ.

fabricated ones—clinging to the multiplicity of their routes of transmission as justification. Everything ultimately became muddled, to the extent that weak reports became deemed as sound (ḥasan and ṣaḥīḥ). Anomalous, conflicting (shādh)[2] reports became sound (maḥfūẓ), and rejected (munkar)[3] reports became accepted (maʿrūf). They even became accommodating towards fabricated and baseless reports instead of regarding them as detested or loathsome.

So what is the correct method for studying ḥadīth?

Qurʾān as Sacred Text, Ḥadīth as Historical Reports

The correct method is that which was practiced by the Successors and those that came after them until the fourth century, which was to receive ḥadīth with its two essential and inseparable parts:

1. The study of its isnād: To not approach ḥadīth as philosophical ideas but as historical reports, which are always referenced to their sources whose veracity is then investigated thoroughly. Historical reports are never accepted until you fully examine them in order to separate the sound from the baseless ones.
2. The study of its matn: to examine the content of ḥadīth reports in order to deeply understand their meaning and to practice them, all of this by linking it with the Book of God in complete clarity and fully reconciling between these two sources.[4]

When the student combines these two matters in this way, he comes to the right way of differentiating between the Qurʾān and ḥadīth: that additional precaution is required with ḥadīth. This precaution is essential to realizing sound knowledge, and this was the approach of the predecessors of our ummah. Know that stripping ḥadīth reports of their isnād is an error of grave proportions

---

[2] A shādh, or anomalous, narration is one that is otherwise sound but conflicts with stronger narrations. In such a conflict the stronger narration is referred to as preserved (maḥfūẓ) and is accepted over the one of lesser strength.

[3] A munkar narration, like the anomalous one, conflicts with stronger evidences, but contains deeper, less benign, contradictions with often negative connotations or meanings. The converse of that, i.e. the strong narration that it is conflicting with, is referred to as maʿrūf, or accepted.

[4] Qurʾān and Sunnah.

which continues to afflict the ummah. Please refer to the chapters 'Ḥadīth and Philosophy' and 'Departure of Scholars from the Way of Ḥadīth Experts' for more details.

Can you let us know which book they should begin with, and how to proceed after that?

They must begin with the Muwaṭṭa' of Imām Mālik through the transmission of Yaḥyā b. Yaḥyā al-Laythī,[5] along with a deep study of its isnāds in order to realize the methodology and caution of Mālik in accepting ḥadīth and examining its contents for comprehension and application. When they complete the Muwaṭṭa' following all of these aspects, they should proceed to the Jāmi' of Abū 'Īsā[6] also studying its isnāds and meanings. They then move on to study Ṣaḥīḥ Muslim and Ṣaḥīḥ Bukhārī, examining their chains and meanings. And then this same methodology is applied to the Sunan of Abū Dāwūd, al-Nasā'ī and Ibn Mājah.

It is also essential for them to study some other seminal works such as the Muqaddimah of Ṣaḥīḥ Muslim, the 'Ilal of Tirmidhī, some portions from the Risālah of Imām Shāfi'ī, Ma'rifah 'Ulūm al-Ḥadīth of Ḥākim, the works of al-Khaṭīb al-Baghdādī, the 'Ilal of Ibn Abū Ḥātim, the 'Ilal of Dāruquṭnī, and the Tārīkh of Bukhārī.

But that would consume so much time! This is what knowledge is: exertion and struggle. Only those are blessed by it who have no other concern and no other preoccupation.

What is your opinion on studying Riyāḍ al-Ṣāliḥīn, Bulūgh al-Marām, and Mishkāt al-Maṣābīḥ?

This is the very same wrong approach which I warned you from. This is exactly what distorted in the minds and thoughts of the people the true meaning

---

[5] The Muwaṭṭa' is transmitted by many famous students of Mālik throughout the world, with slight variations based on when they studied with Imām Mālik (as his work was evolving). The version Dr. Akram is recommending to start with is that of his famous student Yaḥyā of Andalus (d. 234/848), who was one of the last students of Mālik to visit him in Madīnah. He popularized the work in Muslim Spain and contributed to the consolidation of the Mālikī school of jurisprudence in Andalus and North Africa. His version was popular in the West and served as the basis for Ibn 'Abd al-Barr's renowned commentary.

[6] The Jāmi' is a comprehensive ḥadīth compilation inclusive of not only legal rulings, but also additional topics such as tafsīr, aqīdah and heart softeners. The reference here is to the work of Imām Abū 'Īsā Muḥammad b. 'Īsā Tirmidhī (d. 279/892).

of ḥadīth. I am not denying that in the study of isnād-stripped books there is some benefit for the masses who are not students of ḥadīth.

Are not the books of fiqh stripped of isnād? My thoughts on studying fiqh would be the same as my preceding thoughts on studying ḥadīth, only even harsher. I will devote a separate article to this.

Assemblies I Will Never Forget

What specific circles of knowledge left a lasting impact on your life? There were many over time, but I will mention some of the most important ones. First, there were the Niẓāmī lectures at Dār al-ʿUlūm Nadwat al-ʿUlamāʾ, the individual circles of various Nadwah scholars and professors, the academic conferences and lectures at Oxford, and the ḥadīth reading sessions with scholars in Syria, Egypt, Morocco, and Arabia.

Which of these was most impactful on your heart? My teachers from Nadwah have had the greatest role in building my scholarly and intellectual self, and the sessions at Nadwah were highly esteemed and full of benefit. Following that, I learned greatly from the scholarly and academic environment of Oxford, where I increased in new perspectives of thinking and research. But the dearest assemblies to myself and the most impactful on my heart is my association with faithful scholars, researchers, and students in Makkah, Madīnah, and Jeddah. That I know with certainty.

Do you think that your inherent esteem for the holy land has a role in this sentiment? Surely that is one of the reasons for that impact, but there are many other factors, which I will list.

First, there was the purity and sincerity of the individuals with whom I shared in these ḥadīth recital sessions and with whom I developed great closeness and affinity, who were people of noble character, refined tastes, gentle temperaments, and pure hearts. How wonderful was that night I spent with Shaykh Muḥammad ʿAbdullah Āl al-Rashīd, Shaykh Majd Makkī, Muḥammad Abū Bakr Bādhīb, Salmān Abū Ghuddah, and others. What wonderful moments those were when I attended along with twin brothers Aḥmad and ʿAbdullah the lectures of Muḥammad Yūnus in the Ḥaramayn! How fortunate and happy we were!

Second, there was the spiritual environment that engulfed those assemblies in which ḥadīth was recited continually like the never-ending flow of pure water. Those scholars were full of radiant faces who exuded the aroma of real knowledge and piety. They were little concerned with this world and its allure. They were perfectly composed and humble, bold and active, who forbade for themselves certain indulgences that would compromise their character or their valuable time. They were far removed from fruitless argumentation and detested open displays of piety. All of this endeared within them the remembrance of God, recitation of Qurʾān, devotion to hearing ḥadīth reports, and reviewing stories of the pious people of the past. I have witnessed them enveloped in peace, while they invoked blessings upon the Prophet ﷺ at every frequent mention of his blessed name. They would listen with exclusive attention to the ḥadīth reports. I only learned the meaning of attentive listening (istimāʿ) through their noble example.

Third, there were the elevated isnāds of those esteemed teachers. I cannot imagine the kind of joy that I was immersed in when I first met Shaykh ʿAbd al-Raḥmān al-Kattānī, though I had requested ijāzah from him in the past. I had come to his hotel with Shaykh Muḥammad Abū Bakr Bādhīb only to learn that he was leaving in a few hours and was making the farewell ṭawāf[1]. We waited in the hotel for the entire night until he arrived close to his departure time. We heard from him the awaliyyah ḥadīth and read to him Bukhārī's Thulāthiyāt narrations[2]. He granted us general ijāzah, and we were grateful to God for this blessing.

From my senior teachers was the ḥadīth scholar and jurist ʿAbd al-Fattāḥ Rāwah. I visited his home with Shaykh Majd Makkī and heard from him the awaliyyah ḥadīth after which he granted me ijāzah in his Thabt entitled Kitāb al-maṣāʿid al-riwāyah. He had a severe type of hearing impairment and could not hear unless Shaykh Majd Makkī raised his voice to an intense degree. I was reminded of the state of Abū al-ʿAbbās al-Aṣamm who had hearing impairment to the extent that he could no longer hear the braying of donkeys.

In Jeddah, I visited, along with Muḥammad Wāʾil al-Ḥanbalī, the home of Shaykh al-Ḥabīb ʿAbd al-Qādir al-Saqqāf of Hadramawt, who narrates from very early figures such as Shaykh ʿAlī b. Muḥammad al-Ḥabashī and Aḥmad b. Ḥasan al-ʿAṭṭās. I always had a great desire to visit him and had written him for ijāzah previously. We heard the reading to him of the forty ḥadīth connected with Ahl al-Bayt, after which he granted us general ijāzah.

---

[1] Circumambulation around the Kaʿbah.

[2] 22 ḥadīth in the Ṣaḥīḥ that have only 3 intermediaries between Bukhārī and the Prophet ﷺ.

I attended with Aḥmad ʿĀshūr on more than one occasion the lessons of Shaykh Mālik b. al-ʿArabī al-Sannūsī in Madīnah. The first time I met, I heard from him the awwaliyyah ḥadīth and heard the reading of parts of al-ʿArbaʿūn al-ʿAjlūniyyah. He also granted us ijāzah, through the agency of commission (wikālah), from Sayyidah Fāṭimah, better known as Shifā al-Sannūsiyyah, who has ijāzah from Aḥmad al-Rīfī, who narrates from Muḥammad b. ʿAlī al-Sannūsī, representing an extremely high isnād.

With Muḥammad Abū Bakr Bādhīb, we visited the senior scholar Shaykh ʿAbdullah al-Nākhibī at his home in Jeddah. We heard from him the awaliyyah ḥadīth, after which I read to him the first three ḥadīth from Kitāb al-Ṭahārah of Ṣaḥīḥ Muslim and he granted us general ijāzah. His highest isnād is his narration from al-Ḥabīb ʿAlawī b. ʿAbd al-Raḥmān al-Mashhūr: from ʿAbdullah b. Tāhā b. ʿAbdullah al-Ḥaddād: from al-Wajīh al-Ahdal and Aḥmad b. Saʿīd Bāḥanshal: both from Sayyid Sulaymān the father al-Wajīh. Another high chain of his is his narration from his father Sayyid ʿAbd al-Raḥmān b. Muṣṭafā al-ʿAydrūs.

Why such an emphasis on elevated isnāds? Elevated isnāds have great eminence combined with an intoxicating allure. Ḥadīth practitioners have two unique pleasures and one regret, which no one else enjoys. The two intoxicating pleasures are the practice of ḥadīth audition and possessing elevated isnāds, which can lead one to get lost in their allure. Participants would linger on indefinitely if it weren't for pure hearts and fixed goals that set them back on track and cause them to seek their Lord's forgiveness for their slips and falls, for they have no recourse to their Lord save His wonderful ability to pardon and their hope and trust in Him.

PART 6: REMINDERS

Advice to Ḥadīth Seekers

Which group do you ascribe yourself to? My group would be the people of ḥadīth, in whom I seek refuge and to whom I am stubbornly loyal.

Since the Qur'ān is Divine revelation, in wording and in meaning, who do you not ascribe yourself to the people of Qur'ān? The people of ḥadīth are the ones who are devoted to the Prophet's characteristics, life, manner, and conduct, as well as to all the disciplines and sciences relating to his person. These include the Qur'ān, sunnah, fiqh, and all that is connected with God's religion and Sharī'ah. So in reality, those who are committed to ḥadīth are actually committed to the Qur'ān, ḥadīth and fiqh according to the manner of the Prophet ﷺ, Companions, and early Muslims. Any claim of commitment to the Qur'ān alone to the exclusion of ḥadīth reports will result in the rise of innovations that depart from the way of the Prophet ﷺ.

We find you critiquing every group within the Islamic disciplines save for the people of ḥadīth. Is that not partisanship which you never fail to condemn? Why this double standard? You have one for ḥadīth-folk and another for the others? I have love and passion for the people of ḥadīth and seek to live and die upon their way. Loving the people of ḥadīth has settled into my heart and soul. I sing their praises and hide their faults. Love surely blinds. I will not be content with disparaging them or insulting them. However, there are five characteristics I abhor in the people of ḥadīth:

1. *Not Recognizing the Centrality of the Qur'ān*: The Prophet ﷺ made the Qur'ān the base for everything, and his Companions followed suit. The Qur'ān was never dispensable for them nor were they excessive regarding it. The early ḥadīth scholars also followed this trajectory until some later groups of ḥadīth-folk began to diminish the role of the Qur'ān in no small way. They did not deeply study the Qur'ān nor did they ponder over it, and made ḥadīth reports the base for all matters. They did not 'recite the Qur'ān as it ought to be recited.' They did not relate ḥadīth to Qur'ān as subsidiary branches relate to their roots, or peripheral matters to their origin.
2. *Laxity in Ḥadīth Authentication*: Many people of ḥadīth were lacking in their understanding of how early ḥadīth experts authenticated and weakened

reports, until ultimately a formal methodology became crystallized among latter-day ḥadīth scholars which was far removed from the methods of the earliest ḥadīth experts. This created a huge dissonance between early and later experts. The latter methodology, for instance, considered the existence of multiple paths of transmission to elevate gradings of ḥadīth. There are so many reports deemed ḥasan by earlier scholars but ṣaḥīḥ by later ones, or ḍaʿīf by earlier ones and ḥasan by later ones. Later scholars even elevated reports that were shādh or munkar—and even fabricated—to levels of ṣaḥīḥ or ḥasan. I have never seen a group that was more excessive in deeming acceptable those things that were not. They ultimately wound up corrupting this noble discipline. And what a discipline did they wound up corrupting!

3. *Ijāzah and Narration Becoming Goals Rather Than Means:* They could not comprehend the true nature of ḥadīth audition, narration, ijāzah and other terms, and treated them like goals rather than means to an end. This was a major mistake on their part. You find many of them taking from their teachers by way of munāwalah,[1] but this form of munāwalah had no relation to its original at all. For instance, you find them saying, when receiving ijāzah from their teachers, 'qabilnā' ('We accept'). But this form of verbal exchange is only required in contracts such as marriage and sales. Knowledge is not an exchange at all, so what would be the meaning here? This is frivolity and ignorance on their part. Moreover, there arose among them great competition and boasting about the number of books heard and ijāzahs received, which has little to do with actual comprehension. In fact, many individuals without these prolific ijāzahs actually have better understanding and insight about religion than such individuals.

4. *Privileging Narration over Comprehension:* Many of them did not fully understand the meanings of ḥadīth reports. Lack of deep study of the Muwaṭṭaʾ, Ṣaḥīḥayn, and other primary ḥadīth texts led scholars of other disciplines to disparage them as *ḥashawiyyīn.* The fact is that meanings and deeper realities of these reports represent a matter that is far greater than and beyond hearing or reading reports and receiving ijāzah in them. For

[1] Munāwalah is a traditional method of transmission in which a teacher presents a manuscript, book, or other record of his ḥadīth reports to a student for purposes of transmission, usually accompanied by formal ijāzah.

many of these individuals, ḥadīth simply came to represent high or low isnāds, or whether they were reported in musalsal form. They began to boast about the least number of intermediaries between themselves and al-Amīr al-Kabīr, Shāh Walīullah, Kūrānī, Sālim al-Baṣrī, Abū al-ʿAbbās al-Ḥajjār, al-Fakhr b. al-Bukhārī, and others. They did not understand the contents of reports or their arrangements in primary works. They only knew that some reports were continuously connected (musalsal) through Ḥanafī, Mālikī, Shāfiʿī, or Ḥanbalī jurists; or through people of Makkah, Madīnah, or Damascus; or through narrators all named Muḥammad or whose names began with the letter ʿayn, and other such rare and exotic feats.

5. *Ill Manners:* Some of them did not adopt the true manners of the people of ḥadīth and fell into all sorts of sins and evil traits, such as jealousy, rivalry, boycotting one another, compromising one other's rights, calling others by ill titles, slander and gossip. Some of them monopolized certain teachers or became jealous of their peers finding other teachers. Abandoning noble values and ideals is a shame for all scholars, and even more for those who claim to be specialists in the Prophet ﷺ. In fact, their study of ḥadīth did not avail them of anything, and the knowledge wound up becoming a proof against them.

I advise myself and all people of ḥadīth to adorn themselves with the best character traits, to learn portions of other Islamic disciplines in order to rectify ourselves with lasting righteousness, and to avoid crossing limits and bounds. We should pray to God to grant us the essence of knowledge, practice, and sincerity. And we should seek forgiveness from our sins and faults, and turn to Him in repentance.

Departure of Scholars from the Way of Ḥadīth Experts

We attend your lectures, and you point out all sorts of scholarly mistakes in the treatment of the Prophetic sunnah and the failure to fully grasp the approach of the Imāms of ḥadīth. So please inform us of the roots and origins of this error.

There are two matters: that which most scholars fell into and that which only some of them did. First, there were two matters which affected most of them.

Need to Treat Ḥadīth as Historical Reports

First, there is the failure to fully discern the meaning of ḥadīth authentication, whose underlying factor goes back to not apprehending the real nature of ḥadīth. Ḥadīth is basically a historical report, and you cannot arrive at an understanding of its reality or depth without familiarity with the discipline of history: through analyzing reports of its events and occurrences, keeping in view the causes, multifold dimensions and subtle deficiencies of those reports. The Imāms of ḥadīth were thoroughly and utterly proficient in the science of history. Contemplate their reports, discussion and discourse, and you will indeed find my claim to be truthful and correct. Yaḥyā b. Maʿīn, Ibn al-Madīnī, Aḥmad b. Ḥanbal, Bukhārī, Muslim, Nasāʾī, Ibn Abī Ḥātim and others wrote extensively on history and biographies. Bukhārī wrote on history before working on his Ṣaḥīḥ.

Reports can often be contaminated by mistakes, errors, insertions, additions, fabrication, falsehood, and more. These Imāms expended their efforts in scrutinizing reports with precision and proficiency. They reached the farthest extents of caution and diligence in their treatment of narrations, which no scholars of any other discipline managed to reach. Those luminaries did well to classify ḥadīth into ṣaḥīḥ (sound), ḥasan (fair), daʿīf (weak), munkar (rejected), and mawḍūʿ (fabricated). They authored great works on ʿilal (hidden defects of reports) which bore witness to their skill and proficiency in this craft.

Not All Narrators are the Same

It is quite obvious that memorizing one or two legal rulings does not make one a jurist, nor does dealing with an issue or two of logic makes one a logician, nor possessing one or two dirhams makes one rich. This matter is so self-evident that it does not deserve being pointed out. At the same time, unfortunately, most scholars did not observe this crucial difference for narrators of ḥadīth. They deemed equivalent those who were specialists in narration with those who simply narrated an occasional report. How many reports were narrated solely by non-specialists which seasoned experts deemed suspicious to the point of rejection, and yet they attained acceptance among scholars who began to narrate them in their books until the public adopted them wholesale? For that reason, ḥadīth experts stipulated conditions for a narrator such as accuracy, prolonged tutelage under their teachers, and proficiency in this discipline. They were particularly attentive to discrepancies among reporters, especially when one of them differed from others in a solitary manner. They ruled on the strength or weakness of the accuracy of narrators. They frequently described reports as gharīb (solitary), shādh (anomalous), or munkar (rejected),[1] while later scholars frequently elevated these same reports to ṣaḥīḥ or ḥasan based upon the multiplicity of their chains or their being widespread among people.

Recognizing Intra-Narration Mistakes

Similarly, those who reject entire ḥadīth due to such conflicts fail to recognize the nature of this science. A report could fall into discrepancy in one of its peripheral portions while its core remains sound. How many sound reports are found in the books of Bukhārī and Muslim while they have minor discrepancies in some of their portions? Thus, scholars compiled supporting and witnessing reports for these discrepancies, which they sought to point out through these reports. For evidence purposes, they intended to rely on only the established

---

[1] These are all ḥadīth categories that reflect a report differing from others in some way. Gharīb is a neutral judgement on the isnād being solitary (narrated by one or relatively few narrators), while shādh refers to a report, otherwise sound in chain, that conflicts with stronger, or larger group of, chains. Munkar is a weak report that conflicts with stronger ones and is thus more firmly rejected.

portions of these narrations. Imām Ibn Taymiyyah, God have mercy on him, says in his introduction to the Principles of Tafsīr:

> The point here is that when a lengthy ḥadīth is narrated through two different chains without collaboration, then it cannot be a mistake or lie. A lengthy story cannot be one big mistake, but parts of it can contain errors. Therefore, if a person narrates a long and detailed story, and another narrates the exact same story without collusion then both stories cannot be a mistake, just as they cannot be lies. As such, mistakes which occur can be within certain portions of the story, like the ḥadīth in which the Prophet ﷺ bought a camel from Jābir. Whoever contemplates the different chains of this ḥadīth will realize that the ḥadīth is authentic, even though the narrations differ concerning the exact price of the camel. This is also explained by Bukhārī in his Ṣaḥīḥ.[2]

Individual Sunnahs and Ḥadīth are Not Sources of Religion

The second mistake of most scholars was their view of specific sunnah practices as independent sources for this religion, and their forgetting that they were explanations of the Book of God which delineate its generalities and expound on its ambiguities. They fell into mistakes which resemble the error of those who divorce commentaries from their original texts or a structure from its foundation. The erudite scholar ʿAbd al-Ḥamīd Farāhī states in al-Takmīl fī Uṣūl al-Taʾwīl:

> There were many individuals, like most people of narration, who were content with ḥadīth reports that were scrutinized, because they realized that since the speech of the Prophet must agree with the Qurʾān, and the speech of the Companions with the speech of the Prophet, they found in ḥadīth great latitude. Therefore, they made it a foundation due to their lack of comprehension and used it to explain the Qurʾān, until

---

[2] Pg. 94-5. Ibn Taymiyyah, Introduction to the Principles of Tafsīr. Birmingham, UK: Al-Hidaayah Publishing & Distribution Ltd. 2009.

the reigns of the Qur'ān began to be taken by the hands of ḥadīth. They cared little to understand the independent meanings of the Qur'ān but began to explain it in ways that often contradicted its verses. They should have, rather, understood ḥadīth in light of the Qur'ān. Contradictory narrations would have become harmonious if we were to understand them by referring them back to the Qur'ān.

On the other hand, there were some errors which affected only some scholars.

Danger of Treating Prophetic Speech Like Ours

They failed to comprehend the nature of Prophetic speech but relegated it to the speech of ordinary men. The worst offenders in this regard were two types of scholars:

1. Theologians who applied ḥadīth to their theological and creedal views, accepting those ḥadīth which agreed with their views while rejecting those that did not. They began to pit ḥadīth narrations one against another. The Qadarīyyah (advocates of free will), for instance, accepted some ḥadīth reports while rejecting others, and the Jabarites (predeterminists: advocates of divine destiny) did the same, and others followed suit. They sorted out the statements of the Prophet ﷺ on their own accord. Were they to exercise their minds, they would have realized that the Prophetic ḥadīth reports are fully harmonious and congruous, while their own conflicting views needed to be sorted out instead.
2. The jurists who treated the Prophet as a legal scholar (muftī) and converted his ḥadīth to legal verdicts (fatwā) and religious rulings, whereas the Prophet himself was the furthest person from utilizing the terminology of these individuals.

The Way Forward

I advise you to study the books of history and learn the approach of historians. Then you should contemplate over the Book of God, and then the Sunnah as an explanation of the Book. You should be familiar with the speech of the prophets and not treat ḥadīth as matters of theology, fiqh or other views. You should adhere to consulting the books of biographies (rijāl) and hidden defects (ʿilal), examining them deeply so that perhaps God may open for you some of this noble and blessed knowledge.

Slow Down, People of Riwāyah!

Why do you disparage contemporary seekers of transmission (riwāyah) so much? Many of them are wasting their youth and consuming their valuable time and the time of others in their vain pursuit, and will come to regret it but it will be too late.

Did you not interact with such people in your own youth? Yes, I did befriend many such people —and they were the absolute best of my companions whom I would never give up—but they were not like these individuals.

Who are your companions of transmission so that we may meet them and benefit from them? The best of them is the righteous scholar Aḥmad b. ʿAbd al-Malik ʿĀshūr, Shaykh Majd b. Aḥmad Makkī, Shaykh Muḥammad b. ʿAbdullah Āl Rashīd, Shaykh Ḥāmid Akram Bukhārī, Shaykh Niẓām Yaʿqūbī, Shaykh Muḥammad b. Nāṣir al-ʿAjamī, Shaykh ʿAbdullah al-Tūm, Shaykh Muḥammad b. Abū Bakr Bādhīb, Shaykh Muḥammad b. Ziyād al-Tuklah, Shaykh ʿUmar al-Nashūqātī, Shaykh Muḥammad Wāʾil al-Ḥanbalī, Shaykh Khālid al-Sibāʿī, and others.

Tell us about the extent of their expertise and devotion to ḥadīth. They were people of intelligence, high aspirations, and noble character traits. They were keen on attaining audition in reports, and I befriended them while they were already engaged in visiting various scholars to read texts with them for ijāzah. They drank from the pure wells of these scholars, absorbed their knowledge, and followed in their footsteps and manners. They highlighted the virtue of their teachers while hiding their faults. They worked hard and never got tired or bored. They were full of love and mercy. In this environment of love and refined morals, I learned this fine art and developed a fondness for the art of ḥadīth narration and ijāzah. I never forget this bond, and all of these emotions are rekindled whenever we meet again. I am overjoyed in their presence and miss them in their absence, as if part of me were with them.

How does this differ from contemporary people of narration? They differ from them in four areas:

1. My companions entered the domain of knowledge through its proper doors. They learned, for instance, Arabic language through its grammar, morphology, literature and poetry. They learned the Qurʾān,

tafsīr, fiqh, uṣūl al-fiqh, kalām, sīrah, history, and other disciplines, before moving on to the art of narration. Moreover, in this stage of narration, they never forgot their obligation to fully understand the religion of God. Others, however, make their entry into the domain of knowledge through other its proper doors, not learning the arts and disciplines holistically and spending their times in attaining ijāzahs and being devoted to pages and manuscripts. They are not masters of Arabic, literature, or poetry. They claim something which they weren't blessed with and wear the garbs of deception.

2. Our companions learned the intellectual sciences and fine arts, combined knowledge with upright conduct, and adopted the good manners and traits of their teachers. Others do not learn the intellectual sciences and fine arts, and are lazy in prayer, good works, and truthfulness. They are the opposite of their teachers and oppose the lives of the pious.
3. Our companions were sincere and brotherly, ever cooperating in good, loving for others what they loved for themselves. They readily point teachers out to others, and even facilitate such meetings. They circulate the biographies of these teachers as well as the catalogue works (athbāt) and high isnād works. Others are miserly in revealing their teachers, to the point of hiding names, or high isnād works. They do not demonstrate sincerity towards fellow students, and are happy when one of their senior teachers dies so that they can show off their narration from them.
4. Our companions were humble and cordial, while others today are rude and arrogant, always seeking to dismiss others and elevate themselves. They readily exchange insults and disparagement, displaying poor character. Pious people flee from their assemblies and dislike being among them.

What would you advise us then? Learn Arabic and literature, along with acquiring all other sciences, in a manner of humility, gentleness, sincerity and cooperation. Always pray that God blesses your knowledge and practice, and uses you as a means to purify the world upon the Prophetic sunnah and radiant guidance which you have been learning.

Learn Manners, People of Riwāyah!

Students of Prophetic ḥadīth are many types. The best of them are those who study its foundational texts—both primary and secondary ones—in order to master the isnād and mutūn of ḥadīth, its transmitters, the science of defects, and the deeper meanings of the contents of ḥadīth reports, and live the meanings of these ḥadīth in their lives. They are the heirs of the prophets, teachers of good, and callers to the upright path. For these individuals, the presence of abundant chains of narration along with high or rare isnāds would only serve to increase them in beauty and adornment.

However, there are many young people in our times who have not mastered Arabic language, who neither understand God's Book nor Prophetic ḥadīth, who have not learned fiqh or the biographies of the pious. Their portfolios are filled with auditions, recitals, and ijāzahs which are spurious, disconnected, or suspicious. They are devoted to riwāyah with no attention paid to comprehension (dirāyah). They attain these ijāzahs through phone calls and websites to teachers throughout the world who are advanced in age and even senile, who cannot recognize what is being recited to them.

They see these abundant ijāzahs as a virtue. Whenever they learn of a teacher anywhere, they flock to them with poor manners, with little regard for their time, and disturb them tremendously to get what they want.

My advice to the young seekers of this noble discipline is the following:

1. Don't waste your time chasing these ijāzahs which do not represent any real semblance of knowledge. Rather, endeavor to master Arabic, reflect over the Qur'ān, read the biographies of the pious, and study the primary books of ḥadīth, mastering their isnāds, mutūn, transmitters and subtle defects.
2. Turn to your Lord and perfect His worship, for a little bit of knowledge coupled with worship is sufficient and great indeed. Learn a good share of manners before moving on to narration and audition, for the blessing of knowledge lies in its connection with the fear of God and manners. Khaṭīb said: 'The seeker of ḥadīth should be the most well-mannered and humble of all people and the greatest in refinement and religiosity.

He should be the farthest of people from ill-manners and anger due to his ears constantly being filled with reports of the noble manners of the Prophet ﷺ, Companions, his family members, and that of ḥadīth experts and people from the past. They are able to take the best of these reports and leave the weakest ones.'[1]

3. Becomes companions to your teachers in full respect, humility and endearment. Do not call them or text them unless you have their permission. You should realize that they have obligations of teaching, writing, working and taking care of their families. Do not burden them or take them away from their responsibilities. Do not bother them unnecessarily nor anger them. Do not take advantage of them, nor speak ill of them. If you do so, do not rule out the withholding of God's mercy from you and the deprivation of knowledge which you believe you are attaining. Aṣmaʿī said: I heard Shuʿbah say: 'Whenever I learned ḥadīth from any person, I would become his servant so long as he were alive.'[2]

---

[1] *Al-Jāmiʿ li akhlāq al-rāwī*, vol 1, pg 78.

[2] Ibid, vol 1, pg 191.

Index

A

B

C

D

F

G

Ḥ

I

J

K

L

M

O

P

BIBLIOGRAPHY

ʿAbd al-ʿAzīz al-Dihlawī. *The Garden of the Hadith Scholars (Bustān al-muḥaddithīn)*. London: Turath Publishing. 1428/2007.

Al-Qāḍī, Abū Yūsuf Yaʿqūb b. Ibrāhīm. *al-Radd ʿalā siyar al-Awzāʿī*. Hyderabad, India: Iḥyāʾ al-Maʿārif al-Nuʿmānīyyah.

ʿAẓīmābādī, Muḥammad Ashar b. Amīr. *ʿAwn al-maʿbūd sharḥ Sunan Abī Dāwūd*. Beirut: Dār al-Kutub al-ʿIlmīyyah. 1415.

Bayhaqī, Abū Bakr Aḥmad b. al-Ḥusayn. *al-Qirāʾah khalf al-imām*. Beirut: Dār al-Kutub al-ʿIlmīyyah. 1405.

Bayhaqī, Abū Bakr Aḥmad b. al-Ḥusayn. *al-Sunan al-Kubrā*. Beirut: Dār al-Kutub al-ʿIlmīyyah. 1424/2003.

Brown, Jonathan AC. *Hadith: Muhammad's Legacy in the Medieval and Modern World*. Oneworld Publications. 2009.

Bukhārī, ʿAbd al-ʿAzīz b. Aḥmad. *Kashf al-asrār sharḥ uṣūl al-Bazdawī*. Dār al-Kitāb al-Islāmī. 1308.

Bukhārī, Muḥammad b. Ismāʿīl. *Al-Tārīkh al-kabīr*. India: Dāʾirat al-Maʿārif al-ʿUthmānī. 1357.

Dāruquṭnī, Abū al-Ḥasan ʿAlī b. ʿUmar. *Al-ʿilal al-wāridah fī al-āḥādīth al-nabawīyyah*. Riyad: Dār Ṭayyibah. 1405/1985.

—*Al-Ilzāmāt wa al-tatabbuʿ*. Beirut: Dār al-Kutub al-ʿIlmīyyah. 1405/1985.

—*Sunan*. Beirut: Muʾassasat al-Risālah. 1424/2004.

Dhahabī, Shams al-Dīn Muḥammad b. Aḥmad. *Siyar aʿlām al-nubalāʾ*. Beirut, Lebanon: Muʾassasat al-Risālah. 11th edition. 1417/1996.

—*Tārīkh al-Islām*. Beirut: Dār al-Gharb al-Islāmī. 2003.

Al-Fasawī, *Kitāb al-maʿrifah wa al-tārīkh*. Madīnah: Maktabat al-Dār. 1410.

Ḥākim, Abū ʿAbdullah Muḥammad b. ʿAbdullah. *Maʿrifat ʿulūm al-ḥadīth*. Beirut: Dār al-Kutub al-ʿIlmīyyah. 1397/1977.

Al-Hararī, Muḥammad al-Amīn. *Al-Kawkab al-wahhāj wa al-rawj al-bahhāj fī sharḥ ṣaḥīḥ Muslim b. Ḥajjāj*. Jeddah: Dār al-Minhāj. 1430/2009.

Hussain, Ather Shahbaz. *The Nuzhah of Ibn Ḥajar al-ʿAsqalānī: A Translation and Critical Commentary*. PhD Dissertation: The University of Birmingham. May 2012.

Ibn ʿAbd al-Barr. *al-Intiqāʾ fī faḍāʾil al-thalāthat al-aʾimmah al-fuqahāʾ*. Beirut: Dār al-Kutub al-ʿIlmiyyah. 1350.

—*al-Tamhīd li mā fī al-Muwaṭṭaʾ min al-maʿānī wa al-asānīd*. Morocco: Wazārat ʿUmūm al-Awqāf wa al-Shuʾūn al-Islāmī. 1387.

—*Jāmiʿ bayān al-ʿilm wa faḍlihī*. Saudi Arabia: Dār Ibn al-Jawzī. 1414/1994.

—*Al-Istidhkār*. Beirut: Dār al-Kutub al-ʿIlmīyyah. 1421/2000.

Ibn Amīr Ḥāj, Shams al-Dīn Muḥammad b. Muḥammad. *Al-Taqrīr wa al-Taḥbīr*. Beirut: Dār al-Kutub al-ʿIlmī. 1403/1983.

Ibn ʿAsākir, *Tarīkh Damishq*.

Ibn ʿĀṣim al-Andalūsī, Abū Bakr Muḥammad b. Muḥammad b. Muḥammad. *Ḥadāʾiq al-azhār*. Cairo: Dār al-Kutub. 1435/2014.

Al-ʿAsqalānī, Ibn Ḥajar. *Fatḥ al-bārī*. 2nd edition. Egypt: Dār al-ʿĀlamiyyah. 1436/2015.

— *Fatḥ al-bārī*. Beirut: Dār al-Maʿrifah. 1379.

— *Lisān al-Mīzān*. India: Dāʾirah Maʿārif al-Niẓāmī. 1329.

—*al-Majmaʿ al-muʾassis li al-muʿjam al-mufahris*. Beirut: Dār al-Maʿrifah. 1413/1992.

—*Nuzhat al-Naẓar fī Tawḍīḥ Nukhbat al-Fikr fī Muṣṭalaḥ Ahl al-Athar*. Madīnah: Ṭayyibah University. 1429/2008.

—*Tahdhīb al-tahdhīb*. Cairo: Dār al-Kitāb al-Islāmī. 1327.

Ibn Ḥazm, Abū Muḥammad ʿAlī b. Aḥmad. *Al-Iḥkām fī uṣūl al-aḥkām*. Beirut: Dār al-Āfāq al-Jadīdah.

Ibn Kathīr, Abū al-Fidāʾ Ismāʿīl. *Al-Bāʿith al-ḥathīth sharḥ ikthiṣār ʿulūm al-ḥadīth*. Saudi Arabia: Dār Ibn al-Jawzī. 1435.

Ibn Khaldūn, ʿAbd al-Raḥmān b. Muḥammad. *Al-Tārīkh*. Beirut: Dār al-Fikr. 1408/1988.

Ibn Rajab, Zayn al-Dīn ʿAbd al-Raḥmān. *Sharḥ ʿilal al-Tirmidhī*. Jordan: Maktabat al-Manār. 1407/1987.

Ibn Maʿīn, Yaḥyā. *Tārīkh Ibn Maʿīn*. Makkah: Markaz al-Baḥth al-ʿIlmī. 1399/1979.

Ibn al-Qayyim. *Al-Wābil al-ṣayyib min al-kalim al-ṭayyib*. Cairo: Dār al-Ḥadīth. 1999.

Ibn Saʾd, *Ṭabaqāt al-Kubrā*. Beirut: Dār al-Ṣādir. 1968.

Ibn al-Ṣalāḥ, ʿUthmān b. ʿAbd al-Raḥmān. *Muqaddimah Ibn al-Ṣalāḥ*. Beirut: Dār al-Fikr. 1406/1986.

Ibn al-Ṣalāḥ, ʿUthmān b. ʿAbd al-Raḥmān. *An Introduction to the Science of Ḥadīth*. Translated by Eerik Dickinson. Beirut: Garnet Publishing. 2006.

Ibn Taymiyyah, Aḥmad b. ʿAbd al-Ḥalīm. *Majmūʿ al-fatāwā*. Madīnah: Majmaʿ Malik Fahd. 1416/1995.

Ibn Taymiyyah, *al-Muqaddimah fī uṣūl al-tafsīr*. Beirut: Dār Maktabat al-Ḥayāt. 1490/1980.

Al-ʿIrāqī, Abū al-Faḍl Zayn al-Dīn. *al-Taqyīd wa al-īḍāḥ sharḥ muqaddimah Ibn al-Ṣalāḥ*. Madīnah: Maktabah al-Salafīyyah. 1389/1969.

ʿIyāḍ, Abū al-Faḍl al-Qāḍī. *Tartīb al-madārik wa taqrīb al-masālik*. Morocco: Maṭbaʿah Faḍālah al-Muḥammadīyyah. 1965.

Al-Jaṣṣāṣ, Abū Bakr Aḥmad b. ʿAlī al-Rāzī, *al-Fuṣūl fī al-uṣūl*. Kuwait: Ministry of Awqāf. 1414/1994.

Kashmīrī, Muḥammad Anwar Shāh. *Ikfār al-mulḥidīn fī ḍarūriyyāt al-dīn*. Pakistan: al-Majlis al-ʿIlmī. 1424/2004.

Khaṭṭābī, Ḥamd b. Muḥammad. *Maʿālim al-sunan*, Aleppo: Al-Maṭbaʿ al-ʿIlmiyyah. 1351/1932.

Al-Khaṭīb, Abū Bakr Aḥmad b. ʿAlī al-Baghdādī. *al-Jāmiʿ li akhlāq al-rāwī wa ādāb al-sāmiʿ*. Riyad: Maktabah al-Maʿārif. 1403/1983.

—*al-Kifāyah fī ʿilm al-riwāyah*. India: Dāʾirat al-Maʿārif al-ʿUthmānī. 1357.

— *al-Kifāyah fī ʿilm al-riwāyah*. Madīnah: Maktabah al-ʿIlmīyyah. 1357.

— *Sharaf aṣḥāb al-ḥadīth*. Ankara: Dār Iḥyāʾ al-sunnah al-nabawī. 1389/1969.

—*al-Taṭfīl wa ḥikāyāt al-ṭufayliyyīn wa akhbāruhum wa nawādir kalāmihim wa ashʿārihim*. Beirut: Dār Ibn Ḥazm. 1420/1999.

Laher, Suheil Ismail. *Twisted Threads: Genesis, Development and Application of the Term and Concept of Tawātur in Islamic Thought*. Cambridge, Massachusetts: PhD dissertation, Harvard University. April 2014.

Al-Lucknowī, Muḥammad b. ʿAbd al-Ḥayy. *Ẓufar al-amānī bi sharḥ mukhtaṣar al-Sayyid al-Sharīf al-Jurjānī*. Beirut: Dār al-Kutub al-ʿIlmī. 1998.

Al-Mizzī, Abū al-Ḥajjāj Jamāl al-Dīn. *Tahdhīb al-kamāl fī asmāʾ al-rijāl*. Beirut: Muʾassasat al-Risālah. 1400/1980.

Muslim, Abū al-Ḥusayn. *English Translation of Ṣaḥīḥ Muslim*. Riyad: Darrussalam Publishers. 2007.

Nawawī, Sharaf al-Dīn. *Sharḥ al-taqrīb wa al-taysīr li ma'rifat sunan al-bashīr al-nadhīr.* Abū Dhabi: Mu'assasat Baynūnah. 1428/2007.

Al-Qaraḍāwī, Yūsuf. *Kaytfa nata'āmal ma'a al-sunnah al-nabawīyyah.* Cairo: Dār al-Shurūq. 2nd edition. 1423/2002.

Rāmahurmuzī, Abū Muḥammad. *Al-muḥaddith al-fāṣil bayna al-rāwī wa al-wā'ī.* Beirut: Dār al-Fikr. 1404/1984.

Al-Rāzī, Ibn Abī Ḥātim. *'Ilal al-ḥadīth.* Riyad: Maṭābi' al-Ḥumayḍī. 1427/2006.

Al-Sarakhsī, Muḥammad b. Aḥmad. *Uṣūl al-Sarakhsī.* Beirut: Dār al-Ma'rifah.

—*Al-Mabsūṭ.* Beirut: Dār al-Ma'rifah. 1414/1993.

Shāfi'ī, Muḥammad b. Idris. *Al-Risālah.* Edited: Aḥmad Muḥammad Shaykhākir. Egypt: Muṣṭafā al-Bābilī al-Ḥalabī. 1358/1940.

Shāh Walīullah, Aḥmad b. 'Abd al-Raḥīm. *Ḥujjahtullāh al-bālighah.* Beirut: Dār al-Jayl. 1326/2005.

Shākir, Aḥmad Muḥammad. *Jamharat maqālāt al-'all āmah al-shaykh Aḥmad Muḥammad Shākir.* Riyad: Dār al-Riyad. 1426/2005.

—*Kalimat al-Ḥaqq.* Maktabat al-Sunnah. 1408.

Shāshī, Niẓām al-Dīn. *Mukhtaṣar fī uṣūl al-fiqh al-islāmī (Uṣūl al-Shāshī).* Edited: Mohammad Akram Nadwi. Beirut: Dār al-Gharb al-Islāmī. 2000.

Al-Shaybānī, Muhammad b. al-Ḥasan. *Kitāb al-Āthār.* Beirut: Dār al-Kutub al-'Ilmiyyah. 1413/1993.

Al-Shīrāzī, Abū Isḥāq Ibrāhīm b. 'Alī. *Al-Luma' fī uṣūl al-fiqh.* Beirut: Dār al-Kutub al-'Ilmīyyah. 1424/2003.

Slove, Emily. *The Art of Party-Crashing in Medieval Iraq.* New York: Syracuse University Press. 2012.

Suyūṭī, Jalāl al-Dīn. *Tadrīb al-rāwī fī sharḥ taqrīb al-Nawāwī.* Beirut: Maktabah al-Kawthar. 1415.

Tirmidhī, Muḥammad b. 'Īsā. *Al-'Ilal al-kabīr.* Beirut: Maktabah al-Nahḍah al-'Arabīyyah. 1409.

Zarqānī, Muḥammad b. 'Abd al-Bāqī. *Sharḥ al-Zarqānī 'alā Muwaṭṭa' Mālik.* Cairo: Maktabat al-Thaqāfah al-Dīnīyyah. 1424/2003.

Printed in Great Britain
by Amazon

24241535R00155